# Machine Learning with BigQuery ML

Create, execute, and improve machine learning
models in BigQuery using standard SQL queries

**Alessandro Marrandino**

BIRMINGHAM—MUMBAI

# Machine Learning with BigQuery ML

**Group Product Manager**: Kunal Parikh

**Publishing Product Manager**: Sunith Shetty

**Senior Editor**: David Sugarman

**Content Development Editor**: Nathanya Dias

**Technical Editor**: Manikandan Kurup

**Copy Editor**: Safis Editing

**Project Coordinator**: Aparna Ravikumar Nair

**Proofreader**: Safis Editing

**Indexer**: Rekha Nair

**Production Designer**: Prashant Ghare

First published: June 2021

Production reference: 1120521

Published by Packt Publishing Ltd.
Livery Place
35 Livery Street
Birmingham
B3 2PB, UK.

ISBN 978-1-80056-030-7

www.packt.com

# Contributors

## About the author

**Alessandro Marrandino** is a Google Cloud customer engineer. He helps various enterprises on the digital transformation to adopt cloud technologies. He is actively focused on and experienced in data management and smart analytics solutions. He has spent his entire career on data and artificial intelligence projects for global companies in different industries.

*I want to thank the people who have been close to me and supported me, especially my wife, Federica. Thanks to her love and availability, I was able to dedicate most of my free time to writing this book, while we were waiting for the most important person in our life: Eva. Special thanks go to all my family. They have always believed in me and in my passion for technology and data. Just a final remark for my mom: The internet has had some success and there are people working on it!*

# About the reviewers

**Marijan Milovec** currently works as a software developer. He is highly ambitious and interested in software development, DevOps, and software architecture. He is also the lead organizer of the Google Developer Group Zagreb, which focuses on software development, software architecture, artificial intelligence, machine learning, deep learning, data science, DevOps, Docker, Kubernetes, Google Cloud, and more.

**Sathish VJ** is a software architect, technology trainer, and angel investor. He has all the open certifications on Google Cloud, including Google Cloud Machine Learning Engineer, and is also a Google Cloud Authorized Trainer. He runs a YouTube channel, called AwesomeGCP, where he teaches people how to apply Google Cloud to their projects and prepare for certifications.

**Sharmistha Chatterjee** is a data science evangelist with 15+ years of professional experience in the field of machine learning (AI research and productionizing scalable solutions) and cloud applications. She has worked in both Fortune 500 companies, as well as in very early-stage startups. She is currently working as a Senior Manager of Data Sciences at Publicis Sapient where she leads the digital transformation of clients across industry verticals. She is an active blogger, an international speaker at various tech conferences, and 2X Google Developer Expert in Machine Learning and Google Cloud. She is also the Hackernoon Tech award winner for 2020, been listed as 40 under 40. Data Scientist by AIM and '21 tech trailblazers 2021 by Google.

# Table of Contents

# 3
# Introducing BigQuery Syntax

# Section 2: Deep Learning Networks

# 4
# Predicting Numerical Values with Linear Regression

# 5
# Predicting Boolean Values Using Binary Logistic Regression

# 6
# Classifying Trees with Multiclass Logistic Regression

# Section 3: Advanced Models with BigQuery ML

# 7
# Clustering Using the K-Means Algorithm

# 8

# Forecasting Using Time Series

# 9

# Suggesting the Right Product by Using Matrix Factorization

# 10
## Predicting Boolean Values Using XGBoost

# 11
## Implementing Deep Neural Networks

# Section 4: Further Extending Your ML Capabilities with GCP

# 12
## Using BigQuery ML with AI Notebooks

# 13
## Running TensorFlow Models with BigQuery ML

# 14
## BigQuery ML Tips and Best Practices

## Other Books You May Enjoy

## Index

# Preface

**Machine Learning** (**ML**) democratization is one of the fastest growing trends in the AI industry. In this field, BigQuery ML represents a fundamental tool for bridging the gap between data analysis and the implementation of innovative ML models. Through this book, you will have the opportunity to learn how to use BigQuery and BigQuery ML with an incremental approach that combines technical explanations with hands-on exercises. Following a brief introduction, you will immediately be able to build ML models on concrete use cases using BigQuery ML. By the end of this book, you will be able to choose the right ML algorithm to train, evaluate, and use advanced ML models.

## Who this book is for

This book is for data scientists, data analysts, data engineers, and anyone looking to get started with Google's BigQuery ML. You'll also find this book useful if you want to accelerate the development of ML models or if you are a business user who wants to apply ML in an easy way using SQL. A basic knowledge of BigQuery and SQL is required.

## What this book covers

*Chapter 1, Introduction to Google Cloud and BigQuery*, provides an overview of the Google Cloud Platform and of the BigQuery analytics database.

*Chapter 2, Setting Up Your GCP and BigQuery Environment*, explains the configuration of your first Google Cloud account, project, and BigQuery environment.

*Chapter 3, Introducing BigQuery Syntax*, covers the main SQL operations for working on BigQuery.

*Chapter 4, Predicting Numerical Values with Linear Regression*, explains the development of a linear regression ML model to predict the trip durations of a bike rental service.

*Chapter 5, Predicting Boolean Values Using Binary Logistic*, explains the implementation of a binary logistic regression ML model to predict the behavior of a taxi company's customers.

*Chapter 6, Classifying Trees with Multiclass Logistic Regression*, explains the development of a multiclass logistic ML algorithm to automatically classify species of trees according to their natural characteristics.

*Chapter 7, Clustering Using the K-Means Algorithm*, covers the implementation of a clustering system to identify the best-performing drivers in a taxi company.

*Chapter 8, Forecasting Using Time Series*, outlines the design and implementation of a forecasting tool to predict and present the sales of specific products.

*Chapter 9, Suggesting the Right Product by Using Matrix Factorization*, explains how to build a recommendation engine, using the matrix factorization algorithm, that suggests the best product to each customer.

*Chapter 10, Predicting Boolean Values Using XGBoost*, covers the implementation of a boosted tree ML model to predict the behavior of a taxi company's customers.

*Chapter 11, Implementing Deep Neural Networks*, covers the design and implementation of a **Deep Neural Network** (**DNN**) to predict the trip durations of a bike rental service.

*Chapter 12, Using BigQuery ML with AI Notebooks*, explains how AI Platform Notebooks can be integrated with BigQuery ML to develop and share ML models.

*Chapter 13, Running TensorFlow Models with BigQuery ML*, explains how BigQuery ML and TensorFlow can work together.

*Chapter 14, BigQuery ML Tips and Best Practices*, covers ML best practices and tips that can be applied during the development of a BigQuery ML model.

# To get the most out of this book

You will need to have a basic knowledge of SQL syntax and some experience of using databases.

A knowledge of the fundamentals of ML is not mandatory but is advised.

| Software/hardware covered in the book | OS requirements |
| --- | --- |
| Google Cloud Platform | Windows/macOS/Linux |
| Google BigQuery | |
| Google AI Platform Notebooks | |

If you are using the digital version of this book, we advise you to type the code yourself or access the code via the GitHub repository (link available in the next section). Doing so will help you to avoid any potential errors related to the copying and pasting of code.

# Download the example code files

You can download the example code files for this book from GitHub at `https://github.com/PacktPublishing/Machine-Learning-with-BigQuery-ML`. In case there's an update to the code, it will be updated on the existing GitHub repository.

We also have other code bundles from our rich catalog of books and videos available at `https://github.com/PacktPublishing/`. Check them out!

# Code in Action

Code in Action videos for this book can be viewed at `https://bit.ly/3f11XbU`.

# Download the color images

We also provide a PDF file that has color images of the screenshots/diagrams used in this book. You can download it here: `https://static.packt-cdn.com/downloads/9781800560307_ColorImages.pdf`.

# Conventions used

There are a number of text conventions used throughout this book.

`Code in text`: Indicates code words in text, database table names, folder names, filenames, file extensions, pathnames, dummy URLs, user input, and Twitter handles. Here is an example: "Sort the results of a query according to a specific list of fields with the ORDER BY clause."

A block of code is set as follows:

```
UPDATE
    `bigqueryml-packt.03_bigquery_syntax.first_table`
SET
    description= 'This is my updated description'
WHERE
    id_key=1;
```

**Bold**: Indicates a new term, an important word, or words that you see on screen. For example, words in menus or dialog boxes appear in the text like this. Here is an example: "BigQuery supports two different SQL dialects: **standard SQL** and **legacy SQL**."

> **Tips or important notes**
> Appear like this.

# Get in touch

Feedback from our readers is always welcome.

**General feedback**: If you have questions about any aspect of this book, mention the book title in the subject of your message and email us at customercare@packtpub.com.

**Errata**: Although we have taken every care to ensure the accuracy of our content, mistakes do happen. If you have found a mistake in this book, we would be grateful if you would report this to us. Please visit www.packtpub.com/support/errata, selecting your book, clicking on the Errata Submission Form link, and entering the details.

**Piracy**: If you come across any illegal copies of our works in any form on the internet, we would be grateful if you would provide us with the location address or website name. Please contact us at copyright@packt.com with a link to the material.

**If you are interested in becoming an author**: If there is a topic that you have expertise in, and you are interested in either writing or contributing to a book, please visit authors.packtpub.com.

# Reviews

Please leave a review. Once you have read and used this book, why not leave a review on the site that you purchased it from? Potential readers can then see and use your unbiased opinion to make purchase decisions, we at Packt can understand what you think about our products, and our authors can see your feedback on their book. Thank you!

For more information about Packt, please visit packt.com.

# Section 1: Introduction and Environment Setup

This section provides an introduction to machine learning and an overview of the technical tools that will be used in the next sections of the book: Google Cloud Platform, BigQuery, and BigQuery ML, as well as the SQL syntax related to it.

This section comprises the following chapters:

- *Chapter 1, Introduction to Google Cloud and BigQuery*
- *Chapter 2, Setting Up Your GCP and BigQuery Environment*
- *Chapter 3, Introducing BigQuery Syntax*

# 1
# Introduction to Google Cloud and BigQuery

The adoption of the public cloud enables companies and users to access innovative and cost-effective technologies. This is particularly valuable in the big data and **Artificial Intelligence** (**AI**) areas, where new solutions are providing possibilities that seemed impossible to achieve with on-premises systems only a few years ago. In order to be effective in the day-to-day business of a company, the new AI capabilities need to be shared between different roles and not concentrated only with technicians. Most cloud providers are currently addressing the challenge of democratizing AI across different departments and employees with different skills.

In this context, **Google Cloud** provides several services to accelerate the processing of large amounts of data and build **Machine Learning** (**ML**) applications that can make better decisions.

In this chapter, we'll gradually introduce the main concepts that will be useful in the upcoming hands-on activities. Using an incremental approach, we'll go through the following topics:

- Introducing Google Cloud Platform
- Exploring AI and ML services on GCP
- Introducing BigQuery
- Discovering BigQuery ML
- Understanding BigQuery pricing

# Introducing Google Cloud Platform

Starting from 1998 with the launch of **Google Search**, Google has developed one of the largest and most powerful IT infrastructures in the world. Today, this infrastructure is used by billions of users to use services such as **Gmail**, **YouTube**, **Google Photo**, and **Maps**. After 10 years, in 2008, Google decided to open its network and IT infrastructure to business customers, taking an infrastructure that was initially developed for consumer applications to public service and launching **Google Cloud Platform** (**GCP**).

The 90+ services that Google currently provides to large enterprises and small- and medium-sized businesses cover the following categories:

- **Compute**: Used to support workloads or applications with virtual machines such as Google Compute Engine, containers with Google Kubernetes Engine, or platforms such as AppEngine.

- **Storage and databases**: Used to store datasets and objects in an easy and convenient way. Some examples are Google Cloud Storage, Cloud SQL, and Spanner.

- **Networking**: Used to easily connect different locations and data centers across the globe with **Virtual Private Clouds** (**VPCs**), firewalls, and fully managed global routers.

- **Big data**: Used to store and process large amounts of information in a structured, semi-structured, or unstructured format. Among these services are Google DataProc, the Hadoop services offered by GCP, and BigQuery, which is the main focus of this book.

- **AI and machine learning**: This product area provides various tools for different kinds of users, enabling them to leverage AI and ML in their everyday business. Some examples are TensorFlow, AutoML, Vision APIs, and BigQuery ML, the main focus of this book.

- **Identity, security, and management tools**: This area includes all the services that are necessary to prevent unauthorized access, ensure security, and monitor all other cloud infrastructure. Identity Access Management, Key Management Service, Cloud Logging, and Cloud Audit Logs are just some of these tools.

- **Internet of Things** (**IoT**): Used to connect plants, vehicles, or any other objects to the GCP infrastructure, enabling the development of modern IoT use cases. The core component of this area is Google IoT Core.

- **API management**: Tools to expose services to customers and partners through REST APIs, providing the ability to fully leverage the benefits of interconnectivity. In this pillar, Google Apigee is one of the most famous products and is recognized as the leader of this market segment.

- **Productivity**: Used to improve productivity and collaboration for all companies that want to start working with Google and embracing its way of doing business through the powerful tools of Google Workplace (previously GSuite).

## Interacting with GCP

All the services just mentioned can be accessed through four different interfaces:

- **Google Cloud Console**: The web-based user interface of GCP, easily accessible from compatible web browsers such as Google Chrome, Edge, or Firefox. For the hands-on exercises in this book, we'll mainly use Google Cloud Console:

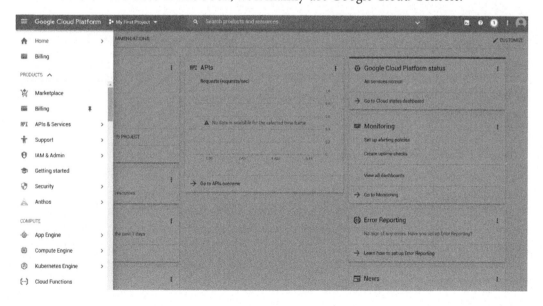

Figure 1.1 – Screenshot of Google Cloud Console

- **Google Cloud SDK**: The client SDK can be installed in order to interact with GCP services through the command line. It can be very useful to automate tasks and operations by scheduling them into scripts.
- **Client libraries**: The SDK also includes some client libraries to interact with GCP using the most common programming languages, such as Python, Java, and Node.js.
- **REST APIs**: Any task or operation performed on GCP can be executed by invoking a specific REST API from any compatible software.

Now that we've learned how to interact with GCP, let's discover how GCP is different from other cloud providers.

# Discovering GCP's key differentiators

GCP is not the only public cloud provider on the market. Other companies have embarked on this kind of business, for example, with **Amazon Web Services** (**AWS**), **Microsoft Azure**, **IBM**, and **Oracle**. For this reason, before we get too deep into this book, it could be valuable to understand how GCP is different from the other offerings in the cloud market.

Each cloud provider has its own mission, strategy, history, and strengths. Let's take a look at why Google Cloud can be considered different from all the other cloud providers.

## Security

Google provides an end-to-end security model for its data centers across the globe, using customized hardware developed and used by Google, and application encryption is enabled by default. The security best practices adopted by Google for GCP are the same as those developed to run applications with more than 1 billion users, such as Gmail and Google Maps.

## Global network and infrastructure

At the time of writing, Google's infrastructure is available in 24 different regions, 74 availability zones, and 144 network edge locations, enabling customers to connect to Google's network and ensuring the best experience in terms of bandwidth, network latency, and security. This network allows GCP users to move data across different regions without leaving Google's proprietary network, minimizing the risk of sending information across the public internet. As of today, it is estimated that about 40% of internet traffic goes through Google's proprietary network.

In the following figure, we can see how GCP regions are distributed across the globe:

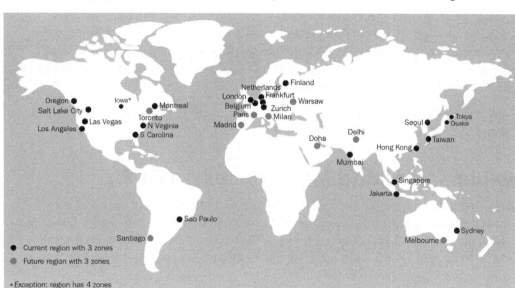

Figure 1.2 – A map of Google's global availability

The latest version of the map can be seen at the following URL: `https://cloud.google.com/about/locations`.

## Serverless and fully managed approach

Google provides a lot of fully managed and serverless services to allow its customers to focus on high-value activities rather than maintenance operations. A great example is BigQuery, the serverless data warehouse that will be introduced in the next section of this chapter.

## Environmental sustainability

100% of the energy used for Google's data centers comes from renewable energy sources. Furthermore, Google has committed to being the first major company to operate carbon-free for all its operations, such as its data centers and campuses, by 2030.

## Pervasive AI

Google is a pioneer of the AI industry and is leveraging AI and ML to improve its consumer products, such as Google Photos, but also to improve the performance and efficiency of its data centers. All of Google's expertise in terms of AI and ML can be leveraged by customers through adopting GCP services such as AutoML and BigQuery ML. That will be the main focus of this book.

Now that we have discussed some of the key elements of GCP as a service, let's look at AI and ML more specifically.

# Exploring AI and ML services on GCP

Before we get too deep into our look at all of the AI and ML tools of GCP, it is very important to remember that Google is an AI company and embeds AI and ML features within many of its other products, providing the best user experience to its customers. Simply looking at Google's products, we can easily perceive how AI can be a key asset for a business. Some examples follow:

- Gmail Smart Reply allows users to quickly reply to emails, providing meaningful suggestions according to the context of the conversation.

- Google Maps is able to precisely predict our time of arrival when we move from one place to another by combining different data sources.

- Google Translate provides translation services for more than one hundred languages.

- YouTube and the Google Play Store are able to recommend the best video to watch or the most useful mobile application to install according to user preferences.

- Google Photos recognizes people, animals, and places in our pictures, simplifying the job of archiving and organizing our photos.

Google proves that leveraging AI and ML capabilities in our business opens new opportunities for us, increases our revenue, saves money and time, and provides better experiences to our customers.

To better understand the richness of the GCP portfolio in terms of AI and ML services, it is important to emphasize that GCP services are able to address all the needs that emerge in a typical life cycle of an ML model:

1. Ingestion and preparation of the datasets

2. Building and training of the model

3. Evaluation and validation

4. Deployment

5. Maintenance and further improvements of the model

In the following figure, you can see the entire AI and ML GCP portfolio:

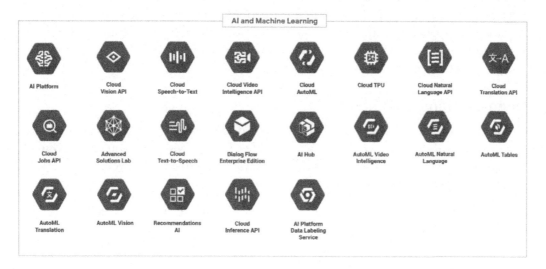

Figure 1.3 – GCP AI and ML services represented by their icons

Each one of the previously mentioned five stages can be fully managed by the user or delegated to the automation capabilities of GCP, according to the customer's needs and skills. For this reason, it is possible to divide the AI and ML services provided by GCP into three subcategories:

- **Core platform services**

- **AI Applications**

- **Solutions**

For each of these subcategories, we'll go through the most important services currently available and some typical users that could benefit from them.

# Core platform services

The core AI and ML services are the most granular items that a customer can use on GCP to develop AI and ML use cases. They provide the most control and flexibility to their users in exchange for less automation; users will also need to have more expertise in ML.

## Processing units (CPU, GPU, and TPU)

With a traditional **Infrastructure-as-a-Service** (**IaaS**) approach, developers can equip their Google Compute Engine instances with powerful processing units to accelerate the training phases of ML models that might otherwise take a long time to run, particularly if complex contexts or large amounts of data need to be processed. Beyond the **Central Processing Units** (**CPUs**) that are available on our laptops, GCP offers the use of high-performance **Graphical Processing Units** (**GPUs**) made by Nvidia and available in the cloud to speed up computationally heavy jobs. Beyond that, there are **Tensor Processing Units** (**TPUs**), which are specifically designed to support ML workloads and perform matrix calculations.

## Deep Learning VM Image

One of the biggest challenges for data scientists is quickly provisioning environments to develop their ML models. For this reason, Google Cloud provides pre-configured **Google Compute Engine** (**GCE**) images that can be easily provisioned with a pre-built set of components and libraries dedicated to ML.

In the following screenshot, you can see how these **Virtual Machines** (**VMs**) are presented in the GCP marketplace:

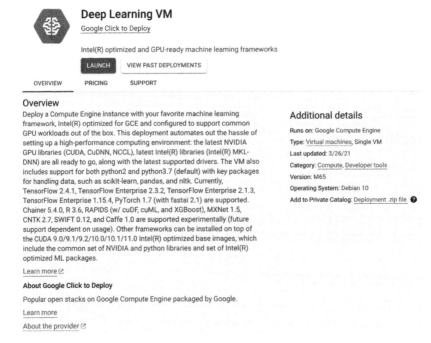

Figure 1.4 – Deep Learning VM in the GCP marketplace

**Deep Learning VM Image** is also optimized for ML workloads and is already pre-configured to use GPUs. When a GCE image is provisioned from the GCP marketplace, it is already configured with the most common ML frameworks and programming languages, such as Python, TensorFlow, scikit-learn, and others. This allows data scientists to focus on the development of the model rather than on the provisioning and configuration of the development environment.

## TensorFlow

**TensorFlow** is an open source framework for math, statistics, and ML. It was launched by Google Brain for internal use at Google and then released under the Apache License 2.0. It is still the core of the most successful Google products. The framework natively supports Python but can be used also with other programming languages such as Java, C++, and Go. It requires ML expertise, but it allows users to achieve great results in terms of customization and flexibility to develop the best ML model.

## AI Platform

**AI Platform** is an integrated service of GCP that provides serverless tools to train, evaluate, deploy, and maintain ML models. With this service, data scientists are able to focus only on their code, simplifying all the side activities of ML development, such as provisioning, maintenance, and scalability.

## AI Platform Notebooks

AI Platform Notebooks is a fully managed service that provides data scientists with a **JupyterLab** environment already integrated and connected with all other GCP resources. Similar to Deep Learning VM Image, **AI Platform Notebooks** instances come pre-configured with the latest versions of the AI and ML frameworks and allow you to develop an ML model with diagrams and written explanations.

All the services described so far require good knowledge of ML and proven experience in hand-coding with the most common programming languages. The core platform services address the needs of data scientists and ML engineers who need full control over and flexibility with the solutions that they're building and who already have strong technical skills.

# Building blocks

On top of the core platform services, Google Cloud provides pre-built components that can be used to accelerate the development of new ML use cases. This category encompasses the following aspects:

## AutoML

Unlike the services outlined in the previous section, **AutoML** offers the ability to build ML models even if you have limited expertise in the field. It leverages Google's ML capabilities and allows users to provide their data to train customized versions of algorithms already developed by Google. AutoML currently provides the ability to train models for images (**AutoML Vision**), video (**AutoML Video Intelligence**), free text (**AutoML Natural Language**), translation (AutoML Translation), and structured data (**AutoML Tables**). When the ML model is trained and ready to use, it is automatically deployed and made available through a REST endpoint.

## Pre-built APIs

Google Cloud provides pre-built APIs that leverage ML technology under the surface but are already trained and ready to use. The APIs are exposed through a standard REST interface that can be easily integrated into applications to work with images (**Vision API**), videos (**Video API**), free text (**Natural Language API**), translations (**Translation API**), e-commerce data (**Recommendations AI**), and conversational scenarios (**Speech-to-Text API**, **Text-to-Speech API**, and **Dialogflow**). Using a pre-built ML API is the best choice for general-purpose applications where generic training datasets can be used.

## BigQuery ML

As **BigQuery ML** will be discussed in detail in the following sections of this chapter, for the moment you just need to know that this component enables users to build ML models with SQL language, using structured data stored in BigQuery and a list of supported algorithms.

None of the building blocks described here requires any specific knowledge of ML or any proven coding experience with programming languages. In fact, these services are intended for developers or business analysts who are not very familiar with ML but want to start using it quickly and with little effort. On the other hand, a data scientist with ML expertise can also leverage the building blocks to accelerate the development of a model, reducing the time to market of a solution.

To see a summary of the building blocks, their usage, and their target users, let's take a look at the following table:

| Building Block | Training Dataset | Algorithm | Target Users |
|---|---|---|---|
| AutoML | Your data | Google's algorithms | Business analysts with no coding skills |
| Pre-Built APIs | Google's data | Google's algorithms | Developers with no ML skills |
| BigQuery ML | Your data | Choice among Google's algorithms | Business analysts with SQL skills |

Figure 1.5 – Building blocks summary table

Now that we've learned the basics of building blocks, let's take a look at the solutions offered by GCP.

# Solutions

Following the incremental approach, building blocks and core platform services are also bundled to provide out-of-the-box solutions. These pre-built modules can be adopted by companies and immediately used to improve their business. These solutions are covered in this section.

## AI Hub

Google Cloud's **AI Hub** acts as a marketplace for AI components. It can be used in public mode to share and use assets developed by the community, which actively works on GCP, or it can be used privately to share ML assets inside your company. The goal of this service is to simplify the sharing of valuable assets across different users, favoring re-use and accelerating the deployment of new use cases.

In the following screenshot, you can see AI Hub's home page:

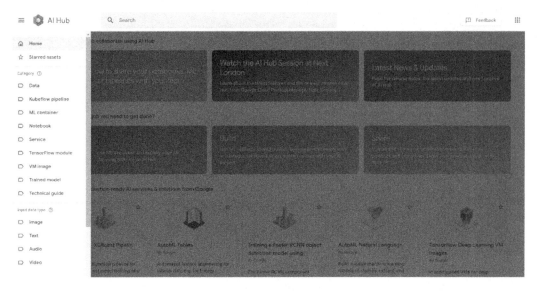

Figure 1.6 – Screenshot of AI Hub on GCP

Now that we've understood the role of AI Hub, let's look at Cloud Talent Solution.

## Cloud Talent Solution

Cloud Talent Solution is basically a solution for HR offices that improves the candidate discovery and hiring processes using AI. We will not go any further with the description of this solution, but there will be a link in the *Further resources* section at the end of this chapter.

## Contact Center AI

**Contact Center AI** is a solution that can be used to improve the effectiveness of the customer experience with a contact center powered by AI and automation. The solution is based on Dialogflow and the Text-to-Speech and Speech-to-Text APIs.

## Document AI

This solution is focused on document processing to extract relevant information and streamline business processes that usually require manual effort. The solution is able to parse PDF files, images, and handwritten text to convert this information into a digitally structured format, making them accessible and researchable.

As can be easily seen from their descriptions, the AI solutions provided by Google are more business-oriented and designed to solve specific challenges. They can be configured and customized but are basically dedicated to business users.

Before going on, let's take a look at the following table, which summarizes the concepts explained in this section and provides a clear overview of the different AI and ML service categories:

| AI and ML Category | Available Products | Target Users | Technical Skills Required |
|---|---|---|---|
| Core platform services | CPU, GPU, TPU Deep Learning VM, TensorFlow, AI Platform, and AI Platform Notebooks | Data scientists | – Proven ML expertise<br>– Programming |
| Building blocks | BigQuery ML, AutoML, and pre – built APIs | Business analysts and developers | – No coding skills apart from API integration<br>– SQL language for BigQuery ML |
| Solutions | Cloud Talent Solution, Contact Center AI and Document AI | Business users | No technical skills is required |

Figure 1.7 – Summary of GCP AI and ML services

Tip

When you need to develop a new use case, we recommend using pre-built solutions and building blocks before trying to reinvent the wheel. If a building block already satisfies all the requirements of your use case, it can be extremely valuable to use it. It will save time and effort during the development and maintenance phases. Start considering the use of core services only if the use case is complex or so particular that it cannot be addressed with building blocks or solutions.

As we've seen in this section, GCP's AI and ML services are extensive. Now, let's take a closer look at the main topic of this book: Google BigQuery.

# Introducing BigQuery

Google BigQuery is a highly scalable, serverless, distributed data warehouse technology built internally by Google in 2006 and then released for public use on GCP in 2010. Thanks to its architecture, it can store petabytes of data and query them with high performance and on-demand scaling. Due to its serverless nature, users who store and query data on BigQuery don't have to manage the underlying infrastructure and can focus on implementing the logic that brings the business value, saving time and resources.

BigQuery is currently used by many large enterprises that leverage it to make data-driven decisions, including Twitter, The Home Depot, and Dow Jones.

# BigQuery architecture

BigQuery has a distributed architecture running on thousands of nodes across Google's data centers. Your datasets are not stored in a unique server but are chunked and replicated across different regions to guarantee maximum performance and availability.

The storage and compute layers are fully decoupled in BigQuery. This means that the query engine runs on different servers from the servers where the data is stored. This feature enables BigQuery to provide great scalability both in terms of data volume and query execution. This decoupled paradigm is only possible thanks to Google's Petabit network, which moves data very quickly from one server to another, leveraging Google's proprietary fiber cables across the globe.

Now let's look deeper into how BigQuery manages storage and the compute engine.

## Storage layer

Unlike traditional data warehouses, BigQuery stores data in columnar format rather than in row format. This approach enables you to do the following:

- Achieve a better compression ratio for each column, because the data in a column is typically homogeneous and simpler to compress.

- Reduce the amount of data to read and get the best possible performance for data warehouse use cases that are usually based on a small selection of columns in a table and aggregating operations such as sums, average, and maximum.

All the data is stored in Google's proprietary distributed filesystem named Google File System (codename Colossus). The distribution of the data allows it to guarantee faster I/O performance and better availability of data in the case of failures. Google File System is based on two different server types:

- **Master servers:** Nodes that don't store data but are responsible for managing the metadata of each file, such as the location and available number of replicas of each chunk that compose a file.

- **Chunk servers:** Nodes that actually store the chunks of files that are replicated across different servers.

In the following diagram, you can see how Google File System manages data:

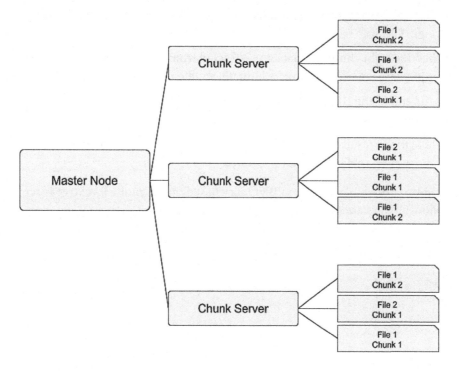

Figure 1.8 – Google File System (Colossus) storage strategy

Now that we've learned how BigQuery handles large volumes of data, let's see how this data can be accessed by the compute layer.

## Compute (query) layer

Fully decoupled from storage, the compute layer is responsible for receiving query statements from BigQuery users and executing them in the fastest way. The query engine is based on Dremel, a technology developed by Google and then published in a paper in 2010. This engine leverages a multi-level tree architecture:

1.  The root node of the tree receives the query to execute.

2.  The root node splits and distributes the query to other intermediate nodes named mixers.

3.  Mixer nodes have the task of rewriting queries before passing them to the leaf nodes or to other intermediate mixer nodes.

4.  Leaf nodes are responsible for parallelizing the reading of the chunks of data from Google File System.

5.  When the right chunks of data are extracted from the filesystem, leaf nodes perform computations on the data and eventually shuffle them across other leaf nodes.

6.  At the end of the computation, each leaf node produces a result that is returned to the parent node.

7.  When all the results are returned to the root node, the outcome of the query is sent to the user or application that requested the execution.

The execution process of a query on BigQuery based on the multi-level tree is represented in the following diagram:

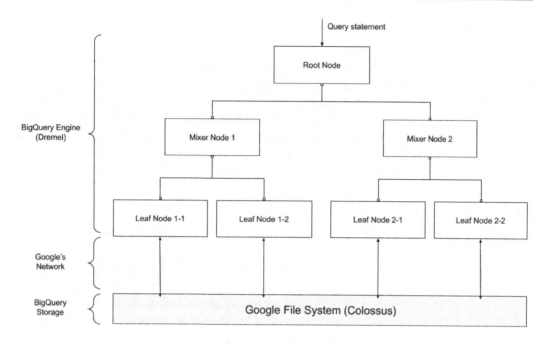

Figure 1.9 – The BigQuery engine is a multi-level tree

Each node provides a number of processing units called BigQuery slots to execute the business logic of the query. A BigQuery slot can be considered a virtual CPU on a Dremel node. The calculation of the slots needed to perform a specific query is automatically managed by BigQuery depending on the complexity of the query and the impacted data volumes.

# BigQuery's advantages over traditional data warehouses

Now that we've learned about the technical architecture underneath BigQuery, let's take a look at how this architecture translates into benefits for the enterprises that use it to become data-driven companies compared to other traditional on-premises data warehouses.

## Serverless

As we have mentioned, BigQuery has a serverless architecture that saves users from having to manage not only the provisioning and maintenance of the servers but also all the maintenance operations related to the upgrading and patching of the operative system and of the database software that supports the functioning of the data warehouse. Thanks to the serverless approach, the user can easily start ingesting data into BigQuery and using it without having to perform capacity planning or any hardware and software provisioning upfront. This is particularly important for prototyping and to enable a fail-fast approach that favors a culture of innovation and experimentation.

## Scalability

It doesn't matter if you need to store megabytes of data or petabytes; BigQuery can provide you with maximum flexibility and scalability in terms of both data storage and processing. Thanks to its multi-tenant architecture, a small or medium-sized business can leverage the same innovative capabilities as the largest enterprises, or they can start with a small use case to scale later, according to business needs. Traditional data warehouse technologies leverage the same servers to store and compute. For this reason, they are not particularly suitable for unbalanced use cases, such as when large volumes of data storage are needed but high computing performance is not required, or vice versa. Thanks to its decoupled architecture, as we've seen in the previous section, BigQuery is designed to independently scale storage and compute power according to the user's actual requirements, reducing the total cost of ownership of the solution.

## Availability

Thanks to its resilient, distributed architecture, BigQuery is able to offer a **Service Level Agreement** (**SLA**) of monthly uptime percentage greater than 99.99%. This very high availability standard is granted by Google without any extra effort from the BigQuery users, who don't need to take care of high availability or disaster recovery strategies.

## Performances

The BigQuery engine offers the ability to query terabytes of data in seconds and petabytes in minutes. This kind of performance is very hard to achieve with a traditional on-premises data warehouse. Higher performance means getting insights faster, as well as processing large volumes of data that very often would be impossible to manage on-premises without huge hardware and software investments. To further improve performance, BigQuery offers the possibility of enabling BigQuery BI Engine. BigQuery BI Engine is an in-memory analytics layer that can be activated on top of BigQuery to execute queries faster, with sub-second latencies.

## Real-time

Traditional data warehouses are designed for long batch operations and are often unable to manage real-time workloads. BigQuery, however, provides a specific interface to ingest data in real time, making it immediately available for analysis. This feature opens up new possibilities to companies that want to accelerate their analytics and overcome the typical approach of data warehouses, which usually involves dealing with the business situation of the day before.

## Format flexibility

BigQuery stores files in a compressed and optimized format in Google File System but provides the option to load data in various formats that are typically used in data lake technologies. Users can load data into BigQuery using Avro, ORC, CSV, and JSON formats.

## Innovative capabilities

BigQuery offers two SQL extensions that are not available in traditional data warehouses:

- **BigQuery GIS**: Provides the ability to easily manage geospatial data with SQL statements to execute geographic calculations and operations

- **BigQuery ML**: Allows users to train, evaluate, and run ML models leveraging SQL language with no programming experience, accelerating the development of innovative use cases with ML

## Security

By default, BigQuery automatically encrypts and decrypts customer's data before storing it in Google File System. BigQuery is also responsible for managing and rotating the encryption and decryption keys. To further improve security, BigQuery provides the option to use **Customer-Managed Encryption Keys** (**CMEKs**). In this case, the keys are managed directly by the customer in Google Cloud Key Management System.

Unauthorized access and use of data can be prevented by setting the right roles in Google **Identity Access Management System** (**IAM**).

## Integration with other GCP services

One of the great benefits of using BigQuery is the native integration with a lot of other GCP services:

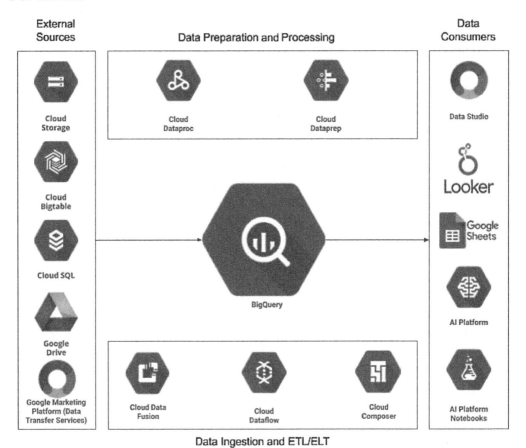

Figure 1.10 – BigQuery integration with other GCP services

As we can see in the preceding screenshot, Google BigQuery can read data from **Google Bigtable**, **Google Cloud Storage**, **Google Cloud SQL**, and **Google Drive** using external tables. This feature can simplify data ingestion into BigQuery from other databases, which can also be performed using ETL/ELT tools such as **Google Dataflow** and **Data Fusion**. When the datasets are stored in BigQuery, they can be accessed from other GCP components, such as **Google DataProc**, **DataPrep** for data processing and preparation, **Data Studio**, **Looker**, and **Google Sheets** for data visualization. BigQuery is integrated with AI Platform Notebooks to allow data scientists and engineers to easily access data from their Jupyter environments.

To summarize, bringing data into BigQuery opens a vast plethora of options that can be used according to the user's needs.

### Rich ecosystem of partners

Beyond the integration with other GCP services, Google's partners provide connectors and integrations with BigQuery, creating a rich data management ecosystem. Some examples include Informatica, Tableau, Fivetran, Talend, and Confluent.

### Public datasets

If you want to start from scratch using BigQuery, you can leverage existing public tables that are available from the **BigQuery Public Datasets Program**. The program contains interesting datasets coming from different industries and different countries about different topics. Some examples that we'll use in the next chapter to train our ML models include transactions from bike sharing services, open data on New York City, and records of taxi trips.

## Interacting with BigQuery

There are different ways to interact with BigQuery. They are:

- The BigQuery web UI in the Google Cloud Console, the graphical user interface accessible from web browsers, represents the easiest way to interact with BigQuery.

- The bq command line, available with the installation of the Google Cloud SDK. It can be used to automate jobs and commands by including them in scripts.

- BigQuery REST APIs. The API layer natively provided by BigQuery can be used to integrate this service with other applications.

- Client libraries to favor the use of the most common programming languages, such as C#, Go, Java, Node.js, PHP, Python, and Ruby.

- JDBC/ODBC drivers, developed by Google's partner, Magnitude Simba Driver, are available for Windows, macOS, and Linux systems.

- Third parties and Google's partners have developed BigQuery connectors for their applications, such as Tableau for business intelligence, Informatica, and Talend for data ingestion and integration.

For our purposes, we'll take a look at the BigQuery web UI available in Google Cloud Console that will be used in the coming chapters to develop with BigQuery ML.

In the following screenshot, you can see how the BigQuery UI appears in the GCP console:

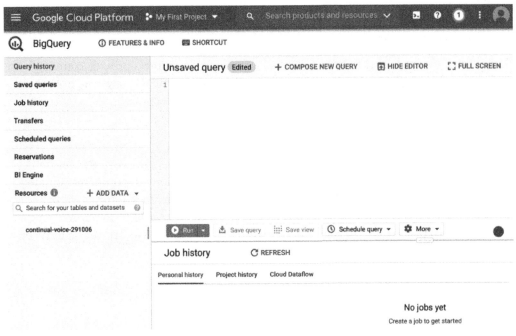

Figure 1.11 – BigQuery web and graphical user interface available in the GCP console

In the left column, the main BigQuery features are available and the datasets are listed and visible to the user. In this case, there is only one dataset.

The remaining part of the screen is occupied by the development canvas with the results and outcomes at the bottom. We'll learn how to use the BigQuery web UI in *Chapter 2, Setting Up Your GCP and BigQuery Environment*, when we'll create a GCP project and start using BigQuery.

## BigQuery data structures

BigQuery structures, such as tables, views, and ML models, are organized in datasets. Each dataset is a container for different structures and can be used to control access to underlying data structures. A dataset is directly linked to the following:

- A GCP project that hosts the dataset itself and is usually linked to the billing account where the storage cost is billed

- A geographic location (regional or multi-regional) that is defined at creation time and cannot be changed later

- A specific name assigned to the dataset that should be unique in the GCP project

In the following diagram, you can see an example of a hierarchy composed of projects, datasets, tables, and BigQuery ML models:

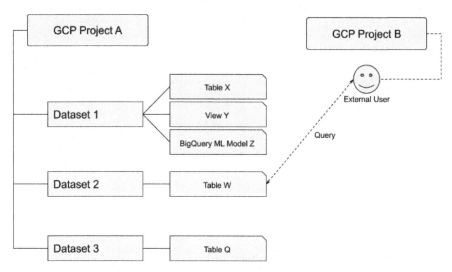

Figure 1.12 – BigQuery hierarchy: datasets, tables, views, and ML models

A dataset hosted in GCP, *Project A*, can also be queried by users linked to another GCP project, *Project B*, if the right permissions are set. In this case, the storage costs are charged to *Project A*, which hosts the dataset structures, while the compute costs are billed on the billing account related to *Project B*. This is exactly what will happen when we use BigQuery public datasets in future chapters for hands-on exercises.

> **Tip**
> Remember, your queries can only include tables that reside in the same region. In BigQuery, you cannot query tables that are stored in different geographic locations. If you want to execute queries on tables located in different regions, you need to export and import the data into a dataset in the same region, passing through Google Cloud Storage.

Now that we've learned the main characteristics of BigQuery, let's focus more specifically on the core of this book: BigQuery ML.

# Discovering BigQuery ML

Developing a new ML model can require a lot of effort and can be a time-consuming activity. It usually requires different skills and is a complex activity, especially in large enterprises. The typical journey of an ML model can be summarized with the following flow:

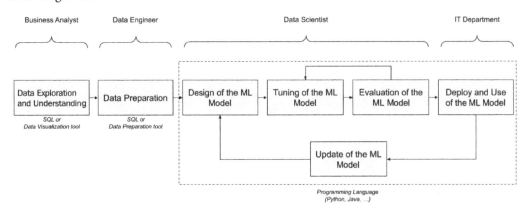

Figure 1.13 – An ML model's typical development life cycle

The first two steps involve preliminary raw data analyses and operations:

1.  In the **Data Exploration and Understanding** phase, the data engineer or data scientist takes a first look at the data, tries to understand the meaning of all the columns in the dataset, and then selects the fields to take into consideration for the new use case.

2.  During **Data Preparation**, the data engineer filters, aggregates, and cleans up the datasets, making them available and ready to use for the subsequent training phase.

After these two first stages, the actual ML developing process starts:

1.  Leveraging ML frameworks such as TensorFlow and programming languages such as Python, the data scientist will engage in the **Design the ML model** step, experimenting with different algorithms on the training dataset.

2.  When the right ML algorithm is selected, the data scientist performs the **Tuning of the ML model** step, applying feature engineering techniques and hyperparameter tuning to get better performance out of the ML model.

3.  When the model is ready, a final **Evaluation** step is executed on the evaluation dataset. This phase proves the effectiveness of the ML model on a new dataset that's different from the training one and eventually leads to further refinements of the asset.

4. After the development process, the ML model is generally deployed and used in a production environment with scalability and robustness requirements.

5. The ML model is also eventually updated in a subsequent stage due to different incoming data or to apply further improvements.

All of these steps require different skills and are based on the collaboration of different stakeholders, such as business analysts for data exploration and understanding, data engineers for data preparation, data scientists for the development of the ML model, and finally the IT department to make the model usable in a safe, robust, and scalable production environment.

BigQuery ML simplifies and accelerates the entire development process of a new ML model, allowing you to do the following:

- Design, train, evaluate, and serve the ML model, leveraging SQL and the existing skills in your company.

- Automate most of the tuning activities that are usually highly time-consuming to get an effective model.

- Ensure that you have a robust, scalable, and easy-to-use ML model, leveraging all the native features of BigQuery that we've already discussed in the *BigQuery's advantages over traditional data warehouses* section of this chapter.

In the following diagram, you can see the life cycle of an ML model that uses BigQuery ML:

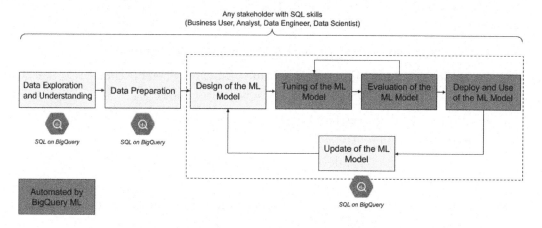

Figure 1.14 – An ML model's development life cycle with BigQuery ML

Now that we've learned the basics of BigQuery ML, let's take a look at the main benefits that it can bring.

# BigQuery ML benefits

BigQuery ML can bring both business and technical benefits during the life cycle of an ML model:

- Business users and data analysts can evolve from a traditional descriptive and reporting approach to a new predictive approach to take better decisions using their existing SQL skills.

- Technical users can benefit from the automation of BigQuery ML during the tuning phase of the model, using a unique, centralized tool that can accelerate the entire development process of an ML model.

- The development process is further sped up because the datasets required to build the ML model are already available to the right users and don't need to be moved from one data repository to another, which carries compliance and data duplication risks.

- The IT department does not need to manage the infrastructure to serve and use the ML model in a production environment because the BigQuery serverless architecture natively supports the model in a scalable, safe, and robust manner.

After our analysis of the benefits that BigQuery ML can bring, let's now see what the supported ML algorithms are.

# BigQuery ML algorithms

The list of ML algorithms supported by BigQuery ML is growing quickly. Currently, the following supervised ML techniques are currently supported:

- **Linear regression**: To forecast numerical values with a linear model

- **Binary logistic regression**: For classification use cases when the choice is between only two different options (Yes or No, 1 or 0, True or False)

- **Multiclass logistic regression**: For classification scenarios when the choice is between multiple options

- **Matrix factorization**: For developing recommendation engines based on past information

- **Time series**: To forecast business KPIs leveraging timeseries data from the past

- **Boosted tree**: For classification and regression use cases with XGBoost

- **AutoML table**: To leverage AutoML capabilities from the BigQuery SQL interface

- **Deep Neural Network (DNN)**: For developing TensorFlow models for classification or regression scenarios, avoiding any lines of code

When the training dataset doesn't contain labeled data, the learning is defined as unsupervised. BigQuery ML currently supports the following:

- **K-means clustering**: For data segmentation of similar objects (people, facts, events)

In addition to what is listed, BigQuery ML allows you to import and use pre-trained TensorFlow models using SQL statements.

# Understanding BigQuery pricing

In this section, the pricing model for BigQuery and BigQuery ML is explained. Since the pricing of GCP services is ever-evolving, we suggest that you consult `https://cloud. google.com/bigquery/pricing` to get the latest updates.

Let's look at the models for BigQuery.

## BigQuery pricing

BigQuery pricing is scalable according to the use of this technology. There are three main cost drivers:

- **Storage**: Price calculated on the volumes of data stored in BigQuery.
- **Compute**: Resources used to query, transform, and process the data or to train, evaluate, and use ML models.
- **Streaming**: Price calculated on the number of records that are ingested through the BigQuery streaming API.

## Storage

BigQuery storage costs are calculated based on the uncompressed size of your datasets. BigQuery offers two layers of storage:

- **Active**: All data stored in tables that have been inserted or updated in the last 90 days is considered active. At the time of writing, active storage is charged at $20.00 per terabyte per month.
- **Long-term**: All data stored in tables that have not been modified in the last 90 days is considered long-term storage. At the time of writing, long-term storage is charged at $10.00 per terabyte per month. The change to long-term storage is automatically applied by Google and does not require any action by the BigQuery user.

> **Tip**
> Thanks to BigQuery long-term storage, it is no longer necessary to transfer archived data to Google Cloud Storage to save money. You can keep your data online and accessible at a very low cost.

## Compute

BigQuery compute costs are calculated based on the volumes of data that are processed by the executed queries. The compute cost can vary according to the model that the customer has chosen:

- **On-demand**: This is the default option. In this case, the user is charged only for the resources that are actually consumed.

- **Flat rate**: This option can be enabled by users or companies that want to have a precise estimation of BigQuery costs and want to keep them stable over time. In this case, a reservation for a specific timeframe is needed and a fixed number of BigQuery slots are assigned to one or multiple GCP projects. As of October 2020, the minimum number of slots that can be reserved is 100 and the minimum time of commitment is 60 seconds. Currently, Google allows you to choose different flat rate options according to the actual requirements. This option can be enabled with a monthly, annual, or flex commitment. The flex option allows you to purchase BigQuery slots for short durations (a minimum of 60 seconds).

> **Tip**
> Keep in mind that you're not charged to store BigQuery public datasets: you pay only to access and query them. For this reason, using BigQuery public datasets can be a cost-effective way to perform tests on BigQuery, paying only for compute and not for storage.

## Streaming

Loading data into BigQuery is usually free, apart from the ingestion processes that happen through the BigQuery streaming API. As of October 2020, you will be charged $0.010 for every 200 MB ingested with this interface. Each row is treated as a minimum of 1 KB.

> **Tip**
>
> If your use case doesn't require you to ingest data in real time, we suggest you use the bulk loading mechanism to ingest data into BigQuery, which is always free of charge.

# BigQuery ML pricing

The pricing model of BigQuery ML is similar to that for BigQuery compute costs. As we saw in the previous section, customers can choose between the following options:

- On-demand (pay-as-you-go) pricing model
- Flat rate pricing model

If the customer has already chosen to activate flat rate mode with a fixed number of BigQuery slots available, BigQuery slots are also leveraged to train, evaluate, and run the BigQuery ML models.

If the customer is using the on-demand pricing model, it is necessary to split the BigQuery ML algorithms into two different categories:

- **External models**: This category includes boosted trees, DNNs, TensorFlow, and AutoML. These models are trained on other GCP services integrated with BigQuery and are charged differently.
- **Internal models**: This category includes all the remaining algorithms mentioned before that are trained directly on BigQuery.

At the time of writing, the pricing of internal models is based on the volumes of data processed during the main stages of the ML life cycle (training, evaluation, and prediction):

| Operation | Price |
| --- | --- |
| Training/Creation | $250.00 per TB processed |
| Evaluation or Prediction | $5.00 per TB processed |

Figure 1.15 – BigQuery ML pricing for internal ML models

The pricing of external models is based on the cost of the external AI Platform resources used for the training of the model plus an additional BigQuery ML fee applied on top:

| Operation | Price |
|---|---|
| Training/Creation | $5.00 per TB pre-processed and passed to the AI Platform component plus the cost of the AI Platform service used for training |
| Evaluation or Prediction | $5.00 per TB processed |

Figure 1.16 – BigQuery ML pricing for external ML models

Prices are always under review and subject to change on GCP. For this reason, we suggest consulting `https://cloud.google.com/bigquery-ml/pricing`.

# Free operations and free tiers

BigQuery offers a wide variety of operations free of charge, as well as free tiers to experiment with this technology at no cost.

The following operations are always free in BigQuery:

- Loading data
- Copying data (apart from the additional storage requested for the copy)
- Exporting data
- Deleting datasets, tables, views, partitions, or functions
- Any metadata operations
- Reading metadata tables and columns
- Creating or replacing **User-Defined Functions (UDFs)**

To encourage experimentation with BigQuery, every month a user has the ability to leverage a free budget of operations under a certain threshold, as seen in the following table:

| Resource | Monthly Free Tier |
|---|---|
| Storage | 10GB |
| Compute for Queries | 1TB |
| Compute for BigQuery ML internal model creation | 10GB |

Figure 1.17 – BigQuery ML free tiers

Now that we've seen the BigQuery free tiers that we can use, let's take a look at the pricing calculator.

## Pricing calculator

If you want to have a good estimation of the cost of using BigQuery with on-demand pricing, you can use the Google Cloud pricing calculator: `https://cloud.google.com/products/calculator`. The following screenshot shows the monthly cost of storing, ingesting through streaming, and processing the following data volumes:

- Uncompressed storage volume: 10 TB
- Volume of streaming inserts: 1 GB

- Data processed by queries: 150 TB:

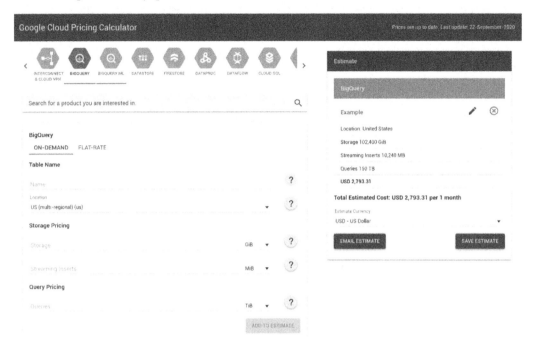

Figure 1.18 – BigQuery pricing calculator

You can use the pricing calculator to estimate the consumption of all the other GCP services to get a better understanding of your GCP costs.

# Summary

Throughout this first chapter, we've taken the first steps into learning what GCP offers, how it is different from other public cloud providers, and how Google is building on its ubiquitous applications such as Gmail and Google Maps to provide great services to companies via GCP.

We've also discovered that Google's proven experience in AI and ML, developed through the making of products such as Google Photos, also forms part of the services of GCP. Each AI and ML service can address various use cases and different types of users according to their skills and background. For example, most technical users, such as data scientists, can leverage TensorFlow to have great flexibility and control over their developed ML models, while business users can use Google's solutions to solve specific challenges with Document AI and Contact Center AI. The intermediate category is composed of AI and ML building blocks; these services can accelerate the development of new ML use cases or spread the usage of innovative techniques through a company.

One of these building blocks is BigQuery: its extension, BigQueryML, enables the development of ML models by leveraging existing SQL skills. The use of BigQuery ML can bring great benefits to companies that want to democratize ML, enabling a large segment of employees to participate by simplifying the heaviest and most time-consuming activities that usually require the involvement of different stakeholders, skills, and tools.

In the next chapter, we will get hands-on by creating a new Google Cloud project and accessing BigQuery for the first time.

# Further resources

- **Google Cloud products**: `https://cloud.google.com/products/`
- **GCP overview**: `https://cloud.google.com/docs/overview`
- **Why GCP is different**: `https://cloud.google.com/free/docs/what-makes-google-cloud-platform-different`
- **Google regions and locations**: `https://cloud.google.com/about/locations`
- **Google's sustainability program**: `https://sustainability.google/commitments/`
- **AI Hub**: `https://aihub.cloud.google.com/?hl=en`
- **Cloud Talent Solution**: `https://cloud.google.com/solutions/talent-solution?hl=en`
- **BigQuery technical architecture**: `https://cloud.google.com/files/BigQueryTechnicalWP.pdf`
- **BigQuery interfaces**: `https://cloud.google.com/bigquery/docs/interacting-with-bigquery`
- **BigQuery ML**: `https://cloud.google.com/bigquery-ml/docs`

# 2
# Setting Up Your GCP and BigQuery Environment

The first steps of using a new public cloud provider can be complex, and sometimes you might feel overwhelmed by all the services and options in front of you. Cloud vendors offer a vast variety of components and resources to solve different use cases. With this plethora of modules, it is not easy to decide which service to use. Fortunately, to create and run a **Google Cloud Platform** (**GCP**) project, you don't have to have specific technical skills or a large budget to invest. Regardless of whether you are a private user or an employee of a large company, GCP offers the possibility to use its cloud services simply by creating an account and a project on the platform. It is also possible to leverage a free trial to get credits and test products for a limited period of time.

The topics covered in this chapter will help to create a solid foundation for your technical environment, and the tasks covered should be performed only once. To avoid any kind of uncertainty and disorientation, in this chapter, you'll be taken step by step through the following activities:

- Creating your GCP account and project
- Activating BigQuery
- Discovering the BigQuery web UI
- Exploring BigQuery public datasets

# Technical requirements

This chapter requires you to have access to a web browser. To perform the steps described in this chapter, we suggest using one of the following:

- Google Chrome
- Firefox
- Microsoft Edge
- Microsoft Internet Explorer 11+
- Safari 8+ (Safari Private Browsing mode is not supported)

Now that you're ready with a supported web browser, let's dive into the creation of a new GCP account and project.

# Creating your GCP account and project

The first step to start using GCP is the creation of a new **GCP account** and a new **project**. A project is a container of multiple GCP resources, and it is usually accessed by users through their accounts. Examples of GCP resources include Google Compute Engine VMs, Google Cloud Storage buckets, App Engine instances, and BigQuery datasets. A GCP project is also linked to a billing account to which all of the costs of services consumption are charged. GCP objects can be organized hierarchically. Projects are the first level of the hierarchy and can be grouped into **folders**. Each folder can have another folder or an **organization** node as a parent. The organization is at the top of the GCP hierarchy and cannot have a parent.

In the following diagram, you can see a hierarchy composed of an organization node, two main folders, and two nested folders linked to three different GCP projects:

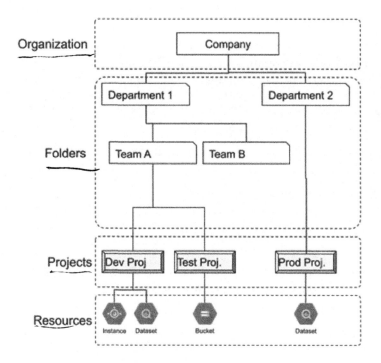

Figure 2.1 – GCP resource hierarchy composed of resources, projects, folders, and an organization

According to GCP best practices, it is suggested that you create different projects to separate different environments, such as **development**, **test**, **quality assurance**, and **production**. Folders are particularly useful to segregate workloads that belong to different departments or different teams within the same company. The creation of an organization node is not required but one can be used to group all the workloads of an entire company or legal entity. The organization and the folder nodes are used to assign uniform policies and permissions across the company's departments with a unique and centralized point of control.

> **Tip**
> To use GCP folders, the creation of an organization node is mandatory. If the organization node is not created, each project will be considered logically separated from the others and cannot be grouped into a folder.

For the hands-on exercises of this book, we'll simply create a GCP project. This is the only necessary item to organize all the BigQuery datasets that we will create throughout the chapters of the book.

Now that we've learned how GCP resources are organized, let's take a look at how to create a new **Google account**.

## Registering a GCP account

To start using GCP, we need at least one user. A user is a **member** configured in the **Identity and Access Management (IAM)** system. The goal of IAM is to grant the right access and permissions to the right members. GCP supports different types of members:

- **Google account**: Any person that may interact with GCP, identified by an email address, such as a Gmail account.

- **Service account**: A technical user, not directly linked to a human user. This is assigned to a GCP service to interact with and access other resources.

- **Google Workspace domain**: A user group created in Google's productivity suite Workspace. It includes multiple members identified by the same domain, such as `user1@companyxyz.com`, `user2@companyxyz.com`, and `user3@companyxyz.com`.

- **Cloud Identity domain**: Similar to the Google Workspace domain, with the only difference being that this group of users doesn't have access to Google's productivity suite.

- **Google group**: Represents a group of accounts. It is linked to an email alias and can be used to assign the same permissions and grants to multiple accounts.

For our purposes, we'll create a simple Google account using the free trial that is offered by Google and available at this address: `https://cloud.google.com/free`:

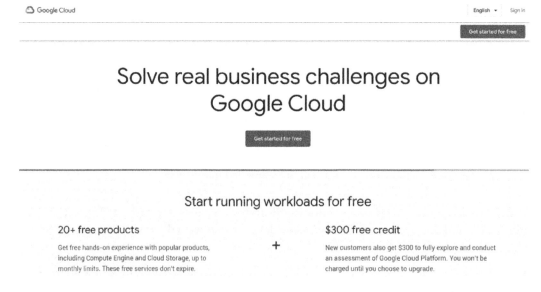

Figure 2.2 – Google Cloud web page to access the GCP free trial

This free option enables you to get started with GCP at no cost and offers the following:

- The possibility to leverage the free tiers of each GCP service, including BigQuery. This option has no expiration.

- A limited credit amount of $300 to overcome the limits of the free tiers or to use other services. This credit expires in 90 days.

If you haven't created a GCP project yet, start by selecting **Get started for free**, or click **Sign In** to access your existing GCP console. For educational purposes, we'll select **Get started for free** to show the entire process of account creation, as shown in the following screenshot:

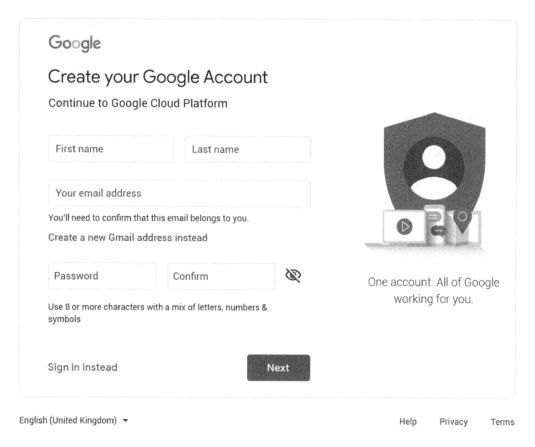

Figure 2.3 – Creation of a Google account for GCP

If you don't have an existing email address, you can directly create a Gmail account during the GCP registration process. For the account creation process, it is necessary to specify your first and last name, an existing or new email address, and a strong password to access GCP.

After accepting the privacy terms, you will be redirected to the GCP registration process, which is basically composed of two steps:

1.  In the first step, you need to select your country, read and agree to the terms of service, and then sign up to receive updates from Google and its partners. As shown on the right-hand side of *Figure 2.4*, the registration page summarizes the main conditions of the free trial:

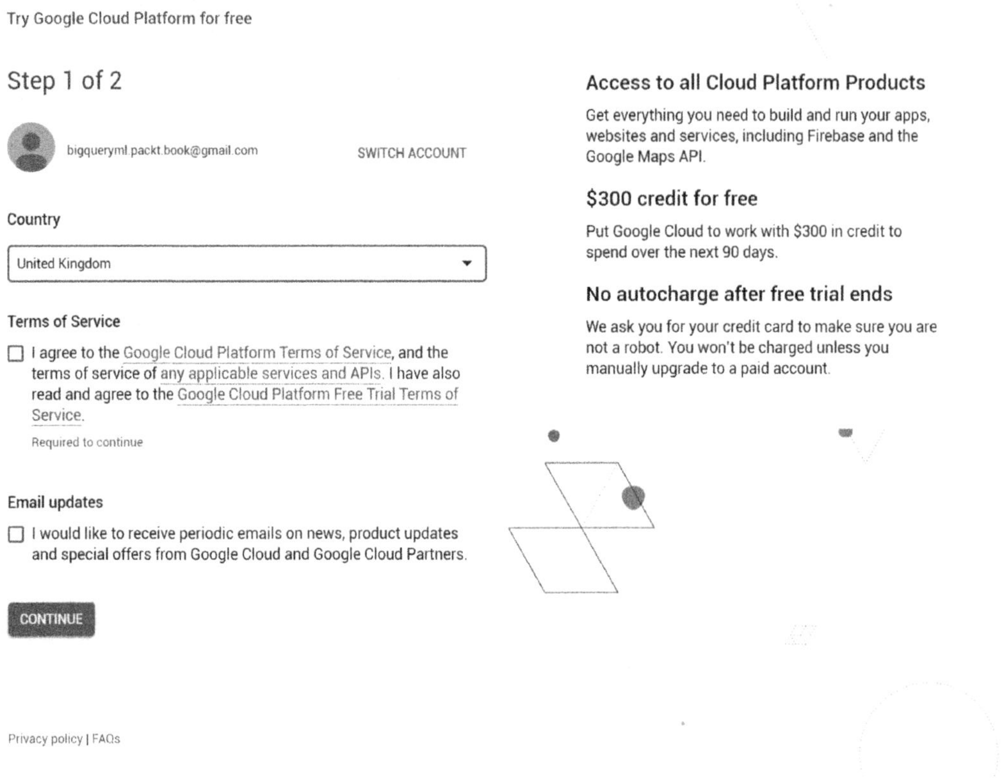

Try Google Cloud Platform for free

## Step 1 of 2

bigqueryml.packt.book@gmail.com                SWITCH ACCOUNT

**Country**

United Kingdom                                                    ▼

**Terms of Service**

☐ I agree to the Google Cloud Platform Terms of Service, and the
terms of service of any applicable services and APIs. I have also
read and agree to the Google Cloud Platform Free Trial Terms of
Service.
  Required to continue

**Email updates**

☐ I would like to receive periodic emails on news, product updates
and special offers from Google Cloud and Google Cloud Partners.

CONTINUE

### Access to all Cloud Platform Products

Get everything you need to build and run your apps,
websites and services, including Firebase and the
Google Maps API.

### $300 credit for free

Put Google Cloud to work with $300 in credit to
spend over the next 90 days.

### No autocharge after free trial ends

We ask you for your credit card to make sure you are
not a robot. You won't be charged unless you
manually upgrade to a paid account.

Privacy policy | FAQs

Figure 2.4 – First step of GCP account creation

2.  The second step requires you to provide all the information that is necessary for the billing of your GCP projects. This step asks for your billing address and a credit card to start using GCP:

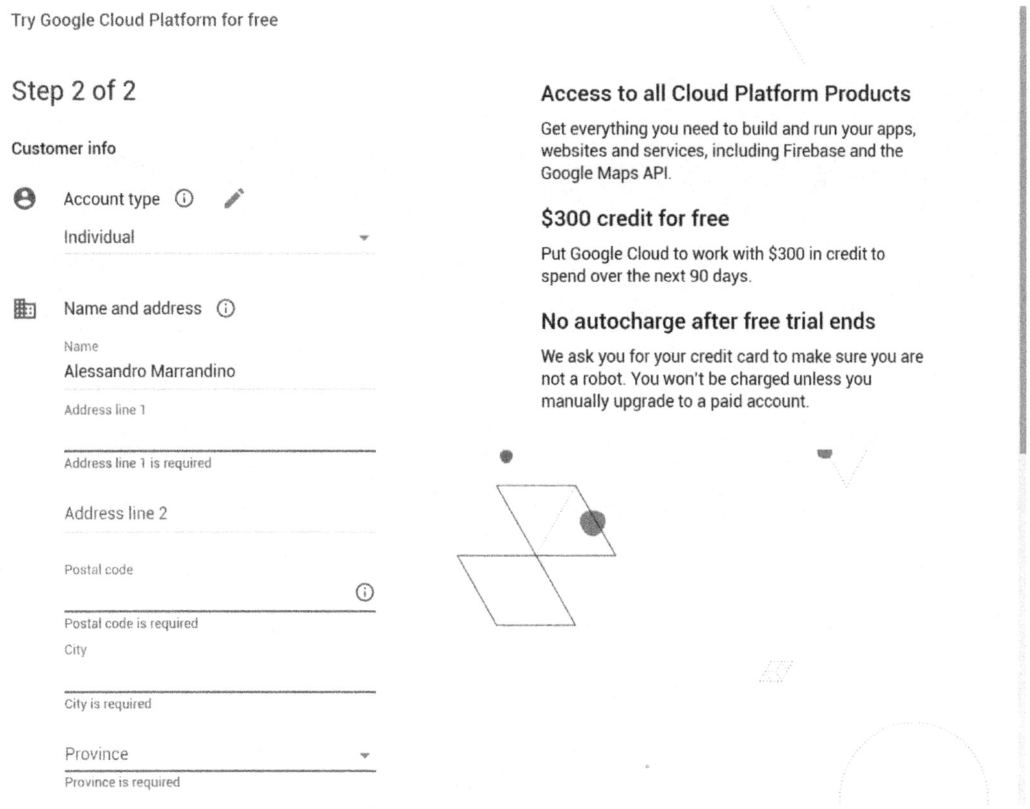

Try Google Cloud Platform for free

## Step 2 of 2

**Customer info**

👤 Account type ⓘ 🖊

Individual    ▾

🏢 Name and address ⓘ

Name
Alessandro Marrandino

Address line 1

Address line 1 is required

Address line 2

Postal code
ⓘ
Postal code is required

City

City is required

Province    ▾
Province is required

**Access to all Cloud Platform Products**

Get everything you need to build and run your apps, websites and services, including Firebase and the Google Maps API.

**$300 credit for free**

Put Google Cloud to work with $300 in credit to spend over the next 90 days.

**No autocharge after free trial ends**

We ask you for your credit card to make sure you are not a robot. You won't be charged unless you manually upgrade to a paid account.

Figure 2.5 – Details to provide to create a GCP account

3.  At the end of the process, select **Start my free trial**; you will be ready to access the home page of Google Cloud Console.

> **Tip**
> Although a credit card is required for the creation of a Google Cloud account, the credit card will not be used until you explicitly decide to upgrade the account from the free tier to the paid version.

Now that we've created our Google account and we have accessed Google Cloud Console for the first time, in the next section we'll explore the main features of this web interface.

# Exploring Google Cloud Console

Google Cloud Console allows users to access and use all the GCP resources using a graphical user interface.

In the following screenshot, you can see Google Cloud Console and its main sections:

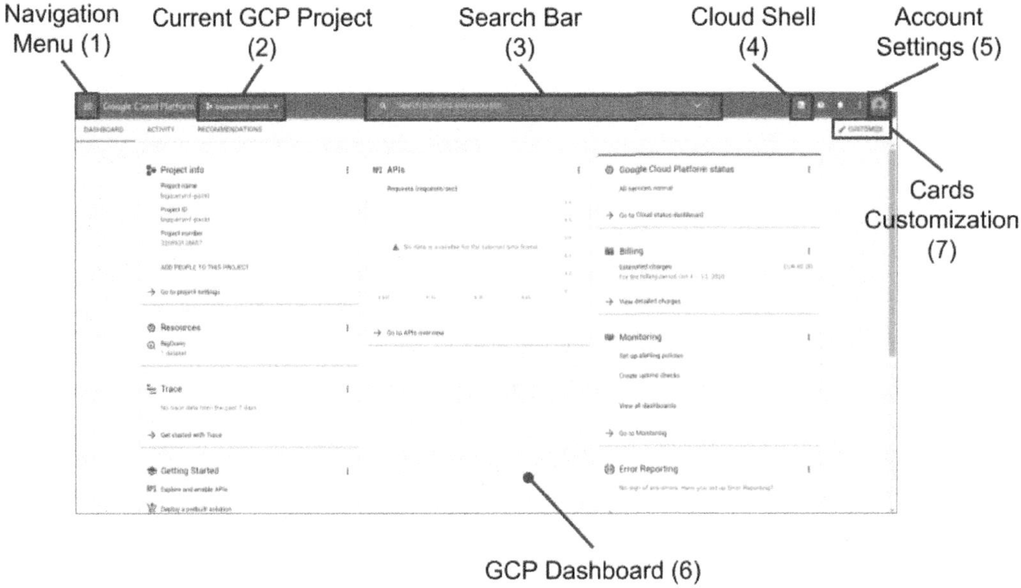

Figure 2.6 – Overview of the functionalities of Google Cloud Console

Starting from the top-left corner, you can see the hamburger button to access the navigation menu (1). This menu allows you to browse among all the GCP resources and select which service to use. Moving to the right, just after the GCP logo, you'll see the name of the current GCP project (2), which shows you which environment is currently in use. The search bar (3), positioned at the top of the page, allows us to look for specific resources or technologies in our project and can be considered an alternative to the navigation menu.

Focusing on the top-right corner, we can find **Cloud Shell** (4). This tool provides the possibility to use, for free, a Linux command line directly from Google Cloud Console. This Linux environment is already pre-configured with the Google Cloud SDK to easily provision and manage resources in your GCP project. Furthermore, it can be used to temporarily store data because it offers 5 GB of capacity at no cost.

Moving further to the left, you can see the account settings (5) function, which is used to access your Google account profile and to log out if needed.

Most of the central area of the screen is occupied by the dashboard (6). It contains some cards, which provide an overview of your GCP project at a glance. The cards are widgets that can be shown or hidden through the **Customize** (7) button on the right.

Now that we've taken a look at the home page of the GCP console, we're ready to create a new GCP project that will host all the hands-on activities of this book.

# Creating a GCP project

As we've explained, a GCP project is a container for all the GCP resources that we use. Each project is identified by the following features:

- **Project name**: An easy-to-remember and readable name chosen during the creation phase. The name doesn't have to be unique; it has a purely descriptive function and can be changed after project creation.

- **Project ID**: This identifier is unique and is assigned by the user or automatically generated by Google during the creation of a new project. Unlike the project name, it cannot be modified. The ID needs to be unique across GCP.

- **Project number**: An identifier that is automatically generated by GCP and cannot be changed by the users. It's also unique across GCP.

Looking at Google Cloud Console in the **Project info** card, all these identifiers can be easily read:

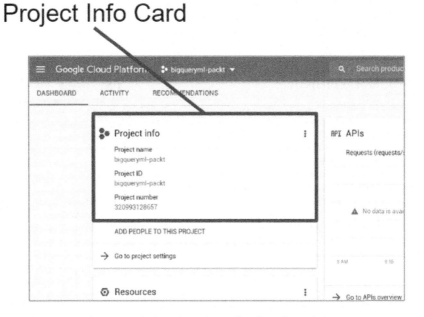

Figure 2.7 – The Project info widget shows the identifiers of a GCP project

By selecting the name of the project that's currently in use, we can access the entire list of GCP projects that we're allowed to access:

Figure 2.8 – By selecting the name of the project in use, it is possible to change it

Clicking opens a pop-up window that allows us to change the current project or to browse the GCP hierarchy of organization, folders, and projects. In our case, the only existing GCP project is **My First Project**, which was automatically created during the registration process.

Let's go through the process of creating a new project:

1.  By selecting the **New Project** button at the top-right corner of the window, it is possible to create a new environment to logically separate cloud workloads. For our purposes, we'll create a dedicated GCP project to host all the hands-on exercises that will follow in the chapters of this book:

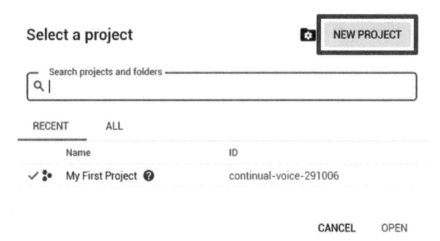

Figure 2.9 – This window allows you to select an existing project or create a new one

2.  In the next step, you are asked to fill in the project name. In this case, we'll use `bigqueryml-packt`, but you can choose another one. This is also the place where it is possible to link your GCP project to a parent object such as an organization or a folder. Upon selecting **Edit**, you have also the opportunity to change the automatically generated project ID. The new project will be created by you clicking the **Create** button:

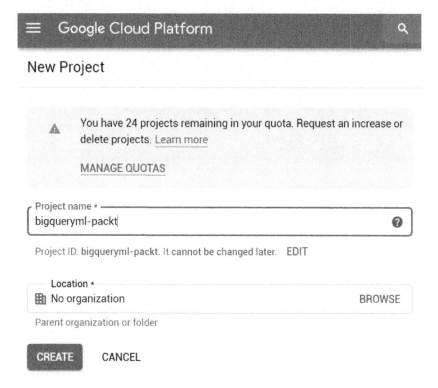

Figure 2.10 – The New Project window allows you to choose the project name, ID, and location

3.  After a few seconds, we will get a notification about the creation of the new project, visible at the top-right corner of the GCP console by clicking on the bell icon:

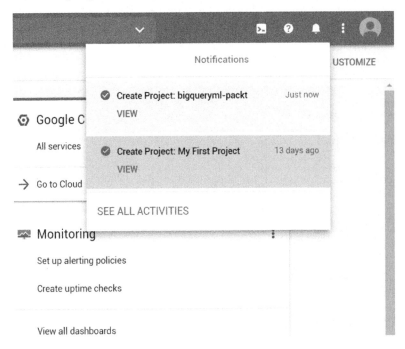

Figure 2.11 – A notification is sent to the GCP user when a new project is created and ready to be used

4.  After creation, the new GCP project is also visible in the project hierarchy and can be selected in order to choose it as the current working environment:

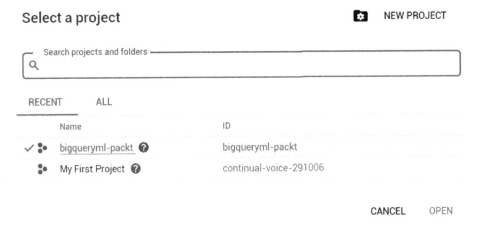

Figure 2.12 – After the project's creation, it is possible to make it the current project

Now that we've created a new project, it is time to start using BigQuery. In the next section, we'll learn how to activate the service before using it.

# Activating BigQuery

Each GCP service can be enabled or disabled according to the customer's needs and the use case that it is required to implement. For our purposes, we'll show the steps that are necessary to activate the BigQuery service, but the same approach can be extended to other GCP technologies:

> **Tip**
> Enabling or disabling a GCP service will not impact the billing of your GCP project. You'll be charged only for the actual usage of GCP components and not for just having a service enabled.

1. The first step is to access the API and services library, which can be easily found in the navigation menu of Google Cloud Console:

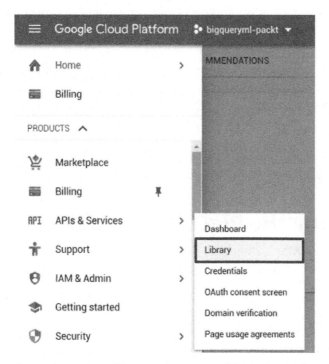

Figure 2.13 – From the navigation menu of the GCP console,
it is possible to access the library of GCP services

This function lets you browse the entire library of GCP services and choose services to turn on or off.

2.  If we search for *bigquery* in the search bar, the first result will be **BigQuery API**:

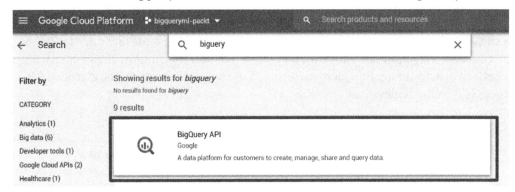

Figure 2.14 – Looking for bigquery using the search bar, it is possible to find the BigQuery API service

3.  Upon clicking on **BigQuery API**, we'll be redirected to a page dedicated to the BigQuery service, where it is possible to read a description of the service, access the BigQuery documentation, and enable the service if that wasn't done before. If the service was disabled, trying to access BigQuery directly from the navigation menu would have redirected us to the same page.

4.  Selecting the **Enable** button, GCP will activate BigQuery, allowing you to start using it. Once the service is effectively enabled, you will be redirected to the dashboard of the service, which shows an overview of the usage statistics and lets you disable this component with the **Disable API** button.

So far, we've created a new Google account and a dedicated GCP project, and we've enabled BigQuery; now it's time to take a look at the BigQuery web interface.

## Discovering the BigQuery web UI

When the BigQuery APIs are enabled, in order to access the BigQuery UI, you can open the GCP navigation menu and select **BigQuery** from the list of Google Cloud services.

At first glance (see the following screenshot), the BigQuery UI might seem complex because it contains a lot of information and buttons. On the left side of the screen, we can see a column occupied by the navigation panel (**1**). This panel is split into two main sections. In the upper one, you can access the following:

- **Query history**, which tracks all the queries previously executed with their execution statuses.

- **Saved queries**, an area to store the queries that you save and use more frequently.

- **Job history**, to keep track of all the bulk load, export, and copy operations with their execution statuses.

- **Transfers** enables us to ingest data into BigQuery, leveraging **BigQuery Data Transfer Service** from **Software as a Service (SaaS)** applications, such as Google Analytics, Google Ads, or Amazon S3.

- **Scheduled queries**, to periodically schedule a query or to monitor queries already scheduled for execution.

- **Reservations,** to reserve BigQuery processing power with the flat-rate pricing model.

- **BI Engine** allows you to activate an in-memory layer on top of BigQuery to further increase performance and get sub-second latencies for reporting activities.

- **Resources** allows you to browse different GCP projects and datasets.

In the lower part of the navigation panel, we can access and browse projects, related BigQuery datasets, and data structures such as tables, views, and machine learning models (**2**):

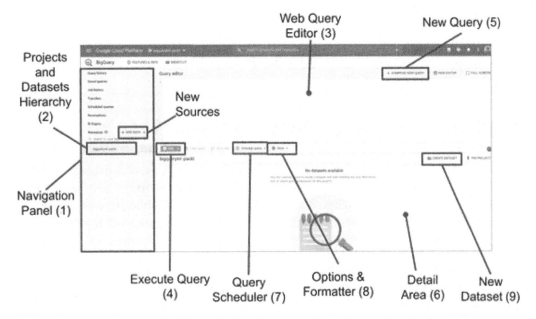

Figure 2.15 – All the functionalities of the BigQuery web interface

At the top center of the web page, you can leverage the web query editor (**3**) to write SQL statements and run these queries using the **Run** button (**4**). The web query editor can be hidden by the developer with the **HIDE EDITOR** button in the top-right corner or cleared by selecting **COMPOSE NEW QUERY** (**5**). Below the query editor, you can visualize the results of the executed queries and the details of each selected item (**6**), such as a dataset or a table. Between the two sections of the web interface, it is possible to access the **Query Scheduler** tool (**7**). Clicking on the **More** button (**8**), it is also possible to access the BigQuery options and the SQL formatter, which is used to make SQL queries readable.

On the right-hand side of the **bigqueryml-packt** panel, you can select/click **CREATE DATASET** (**9**) to create a new BigQuery dataset.

> **Tip**
>
> Among the BigQuery options, you can find the options to enable or disable the BigQuery cache. If the cache is enabled, BigQuery tries to use cached results if they are available. If the result of a query is already in the cache, the query is not executed. The cache is used to save computational resources and get high performance. If a query contains non-deterministic functions, such as CURRENT_TIMESTAMP() and NOW(), the cache is not used and BigQuery will execute the query statement.

In this section, we've analyzed all the main features available in the BigQuery web interface. Now, we can start exploring the **BigQuery public datasets** and understand how to use them in our projects.

# Exploring the BigQuery public datasets

Collecting large volumes of data is fundamental to developing machine learning use cases. This kind of activity is considered one of the most painful jobs in the data management field. In fact, it requires tools and best practices to regularly monitor and gather information from the physical world to translate it into data. Thanks to the **Cloud Public Datasets Program**, we are allowed to use data that has already been collected and ingested into BigQuery.

The **BigQuery public datasets** are available in the **Datasets** section of the **Google Cloud Marketplace** and are publicly available and ready to use for all GCP users. A list of all the datasets is reachable at this URL: https://console.cloud.google.com/marketplace/browse?filter=solution-type:dataset. The datasets are provided not only by Google but by large companies and public organizations that contribute to the maintenance of this multidisciplinary set of around 200 datasets. Some of the contributors are GitHub, NOAA, NASA, the City of Chicago, the University of Oxford, and the USA Department of Transportation.

The public datasets are also directly accessible from the BigQuery UI. In the next few pages, we'll discover step by step what we should do to start using them.

## Searching for a public dataset

From the BigQuery UI, we can select the **Add Data** button in the navigation menu and then click on **Explore public datasets** to open an overlay window that will show the BigQuery public datasets divided by category of interest.

In the following screenshot, you can see some BigQuery public datasets:

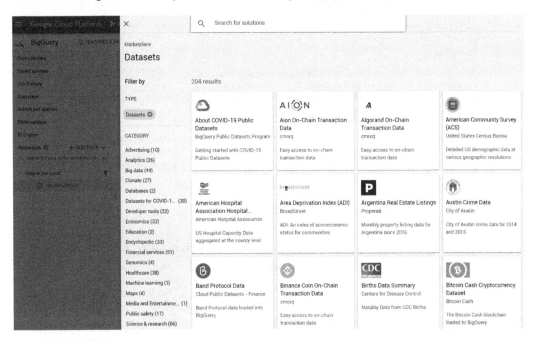

Figure 2.16 – The BigQuery public datasets embedded view in the main BigQuery UI

From this screen, you can scroll up and down to explore the available datasets, use the search bar to look for a specific topic, or use the **Category** menu to filter the topics.

For our purposes, we'll look for the open data related to **Chicago Taxi Trips**, published by the City of Chicago. To find this dataset, the suggestion is to search the keywords Chicago taxi and select the only item that will appear with the name **Chicago Taxi Trips**.

In the following screenshot, you can see a description of the dataset:

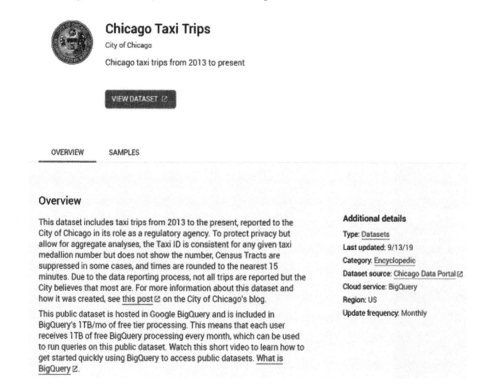

**Chicago Taxi Trips**
City of Chicago

Chicago taxi trips from 2013 to present

VIEW DATASET ↗

OVERVIEW        SAMPLES

**Overview**

This dataset includes taxi trips from 2013 to the present, reported to the
City of Chicago in its role as a regulatory agency. To protect privacy but
allow for aggregate analyses, the Taxi ID is consistent for any given taxi
medallion number but does not show the number, Census Tracts are
suppressed in some cases, and times are rounded to the nearest 15
minutes. Due to the data reporting process, not all trips are reported but the
City believes that most are. For more information about this dataset and
how it was created, see this post ↗ on the City of Chicago's blog.

This public dataset is hosted in Google BigQuery and is included in
BigQuery's 1TB/mo of free tier processing. This means that each user
receives 1TB of free BigQuery processing every month, which can be used
to run queries on this public dataset. Watch this short video to learn how to
get started quickly using BigQuery to access public datasets. What is
BigQuery ↗.

**Additional details**

Type: Datasets
Last updated: 9/13/19
Category: Encyclopedic
Dataset source: Chicago Data Portal ↗
Cloud service: BigQuery
Region: US
Update frequency: Monthly

Figure 2.17 – The Chicago Taxi Trips public dataset overview, accessible from the
Google Cloud Marketplace

In the **Overview** section, the dataset is described, and additional information is provided
on the right. In this particular case, we can read that the dataset is updated monthly and is
published on the Chicago Data Portal.

Upon clicking the **View Dataset** button, we'll be redirected to the BigQuery UI where we
can access the `bigquery-public-data` project. Browsing this GCP project, you'll find
the `chicago_taxi_trips` dataset, which contains only one table: `taxi_trips`.

## Analyzing a table

Clicking on the table name will enable you to go deeper into some aspects of the
`taxi_trips` data. In the **Schema** tab, we can explore what the fields that compose the
selected table are. Some columns are defined as **REQUIRED** and others are **NULLABLE**.
Thanks to the publisher of the dataset, this table is also well documented, and we can read
a short description of each field. This kind of information will help us during the first
stages of the implementation of a new use case before building a machine learning model:

taxi_trips                                                                    ⊕ QUERY TABLE

Schema    Details    Preview

| Field name | Type | Mode | Policy tags ⓘ | Description |
|---|---|---|---|---|
| unique_key | STRING | REQUIRED | | Unique identifier for the trip. |
| taxi_id | STRING | REQUIRED | | A unique identifier for the taxi. |
| trip_start_timestamp | TIMESTAMP | NULLABLE | | When the trip started, rounded to the nearest 15 minutes. |
| trip_end_timestamp | TIMESTAMP | NULLABLE | | When the trip ended, rounded to the nearest 15 minutes. |
| trip_seconds | INTEGER | NULLABLE | | Time of the trip in seconds. |
| trip_miles | FLOAT | NULLABLE | | Distance of the trip in miles. |
| pickup_census_tract | INTEGER | NULLABLE | | The Census Tract where the trip began. For privacy, this Census Tract is not shown for some trips. |
| dropoff_census_tract | INTEGER | NULLABLE | | The Census Tract where the trip ended. For privacy, this Census Tract is not shown for some trips. |

Figure 2.18 – The table schema is accessible simply by selecting the table name
from the navigation menu

To deep dive into the technical details of the table, we can move to the **Details** tab. This
section shows relevant information such as the following:

- The table size in GB.

- The number of rows in the table.

- The creation date of the table and also the last time that it was updated.

- The BigQuery region in which the table is stored. In this case, the data is stored
  in the multi-region US.

---

**Tip**

**Number of Rows** and **Last Modified Date** give fundamental information
for machine learning purposes. To train effective models, we need to be sure
that we have enough records and that those records aren't obsolete. Using an
insufficient number of records or old data can produce low-quality machine
learning models.

---

The **Preview** tab gives us the last available information that we can gather from the table.
This functionality allows us to take a view of a sample of data stored in the table and
understand the content at a glance.

In the following screenshot, you can visualize the records of the table using the **Preview** feature:

| | | | Q QUERY TABLE | COPY TABLE | DELETE TABLE | EXPORT |
|---|---|---|---|---|---|---|
| taxi_trips | | | | | | |

Schema    Details    Preview

| Row | unique_key | taxi_id | trip_start_time |
|---|---|---|---|
| 1 | ce4c12b3fa886579a20b5ad2f22ebf7e195cc037 | 9b7291d09194ffcd0bc0d27589b7e8a44ff1904f592c5cc10c6346ef734b98b4969e293efc221bea11211167963992b3ebc01f779d164c67c13af5f2239028a2 | 2015-09-02 |
| 2 | 424d3834d804ba5ce84862c3972474dd6525c686 | 623c452c15d06a0ce93dda0703872746dd06750a9952dd6180733eebef7cc5e7149706dda5e9c2513c2bd38a5e18dac5746bc7fabaf019e06bc735d97053a06d | 2016-01-05 |
| 3 | 8286c2e96b922b04d45f075bd1729e0014db139d | fa009aab0cbf98afe9f7fdd040ffbdaeaf0f11370dc24a1e3e6cdff63c741407ebe2f2f9658122a63c480ced0cd50a76741e5cf9d602f3e72079b09bf5bddfd7 | 2015-09-15 |
| 4 | 088f33c4e191ffea5d9ab152a8c468dc30a3b44e | b7c0e0732dc451395225bdd8f7dbc6e83ff14b172f4c16255f1f0fd30e47ea67fd30d961e836cfc2945e549e18582adddcb196722df7abf856ba6b1d68e13ff0 | 2015-08-22 |
| 5 | d81f52f8ec80328f6edc32a3883a012fb84eb982 | ad33dffdd6cd00795ea1a00a6a6db1a38482075d532b55e712741e9b4a2541375fcf642d01d35b51646d2a07b49376f167b5ddd1f7b0a5354afe07f514108365 | 2015-09-01 |
| 6 | 4dc05edb127cc330046038eedbef57fe9d456d96 | 38aa3432a4d83f7e9765908ff1bdf10ada6b21ffc6ba0e005c4cf078e74cfe651e5849b945f632e2c7f3338b938a3a902130f9da715714423bf3072cefd89be2 | 2015-09-06 |
| 7 | 10827de46a0e85916d9b63a43ff9436b9e68c181 | bbae5426953eda048ae808d6e455e6a6deaf2825313dbd54f77eaec894804f119c333e5e252798133b66f7ef1bff94ee185c1482b919e76c5d337677077a33e8 | 2015-09-01 |

Figure 2.19 – The Preview tab presents a sample of records from the taxi_trips table

> **Tip**
> Accessing information from the **Details** and **Preview** tabs doesn't impact the billing of your project. To get the count of the records in a table, we suggest you use **Number of Rows** in the **Details** tab instead of performing a SELECT COUNT (*) query. To view a sample of the records, it is recommended to use the **Preview** function in place of executing SELECT * on the table.

# Summary

Throughout this second chapter, we've taken the first steps into GCP. Before starting the registration process, we look at the hierarchy of GCP resources, composed of multiple projects, folders, and an organization node.

After that, we learned how to create a new account and leverage the free trial offered by Google. Then, we explored Google Cloud Console from the web browser and created a new GCP project that we'll use in the next chapters to host our machine learning use cases.

Upon completing the setup operations, we enabled the BigQuery API to start accessing this serverless analytic data warehouse.

Since BigQuery provides a lot of different functions, we introduced each of them gradually, exploring their utility. One of the most important functions is adding public datasets to our console. This capability enables us to access and use tables that have already been compiled by companies and public institutions. The datasets are ready to use and can be leveraged to develop our use cases.

For this chapter, we focused on a table with information about taxi trips, published by the City of Chicago. This table offered us the opportunity to explore the technical details of a table and how to preview the data in it.

In the next chapter, we will write our first SQL statements to become confident with all the basic operations that will be extremely valuable during the development of machine learning models.

# Further reading

The following links will offer you more resources on this chapter:

- **Google Cloud trial**: https://cloud.google.com/free
- **Enabling an API in GCP**: https://cloud.google.com/endpoints/docs/openapi/enable-api
- **BigQuery web interface**: https://console.cloud.google.com/bigquery
- **BigQuery web interface documentation**: https://cloud.google.com/bigquery/docs/bigquery-web-ui
- **BigQuery public datasets marketplace**: https://console.cloud.google.com/marketplace/browse?filter=solution-type:dataset
- **BigQuery public datasets documentation**: https://cloud.google.com/bigquery/public-data
- **Data portal of the City of Chicago**: https://data.cityofchicago.org/

# 3
# Introducing BigQuery Syntax

The BigQuery dialect is compliant with the standard ANSI 2011 and is quite easy to learn for people who know other dialects and have experience with SQL. The main differences in terms of syntax are represented by BigQuery extensions, which allow us to use advanced features such as **Machine Learning** (**ML**). Bringing ML capabilities into SQL allows different roles to access it. This approach has the clear goal of democratizing the use of ML across different functions within a company, generating as much value as possible. With BigQuery ML, Google Cloud is filling the gap between tech-savvy people with ML skills and business analysts who know the company's data very well and have been working on it for years.

To build your confidence with the BigQuery environment and its dialect, we'll go through the following topics:

- Creating a BigQuery dataset
- Discovering BigQuery SQL
- Diving into BigQuery ML

# Technical requirements

This chapter requires access to a web browser and the following:

- A GCP account to access Google Cloud Console

- A GCP project to host the BigQuery datasets

Now that we're ready with the technical requirements, let's dive into the creation of a BigQuery dataset.

Check out the following video to see the Code in Action: `https://bit.ly/3vR8I7f`

# Creating a BigQuery dataset

Before jumping into the BigQuery syntax, it is necessary to create a new BigQuery dataset that will employ the data structures created in the next sections. For each hands-on chapter, we'll create a new dataset to segregate each use case and maintain a logical separated structure:

1.  Access the BigQuery UI by browsing to the GCP Navigation menu from the GCP console and selecting the **BigQuery** service.

2.  After selecting the right GCP project in the navigation menu of the BigQuery UI, it is possible to click on the **Create Dataset** button:

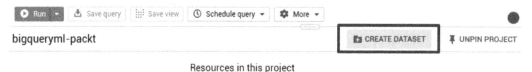

Resources in this project

Figure 3.1 – Creation of a new BigQuery Dataset

3.  In the overlay window that appears on the right of the screen, choose the **Dataset ID** that you prefer and leave all the other options configured with default values. To host the data structures of this chapter, we suggest using the name `03_bigquery_syntax`. Then, select **Create dataset**:

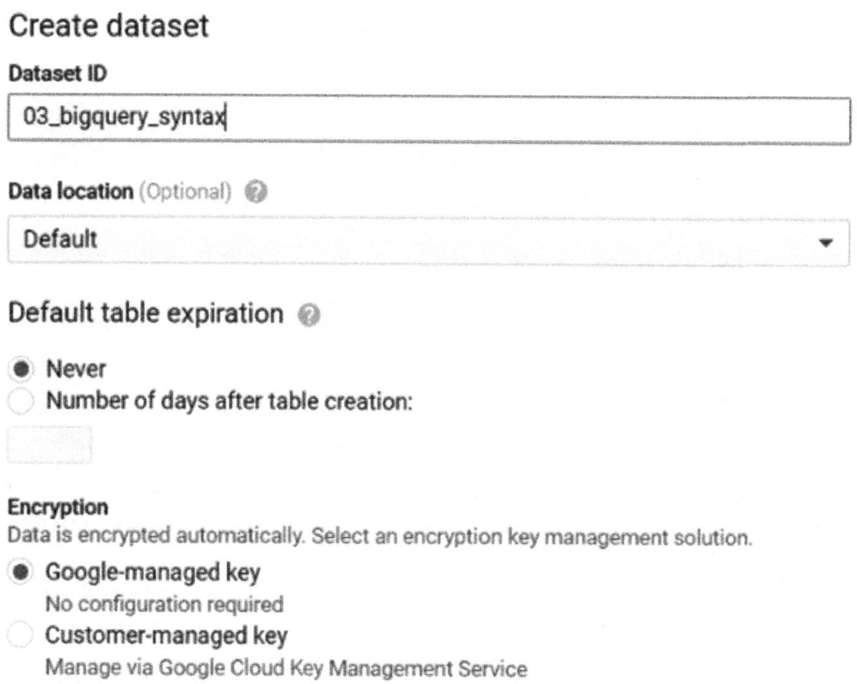

## Create dataset

**Dataset ID**

03_bigquery_syntax

**Data location** (Optional) @

Default ▼

### Default table expiration @

● Never

○ Number of days after table creation:

[ ]

**Encryption**

Data is encrypted automatically. Select an encryption key management solution.

● Google-managed key

No configuration required

○ Customer-managed key

Manage via Google Cloud Key Management Service

Figure 3.2 – Create dataset screen

Now that we've created our first BigQuery dataset, let's take an overview of the main characteristics of the BigQuery SQL syntax.

# Discovering BigQuery SQL

BigQuery supports two different SQL dialects: **standard SQL** and **legacy SQL**. In this book, we'll use Standard SQL, but it could be useful to know what Legacy SQL is and how to enable it if you want to test queries coming from legacy applications.

As we have already mentioned, BigQuery was developed as an internal product within Google and was initially realized to process log records. The query engine Dremel was able to support a limited set of SQL operations that are now defined as Legacy SQL.

In the following screenshot, you can see how to change the **SQL dialect**:

Figure 3.3 – Screenshot of the Query Settings menu to change SQL dialect

By default, the BigQuery UI is configured to use Standard SQL, but you are allowed to change the SQL dialect by using the specific option located in the **Query Settings** of the BigQuery web interface, or by prefacing your queries with the `#legacySQL` keyword in the first line of your SQL statement. The **Query Settings** button is available under the **More** button in the BigQuery UI.

> **Tip**
> To develop new use cases, we suggest that you adopt BigQuery Standard SQL, but keep in mind that you could find existing applications that are still based on Legacy SQL. If you find a query that is not validated by the Query Editor, try to switch to Legacy SQL before intervening on the SQL statement.

## CRUD operations

In this paragraph, we'll learn how to perform the basic commands in order to **Create, Read, Update and Delete** (**CRUD**) objects in BigQuery. This is not an exhaustive view of all the operations that you can use with BigQuery, but the goal of this section is to provide you with the minimum knowledge needed to effectively face the next hands-on chapters of this book.

## Create

This category of statements is generally used to create objects in BigQuery such as tables, views, **User-Defined Functions (UDFs)**, and machine learning models, or to insert new records into an existing table:

1.  As a first step, let's create a new empty table in BigQuery:

```
CREATE TABLE
  `bigqueryml-packt.03_bigquery_syntax.first_table`
  ( id_key INT64,
    description STRING);
```

The first two words of the query statement, CREATE TABLE, are self-explanatory and are used to start the creation of a new table. After that, we can find the identifier of the object that we're creating. It is composed by the concatenation of the following strings separated by the . character:

*   The name of the GCP project: bigqueryml-packt

*   The identifier of the BigQuery dataset: 03_bigquery_syntax

*   The name of the table to create: first_table

The string of the identifier is also enclosed by the backtick character, `. This character delimits the beginning and the end of the name of our object.

Between the two round brackets, you can see the list of fields with their data type separated by the comma character. In this example, the table contains only two fields: the numerical id_key and the textual description.

> **Tip**
> If a table with the same name already exists, it is possible to create a new table replacing the existing one using the CREATE OR REPLACE TABLE keywords. This technique is particularly useful when you need to periodically schedule your scripts running them multiple times. These keywords automatically clean the results of the previous executions.

2. Now that we've created our first empty table, let's INSERT our first record:

```
INSERT INTO
    `bigqueryml-packt.03_bigquery_syntax.first_table`
VALUES
  ( 1,
    'This is my first record inserted in BigQuery' );
```

For the insertion of a new record into our first_table, we've used the INSERT INTO and VALUES keywords. Between the round brackets, we've listed the actual values to insert. In this case, we've chosen the integer number 1 as id_key and the string 'This is my first record inserted in BigQuery' in single quotes.

3. On top of a table, it is possible to create a **view**. The view doesn't contain any records but allows you to access the records of an underlying table with a specific business logic:

```
CREATE VIEW
    `bigqueryml-packt.03_bigquery_syntax.first_view` AS
  SELECT * FROM
    `bigqueryml-packt.03_bigquery_syntax.first_table`;
```

The CREATE VIEW statement is similar to the CREATE TABLE one, the only difference being that the view structure is based on the SELECT statement that follows the AS keyword. In this case, first_view has the same structure as first_table and doesn't apply any filters or transformations on the records stored in the table.

## Read

Read operations are mainly based on SELECT statements and can be applied to different database objects such as tables and views.

Let's execute a SELECT statement on the first_table table:

```
SELECT
  *
FROM
  `bigqueryml-packt.03_bigquery_syntax.first_table`
WHERE
  id_key=1;
```

To read data from a table or a view, it is necessary to use the SELECT keyword, followed by the list of the fields to read or the wildcard *, then the keyword FROM and the identifier of the source data structure. It is also possible to include a WHERE clause to express all the logical filters that we want to apply. In this case, we're picking up only the records with id_key=1 that corresponds to the only record that we've previously inserted into the table.

> **Tip**
>
> Using the wildcard * is not recommended, especially on tables with a large number of columns. Since BigQuery has columnar storage, selecting only the fields that are really needed can dramatically improve the performance and decrease the computational cost of the query.

With hierarchical queries with nested SELECT statements, the WITH clause can be used to improve the readability of the query:

1.  As the first step, let's create a nested SELECT statement:

```
SELECT COUNT(*) FROM (
    SELECT
    *
    FROM
        `bigqueryml-packt.03_bigquery_syntax.first_table`
    WHERE
        id_key=1
);
```

2.  After that, we can rewrite the same logic using the WITH clause. The query becomes this:

```
WITH records_with_clause AS (SELECT *
    FROM
        `bigqueryml-packt.03_bigquery_syntax.first_table`
    WHERE
        id_key=1)

SELECT COUNT(*) FROM records_with_clause;
```

In the second query, the `WITH` clause embeds the logic that follows the `AS` keyword and is enclosed by round brackets. After the definition of the `WITH` clause with the name `records_with_clause`, the logic of this query can be recalled in the next `SELECT COUNT` statement.

> **Tip**
> The `WITH` clause doesn't create a temporary table. Using the `WITH` clause improves the readability of the query, especially if there are many nested `SELECT` statements, but it doesn't affect the performance of the query.

BigQuery offers the possibility to leverage many other operators that will not be described in detail in this chapter because they will not be extensively used in the hands-on exercises. These additional operators allow you to do the following:

- Sort the results of a query according to a specific list of fields with the `ORDER BY` clause.

- Apply aggregations on the query results with `COUNT`, `SUM`, `MAX`, `AVG`, and the `GROUP BY` and `HAVING` clauses.

- Manage the array data type using `NEST`, `UNNEST`, `ARRAY_AGG`, and `ARRAY_LENGTH`.

- Join two or more tables with `INNER JOIN`, `LEFT OUTER JOIN`, `RIGHT OUTER JOIN`, and `CROSS JOIN`.

## Update

Although BigQuery was born as an analytic tool, update operations such as `UPDATE` and `MERGE` are supported and can be used to change existing records in BigQuery tables.

In order to change the value of a record or a set of records, we can use the `UPDATE` statement in the following way:

```
UPDATE
    `bigqueryml-packt.03_bigquery_syntax.first_table`
SET
    description= 'This is my updated description'
WHERE
    id_key=1;
```

In the first two lines of code, the UPDATE keyword is followed by the identifier of the table on which the operation should be applied. After that, the SET keyword defines the columns that should be changed. In this case, the description will be modified.

The WHERE clause allows you to apply the UPDATE operations only to the records that match the filter. In this case, only the records with an id_key equal to 1.

The other powerful statement to update a table is the MERGE function. This function can combine the records of two different tables applying insert, update, and delete operations in a single SQL statement.

## Delete

Delete operations are particularly useful to delete records or remove objects from BigQuery preventing storage costs:

1.  As a first step, we can delete a record from the first_table table, using the DELETE statement as follows:

```
DELETE
      `bigqueryml-packt.03_bigquery_syntax.first_table`
WHERE
      id_key=1;
```

If we analyze the SQL code, we can see that the DELETE keyword is followed by the identifier of the table on which the operation should be applied. The WHERE clause filters the set of records to delete. In this case, only the record with an id_key equal to 1 is affected.

2.  Another way to remove records from a table is using the TRUNCATE TABLE operator. This function allows you to remove all the records with a single statement:

```
TRUNCATE TABLE
    `bigqueryml-packt.03_bigquery_syntax.first_table`;
```

After the TRUNCATE, our first_table will continue to exist but will not contain any records.

3.  To delete the entire table, including its structure, we can use the DROP TABLE keywords:

```
DROP TABLE
    `bigqueryml-packt.03_bigquery_syntax.first_table`;
```

Dropping a table removes it from the dataset, making the data structure inaccessible. If we explore the list of objects of the 03_bigquery_syntax dataset, we can see that the first_table table is no longer visible:

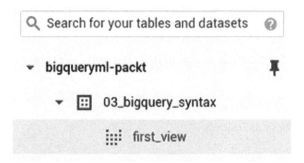

Figure 3.4 – The table that was affected by the DROP TABLE statement is no longer visible

In this case, an interesting aspect is that first_view, created on top of the first_table table, is still visible.

4.  If we try to execute a SELECT statement on it, the following error will be raised:

## Query failed

#### Job information

⊖ Not found: Dataset bigqueryml-packt:03_bigquery_syntax was not found in location US

```
1  SELECT * FROM `bigqueryml-packt.03_bigquery_syntax.first_view`;
```

Figure 3.5 – Querying a view when the underlying table was dropped raises an error

The error, generated by BigQuery, notifies the user that the underlying table is no longer available and cannot be found.

5. To keep our dataset consistent, it is better to also drop the view with the DROP VIEW statement:

```
DROP VIEW
   `bigqueryml-packt.03_bigquery_syntax.first_view`;
```

Dropping a view is similar to dropping a table, but this operation affects only the metadata because the view doesn't actually store any records.

In this section of the chapter, we've discovered the main operations that we can do with BigQuery SQL; now it's time to dive into BigQuery ML and its syntax.

# Diving into BigQuery ML

Developing an ML model in BigQuery involves three main steps:

1. **Model creation**, where you are required to choose the **features** and **labels** of your ML model and the options to tune the ML model. At this stage, BigQuery runs the training of the ML model on the training set that you've chosen.

2. **Model evaluation** allows you to test the model trained in the previous step on a different set of records to prevent any **overfitting**.

3. **Model use**: when the ML model is ready, we can apply it to a new dataset in order to make predictions or classifications of the labels according to the available features.

In the next paragraphs, we'll take a look at the syntax of these three stages and how these statements are built using stubs of code.

## Creating the ML model (training)

When you've identified the ML use case and also the set of records to train your model, you can start training the model with the following query:

```
CREATE MODEL`<project_name>.<dataset_name>.<ml_model_name>`
TRANSFORM (<list_of_features_transformed>
OPTIONS (<list_of_options>)
AS <select_statement>;
```

Very similarly to the creation of a BigQuery table, the statement to train a new model consists of the following:

- The CREATE MODEL keywords.

- Then the name of the new ML model. This identifier is composed of the concatenation of the project name, dataset name, and ML model name, separated by the . character and enclosed by backticks.

- The TRANSFORM clause is not mandatory but is very useful. It allows us to list all the preprocessing transformations applied to the features before training. Putting the preparation functions here allows us to automatically apply the same actions during the actual use of the model.

- A list of OPTIONS requires us to specify the model_type that we want to use, such as linear regression or logistic regression. This list of options is also used to select the list of labels of the ML model through the input_label_cols keyword. Other options can be used to tune the ML model and will be explained in the next chapters of the book, with the hands-on exercises.

- The AS keyword followed by the SELECT statement. This statement defines the set of records on which the ML model will be trained.

In addition to the CREATE MODEL statement, we can also use the following:

- CREATE OR REPLACE MODEL to create a new model or replace the existing one with the same name.

- CREATE MODEL IF NOT EXISTS to train the new model only if a model with the same name doesn't exist.

Now that we've understood how to create an ML model in BigQuery ML, let's take a look at the next phase: the evaluation of the model.

## Evaluating the ML model

After training an ML model on a set of records, it is extremely important to evaluate its performances on a second dataset that's different from the training one to avoid any **overfitting**.

> **Important note**
>
> With the term overfitting, we refer to a situation that could happen when the ML model learns very well from the training dataset but performs negatively on new ones. This usually happens when the model adheres too much to the details of the training dataset and remains conditioned by the noise present in it.

According to the ML algorithm that we've chosen during the model creation, we can choose among different evaluation functions.

## Evaluate function

This function can be used with linear regression, logistic regression, *k*-means clustering, matrix factorization, and time-series models based on ARIMA:

```
SELECT *
FROM ML.EVALUATE(
    MODEL `<project_name>.<dataset_name>.<ml_model_name>`,
        `<project_name>.<dataset_name>.<evaluation_table>`
    , STRUCT(<threshold> AS threshold));
```

The `ML.EVALUATE` function returns only one record with the key performance indicators of the ML model that we've trained and evaluated. The indicator it returns depend on the model type. The query stub is composed of the following:

- An initial `SELECT *` statement that allows us to retrieve all the fields returned by the evaluation stage.

- The call of the evaluation function from the `ML` package: `ML.EVALUATE`.

- The identifier of the ML model with the syntax that we already know very well: project, dataset, and model name.

- The `<evaluation_table>` on which the ML model will be evaluated. This table can be replaced by a `SELECT` statement and is not mandatory. If you don't provide the table for the evaluation stage, BigQuery will use the entire training set or a portion of it to evaluate your ML model.

- An optional `<threshold>` that can be used to evaluate logistic regression models. If this value is not specified, BigQuery will use `0.5` as the default value.

> **Tip**
>
> To use the ML.EVALUATE function, the name of the fields of the evaluation set should correspond to the name of the fields of the training dataset that we've used during the model creation.

## Confusion matrix function

This function returns a confusion matrix to evaluate the performances of logistic regression and multiclass logistic regression models:

```
SELECT *
FROM ML.CONFUSION_MATRIX(
    MODEL `<project_name>.<dataset_name>.<ml_model_name>`,
        `<project_name>.<dataset_name>.<evaluation_table>`
    , STRUCT(<treshold> AS threshold));
```

This function returns two rows and two columns that contain the number of false positives, false negatives, true positives, and true negatives. Compared to the EVALUATE function, the only difference in terms of syntax is represented by the use of the ML.CONFUSION_MATRIX function.

## ROC curve function

This function can be used only with logistic regression models and returns multiple records according to the array of thresholds that are passed as input to the function:

```
SELECT *
FROM ML.ROC_CURVE(
    MODEL `<project_name>.<dataset_name>.<ml_model_name>`,
        `<project_name>.<dataset_name>.<evaluation_table>`
    , GENERATE_ARRAY(<treshold_1>, <treshold_2>, <treshold_n>
));
```

The only meaningful difference that we can see from the other evaluation functions that we analyzed in the previous paragraphs is the presence of an array of thresholds. The GENERATE_ARRAY function creates an array that contains the values of the thresholds separated by the comma character and enclosed by round brackets.

The output of this function includes the threshold passed in input, the recall value, the rate of false positives, and the number of true positives, false positives, true negatives, and false negatives.

We have been through all the evaluation techniques of BigQuery ML models, now it's time to see how to apply them and get the results.

## Using the ML model

When we're satisfied with the performance of our ML model, the next step is to use it to achieve our outcomes and finally get business value from the implementation.

### Predict function

This function is applicable to linear regression, logistic regression, multiclass logistic regression, *k*-means clustering, and imported TensorFlow models:

```
SELECT *
FROM ML.PREDICT(
    MODEL `<project_name>.<dataset_name>.<ml_model_name>`,
        `<project_name>.<dataset_name>.<features_table>`
    , STRUCT(<treshold> AS threshold));
```

The query is composed of the following:

- The SELECT * FROM statement to get all the records and fields returned by ML.PREDICT function.

- The ML.PREDICT keyword, which accepts as input the name of the ML model to use for the prediction (<ml_model_name>) and the table (<features_table>) that contains the features to execute the predictions.

- Optionally, you can use a <threshold> value for the logistic regression models followed by the AS threshold keywords.

The ML.PREDICT function generates and returns a record for each row present in <features_table>. Each row is composed of the features and the predicted labels.

### Forecast function

This function can only be used for time-series ML models:

```
SELECT *
FROM ML.FORECAST(
    MODEL `<project_name>.<dataset_name>.<ml_model_name>`,
    STRUCT(<horizon_value> AS horizon,
        <confidence_value> AS confidence_level));
```

Unlike the PREDICT statement, it doesn't require a table as input. It allows us to choose the following:

- A specific <horizon_value>. The horizon represents the number of time points that should be forecast. If you don't specify this value, BigQuery will use 3 as the default.

- A confidence_level, which represents the percentage of the forecast values that reside in the interval of the prediction.

### Recommend function

This function can only be used for matrix factorization ML models. It returns a rating for each combination of user and item in the <user_item_table> table or in the training table:

```
SELECT *
FROM ML.RECOMMEND(
    MODEL `<project_name>.<dataset_name>.<ml_model_name>`,
        (`<project_name>.<dataset_name>.<user_item_table>`));
```

The query is composed of the following:

- The SELECT * FROM statement to get all the records and fields that come from the outcome of the ML.RECOMMEND function.

- The ML.RECOMMEND keyword, which accepts as input the name of the ML model to use for the prediction (<ml_model_name>) and, optionally, the input table (<user_item_table>), which contains the user and items. If the table is not provided, BigQuery will use the entire training table for the recommendation.

We've learned how to apply a BigQuery ML model; if the model is no longer needed, it is best to delete it to save resources. Let's take a look at how we can do that.

### Deleting an ML model

Deleting an ML model is quite straightforward, and the syntax is very similar to the cancellation of a table:

```
DROP MODEL `<project_name>.<dataset_name>.<ml_model_name>`;
```

With the DROP MODEL keywords followed by the identifier of the BigQuery ML model, you can remove the asset from your dataset.

You can also use the `DROP MODEL IF EXISTS` keywords, which prevents errors if the BigQuery ML model has been already deleted. This operation removes the model only if it is present in the dataset:

```
DROP MODEL IF EXISTS
`<project_name>.<dataset_name>.<ml_model_name>`;
```

When the model is deleted, we can be sure that no resources are consumed to keep it active in BigQuery.

## Summary

In this chapter, we've learned the main aspects of the BigQuery syntax. After the creation of a dataset, we've discovered how to create tables, insert records, and read the rows stored in a table. You've also learned how to update existing records and how to remove rows and delete objects that are no longer useful, such as tables and views.

Completing the overview of the BigQuery SQL syntax, we dived into the main stages of the life cycle of an ML model. The three main phases to realize a use case are the creation, the evaluation, and the use of the ML model. For the training phase, we have found out how to train and create a new model using SQL. After that, we went through all the functions that can be used to monitor the effectiveness of a trained model, evaluating its key performance indicators. Finally, we saw how to use a trained model on a new dataset to infer the results and get predictions, forecasts, or recommendations. At the end of the chapter, we also learned how to delete BigQuery ML models that are no longer useful.

Now that we have a clear understanding of the syntax and all the capabilities that we can use in BigQuery, it's time to apply all these concepts to our first hands-on use case. In the next chapter, we will develop our first BigQuery ML model to predict the estimated duration of a bike trip for an important bike rental service in New York City.

## Further resources

- **BigQuery datasets**: https://cloud.google.com/bigquery/docs/datasets
- **BigQuery SQL syntax**: https://cloud.google.com/bigquery/docs/reference/standard-sql/query-syntax
- **BigQuery data types**: https://cloud.google.com/bigquery/docs/reference/standard-sql/data-types

- **Create model syntax**: `https://cloud.google.com/bigquery-ml/docs/reference/standard-sql/bigqueryml-syntax-create`

- **Evaluate syntax**: `https://cloud.google.com/bigquery-ml/docs/reference/standard-sql/bigqueryml-syntax-evaluate`

- **Confusion matrix syntax**: `https://cloud.google.com/bigquery-ml/docs/reference/standard-sql/bigqueryml-syntax-confusion`

- **ROC curve syntax**: `https://cloud.google.com/bigquery-ml/docs/reference/standard-sql/bigqueryml-syntax-roc`

- **Predict syntax**: `https://cloud.google.com/bigquery-ml/docs/reference/standard-sql/bigqueryml-syntax-predict`

- **Forecast syntax**: `https://cloud.google.com/bigquery-ml/docs/reference/standard-sql/bigqueryml-syntax-forecast`

- **Recommend syntax**: `https://cloud.google.com/bigquery-ml/docs/reference/standard-sql/bigqueryml-syntax-recommend`

# Section 2: Deep Learning Networks

In this section, regression machine learning models are explained and presented with real hands-on examples using BigQuery ML.

This section comprises the following chapters:

- *Chapter 4, Predicting Numerical Values with Linear Regression*
- *Chapter 5, Predicting Boolean Values Using Binary Logistic*
- *Chapter 6, Classifying Trees with Multiclass Logistic Regression*

# 4
# Predicting Numerical Values with Linear Regression

Predicting numerical measures could be extremely valuable for companies that need to plan their strategies in terms of budgets and resources. In most industries, predicting numbers could bring huge business advantages over their competition, and also enable new business scenarios.

Born from the statistics discipline, linear regression became one of the most well-known machine learning techniques to perform this kind of task. In data science, linear regression models are used to find and quantify the relationships between causes and effects among different variables. This kind of model can be very useful in different business scenarios where it's needed to make predictions on numerical measures.

In this chapter, we'll go through all the steps required to build a linear regression model while leveraging BigQuery ML, which simplifies and accelerates all the stages of the development process.

By following a gradual and incremental approach, we'll cover the following topics:

- Introducing the business scenario
- Discovering linear regression
- Exploring and understanding the dataset
- Training the linear regression model
- Evaluating the linear regression model
- Utilizing the linear regression model
- Drawing business conclusions

Let's get started!

# Technical requirements

This chapter requires you to access to a web browser and be able to leverage the following:

- A GCP account to access Google Cloud Console
- A GCP project to host the BigQuery datasets

Now, let's dive into the analysis and development parts of our BigQuery ML linear regression model.

Check out the following video to see the Code in Action: `https://bit.ly/2Rru9wA`

# Introducing the business scenario

Imagine being one of the business analysts that works for a large company in New York City. Your company manages the nation's largest bike sharing program. It leverages 10,000 bikes and has realized 600 stations across different New York areas: Manhattan, Brooklyn, Queens, and Jersey City.

The following is a picture from a bike sharing station in New York City:

Figure 4.1 – New York City bike sharing service by Citi Bike

Thanks to the vision and spirit of innovation of the company, huge amounts of data has been collected since 2013 and is still updated every day. This data contains a lot of information about the usage of the service and can be used to extract very interesting statistics.

At the time of writing, the bike sharing service is available for all the customers that have signed up for a weekly, monthly, or yearly subscription. However, this is not accessible to and convenient for people that only stay for a few days in the city, such as tourists or business travelers.

Considering the large number of people staying in New York City for only a few days, the company wants people to be able to rent a bike for only a few hours. For this reason, management is thinking about the possibility to enable a new pay-as-you-go rental option.

The company's goal is to create a fully digital experience for this segment of customers and is thinking about the development of a new mobile application. If the customer indicates their departure and arrival station in advance, the mobile application should be able to predict the average trip time and a cost estimation for the ride. Thanks to this feature, the customers would know in advance if the trip time is compatible with their time schedule and if it's cheaper compared to other public transportation services.

One of the managers of the company may ask you to use **Machine Learning (ML)** to develop the prediction system that will be introduced to the new mobile application. The ML system should predict the trip time of a bike rental using the data that has already been collected and stored in a BigQuery public dataset.

Now that we've explained and understood the problem statement, let's take a look at the machine learning technique that we can use to predict a numerical value such as the duration of a trip.

# Discovering linear regression

**Linear regression** is one of the simplest techniques that we can apply when we have a continuous numerical value to predict. It is a well-known algorithm that was initially introduced in statistics to analyze the correlation between different variables.

> **Important note**
> In statistics, the term regression means that two variables are correlated. This term describes a cause and effect relationship. The cause is called the **independent variable**, while the effect is called the **dependent variable**. The dependent variable can be calculated as a function of the independent variable.

The following diagram shows the graphical representation of a simple linear relationship between two variables:

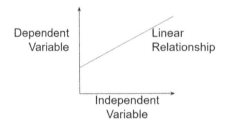

Figure 4.2 – Representation of simple linear regression

A linear regression model tries to predict the label by finding the best linear relationship between the label and its features. If the machine learning model uses only one input variable, the model is defined as **simple linear regression**. If the ML model is based on multiple features, it is called **multivariate linear regression**.

In our business scenario, the duration of a ride can be expressed with a numeric value, so we can use the linear regression approach to train our ML model. An example of simple linear regression is represented by the possibility to leverage only one variable, such as the distance between the start and stop station, to predict the outcome. Multivariate linear regression is based on multiple input variables. In our scenario this could be the distance between the start and stop stations, the age of the rider, and the day of the week when the rent occurred.

Training a linear regression model means trying to find the values of the coefficients that can be used in the linear equation between the input variables, called features, and the output variable, called the label.

We won't go through all the details of linear regression in this book, but we can mention some examples of linear relation to better understand this concept. In real life, we can find a lot of measures that can be well-estimated with linear regression, such as the following:

- The weight of a person is dependent on their height.
- The revenues of a company are a function of the number of customers.
- The quantity of fuel consumed by a plane is conditioned by the distance traveled.

Now that we've learned the basics of linear regression, it's time to take a look at the dataset that we'll use to build our machine learning model.

# Exploring and understanding the dataset

Before diving into the machine learning implementation, it's necessary to analyze the data that is available for our use case. Since machine learning training is based on examples, we need to clearly understand what data to consider and check the quality of the available records.

> **Tip**
> Data scientists and business analysts spend a lot of time and resources getting a clear understanding of the datasets, checking their quality, and preparing them. Although these operations don't seem to be directly linked to the realization of a machine learning algorithm, they are essential if you wish to get solid results. The actual training of the model is the last mile of a longer journey that begins with comprehending data, the control of its quality, and preparing it.

Let's start by getting a clear understanding of the information that we have in our dataset to build our use case.

# Understanding the data

To have a clear understanding of the dataset that we're going to be using for the implementation of this use case, we need to do the following:

1. Log into Google Cloud Console and access the BigQuery user interface from the navigation menu:

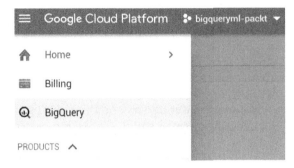

Figure 4.3 – Accessing the BigQuery service from the GCP console

2. Create a new dataset under the project that we created in *Chapter 2, Setting Up Your GCP and BigQuery Environment*. To do this, we need to select our GCP project in the BigQuery navigation menu and click on the **Create Dataset** button. For this scenario, we'll choose the name 04_nyc_bike_sharing, keeping all the other options with default values:

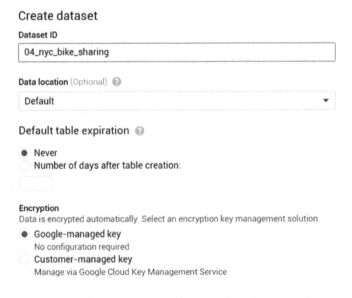

Figure 4.4 – Creating the new BigQuery dataset to host the assets of our use case

This dataset will contain our BigQuery ML model and all the intermediate tables that we'll create in the next steps of this chapter.

Once the dataset has been created, it will be visible in the BigQuery navigation menu, as shown in the following screenshot:

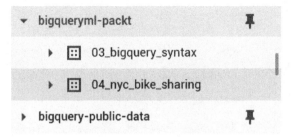

Figure 4.5 – The new dataset is available within the GCP project and
visible in the BigQuery navigation menu

3. Open the **bigquery-public-data** GCP project that hosts all the BigQuery public datasets and browse the items until you find the **new_york_citibike** dataset. In this public dataset, we will see two BigQuery tables: **citibike_stations** and **citibike_trips**. The first table is a registry of the stations of our bike sharing service, while the second one is the most interesting for our use case. We can start analyzing it now:

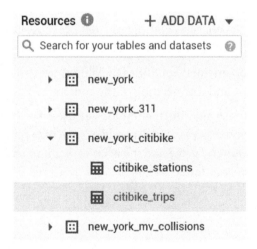

Figure 4.6 – The New York Citi Bike Public dataset contains two
different tables that can be used for our business scenario

4. Let's click on the **citibike_trips** table in the BigQuery navigation menu to access the schema of the table:

## citibike_trips

QUERY TABLE

Schema    Details    Preview

| Field name | Type | Mode | Policy tags | Description |
| --- | --- | --- | --- | --- |
| tripduration | INTEGER | NULLABLE | | Trip Duration (in seconds) |
| starttime | DATETIME | NULLABLE | | Start Time, in NYC local time. |
| stoptime | DATETIME | NULLABLE | | Stop Time, in NYC local time. |
| start_station_id | INTEGER | NULLABLE | | Start Station ID |
| start_station_name | STRING | NULLABLE | | Start Station Name |
| start_station_latitude | FLOAT | NULLABLE | | Start Station Latitude |
| start_station_longitude | FLOAT | NULLABLE | | Start Station Longitude |
| end_station_id | INTEGER | NULLABLE | | End Station ID |
| end_station_name | STRING | NULLABLE | | End Station Name |

Figure 4.7 – The structure of the citibike_trips table lists all the fields that can be used as labels and features

The table is well-documented and for each column, we can easily understand the name, the datatypes, and the meaning of the content.

This table contains relevant information for our use case: the **tripduration** field indicates the duration expressed in seconds of each bike rental. The value of **tripduration** is a numeric value and it's what we want to predict in our business scenario, so it will be our **label**.

All the other fields in the table are potential **features**. In fact, we have information about the starting and stopping stations, when the trip happened, and some insights into the customer, such as their age. All these columns could be good candidates for features since the position of the stations is directly related to the distance to go through and affects the duration of the trip. Also, the moment the ride begins could affect the duration because, on some, days the streets could be busier. Then, from a customer perspective, we might guess that young people ride faster than old people. From a schema perspective, we can conclude that this table represents a good dataset for developing our machine learning model, but we need to check our initial guesses further.

5. As the next step, let's take a look at how many records we have in the table and if they're enough for our purposes.

   Clicking on the **Details** tab, we can see that the table contains more than 58 million records:

## citibike_trips

Schema    Details    Preview

### Description ✏

None

### Table info ✏

| | |
|---|---|
| Table ID | bigquery-public-data:new_york_citibike.citibike_trips |
| Table size | 7.47 GB |
| Long-term storage size | 7.47 GB |
| Number of rows | 58,937,715 |
| Created | Apr 12, 2017, 9:40:35 PM |
| Table expiration | Never |
| Last modified | Sep 11, 2018, 3:29:21 AM |
| Data location | US |

Figure 4.8 – The Details tab of the citibike_trips table shows the number of records that are available

We can be extremely confident about building an ML model with this huge amount of data.

In this section, we understood how much information we can obtain just by analyzing the metadata provided by BigQuery in its user interface. Now, it's time to look at the actual data in this table and use it effectively.

## Checking the data's quality

The quality of data is fundamental to building robust machine learning models. An ML model learns from examples. If the examples present incorrect data, the model will inevitably learn from these errors and apply them during the actual usage.

Let's start analyzing the dataset that will be used to build our ML model:

1. Frist of all, we will focus on the `tripduration` field. This is the column that we want to predict with our machine learning model and represents our label:

```
SELECT COUNT(*)
FROM
    `bigquery-public-data.new_york_citibike.citibike_trips`
WHERE
    tripduration is NULL
    OR tripduration<=0;
```

This query statement counts the number of rows with a `tripduration` that's empty or less than zero. Although the table description reported that the dataset only contains trips with a duration greater than 1 minute, we can immediately notice that the outcome of this query is a number greater than 0. In fact, we can find more than five million records with the `tripduration` field not properly valued. Since we cannot train a model on an empty or wrong value of the label, we'll need to exclude these records from our use case.

2. Next, we'll inspect the minimum and the maximum value of the `tripduration` field to evidence any outlier that can cause poor performance for our machine learning model:

```
SELECT  MIN (tripduration)/60 minimum_duration_in_
minutes,
        MAX (tripduration)/60  maximum_duration_in_
minutes
FROM
    `bigquery-public-data.new_york_citibike.citibike_trips`
WHERE
```

```
tripduration is not NULL
AND tripduration>0;
```

While the minimum rental time is an expected value of 1 minute, we can see that the maximum value is not compatible with the normal functionality of a bike sharing service. In fact, the maximum duration is more than 300,000 minutes, which is approximately equivalent to a rental period of more than 225 days.

In the following screenshot, you can see the result of the query:

**Query results**        ⬇ SAVE RESULTS        📈 EXPLORE DATA  ▼

Query complete (0.7 sec elapsed, 405.2 MB processed)

Job information    Results    JSON    Execution details

| Row | minimum_duration_in_minutes | maximum_duration_in_minutes |
|-----|------------------------------|------------------------------|
| 1   | 1.0                          | 325167.48333333334           |

Figure 4.9 – The results of the query, evidencing the presence of outliers in the tripduration column

While preparing our datasets, we'll take all these factors into considerations to avoid any impact on the machine learning model.

3.  Then, we can apply a similar check to all the columns that are potential features of our machine learning model, excluding the records that present a non-significant value of `tripduration`:

```
SELECT   COUNT(*)
FROM
    `bigquery-public-data.new_york_citibike.citibike_trips`
WHERE
    (tripduration is not NULL
    AND tripduration>0) AND (
    starttime is NULL
    OR start_station_name is NULL
    OR end_station_name is NULL
    OR start_station_latitude is NULL
    OR start_station_longitude is NULL
    OR end_station_latitude is NULL
    OR end_station_longitude is NULL);
```

With this query statement, we're only focusing on the records with a rental duration greater than zero and not empty. The goal of the query is to check that all the other potential features are not empty fields.

In this case, the query returns a count of zero. For this reason, we can be confident that, excluding the rows where `tripduration` is NULL, we'll get meaningful values for the other columns.

4.  After that, we can analyze the `birth_year` column, which represents the birth year of the customer that is using the bike sharing service:

```
SELECT   COUNT(*)
FROM
    `bigquery-public-data.new_york_citibike.citibike_trips`
WHERE
    (tripduration is not NULL
    AND tripduration>0)
    AND ( birth_year is NULL);
```

The `SELECT COUNT (*)` statement looks for records where the customer's birth year is empty. The query filters the records where `tripduration` is NULL or less than zero.

Upon executing the query, we can immediately notice that there are more than five million records that contain a NULL value for `birth_year`. We'll need to filter these records in the following stages of our use case.

> **Tip**
> To accelerate the process of composing a SELECT statement on a table and to avoid any typos, BigQuery allows you to use the **Query Table** button, which automatically generates a SQL stub where you need to choose only the fields to extract. In addition, you can also select the table name from the navigation menu, or the column name from the **Schema** tab, to automatically include the name of the selected object in the SQL query that you're composing.

Now that we've performed some quality checks on our dataset, let's focus on segmenting the rows into three different tables: training, evaluation, and prediction.

# Segmenting the dataset

One of the main principles of developing a machine learning model is based on segmenting our dataset into train and evaluation sets, and then using the ML model on different records.

Let's start segmenting the dataset by performing the following steps:

1. To understand how the data is distributed across the years and months, we can use the following query statement:

```
SELECT
    EXTRACT (YEAR FROM starttime) year,
    EXTRACT (MONTH FROM starttime) month,
    count(*) total
FROM
    `bigquery-public-data.new_york_citibike.citibike_trips`
WHERE
    EXTRACT (YEAR FROM starttime)=2017 OR
    EXTRACT (YEAR FROM starttime)=2018
    AND (tripduration>=3*60 AND tripduration<=3*60*60)
    AND  birth_year is not NULL
    AND birth_year < 2007
GROUP BY
    year, month
ORDER BY
    year, month asc;
```

The SELECT statement extracts the year and the month from the starttime field, which indicates the exact moment when the bike trip started.

To extract a portion of the entire timestamp, we can use the EXTRACT function, which accepts a parameter such as YEAR, MONTH, QUARTER, WEEK, DAYOFYEAR, or DAYOFWEEK as input, followed by the FROM keyword and the field that contains the date expression.

The query already excludes all the bad records that we found in the previous section and focuses on 2017 and 2018.

To exclude outliers in the tripduration column, we're only taking into consideration the rows with a minimum rental time of 3 minutes and a maximum of 3 hours.

We can also add a filter to the year of birth of our customers, by filtering all the records with an empty `birth_year` and ignoring all the customers born after 2007.

The query counts the number of rows segmenting the results per year and month with the GROUP BY clause and orders these periods in ascending mode, as specified in the ORDER BY clause.

In the following screenshot, you can see the query's result:

| Query results | ↧ SAVE RESULTS |
|---|---|

Query complete (0.0 sec elapsed, cached)

| Job information | Results | JSON | Execution details |
|---|---|---|---|

| Row | year | month | total |
|---|---|---|---|
| 1 | 2017 | 4 | 1315404 |
| 2 | 2017 | 5 | 1523268 |
| 3 | 2017 | 6 | 1731594 |
| 4 | 2017 | 7 | 1735599 |
| 5 | 2017 | 8 | 1816498 |
| 6 | 2017 | 9 | 1878098 |
| 7 | 2017 | 10 | 1897592 |
| 8 | 2017 | 11 | 1330649 |
| 9 | 2017 | 12 | 889967 |
| 10 | 2018 | 1 | 668885 |
| 11 | 2018 | 2 | 782785 |
| 12 | 2018 | 3 | 909781 |
| 13 | 2018 | 4 | 1224906 |
| 14 | 2018 | 5 | 1728078 |

Figure 4.10 – The results of the query describe the segmentation on a monthly basis

From the results of the query, we can see that the dataset goes from April 2017 until May 2018. We can use a rule of thumb and keep 80% of the data for training, 10% for evaluation, and the remaining 10% for prediction. By applying this rule to our dataset, we'll use the first 11 months for the training stage, the following 2 months for the evaluation stage, and the last month for the prediction stage.

2.  Applying what we decided on in the previous step, let's create a table that contains only the rows that will be used to train our BigQuery ML model:

```
CREATE OR REPLACE TABLE `04_nyc_bike_sharing.training_
table` AS
  SELECT
    tripduration/60 tripduration,
```

```
                        starttime,
                        stoptime,
                        start_station_id,
                        start_station_name,
                        start_station_latitude,
                        start_station_longitude,
                        end_station_id,
                        end_station_name,
                        end_station_latitude,
                        end_station_longitude,
                        bikeid,
                        usertype,
                        birth_year,
                        gender,
                        customer_plan
    FROM
        `bigquery-public-data.new_york_citibike.citibike_
    trips`
    WHERE
        (
            (EXTRACT (YEAR FROM starttime)=2017 AND
             (EXTRACT (MONTH FROM starttime)>=04 OR
              EXTRACT (MONTH FROM starttime)<=10))
            OR (EXTRACT (YEAR FROM starttime)=2018 AND
             (EXTRACT (MONTH FROM starttime)>=01 OR
              EXTRACT (MONTH FROM starttime)<=02))
        )
        AND (tripduration>=3*60 AND tripduration<=3*60*60)
        AND birth_year is not NULL
        AND birth_year < 2007;
```

The result of the query is stored in the new `04_nyc_bike_sharing.
training_table` table that we created to support the following steps of
our use case.

The SELECT statement extracts all the fields inside the citibike_trips table
from the BigQuery public dataset, converting the value of tripduration from
seconds into minutes.

The WHERE clause allows us to consider only the months that we want to use for the training stage. The time frame goes from April 2017 to February 2018. We've also applied the filters that come from the data quality checks in the same clause.

3.  Now that we've delimited the training dataset, we can create another table dedicated to the records that will be used to evaluate our machine learning model:

```
CREATE OR REPLACE TABLE `04_nyc_bike_sharing.evaluation_
table` AS
SELECT
    tripduration/60 tripduration,
                    starttime,
                    stoptime,
                    start_station_id,
                    start_station_name,
                    start_station_latitude,
                    start_station_longitude,
                    end_station_id,
                    end_station_name,
                    end_station_latitude,
                    end_station_longitude,
                    bikeid,
                    usertype,
                    birth_year,
                    gender,
                    customer_plan
            FROM
        `bigquery-public-data.new_york_citibike.citibike_
trips`
            WHERE
    (EXTRACT (YEAR FROM starttime)=2018 AND
        (EXTRACT (MONTH FROM starttime)=03 OR
         EXTRACT (MONTH FROM starttime)=04))
    AND (tripduration>=3*60 AND tripduration<=3*60*60)
    AND  birth_year is not NULL
    AND birth_year < 2007;
```

The query is very similar to the statement that was used to create the training table. The only difference is related to the period we selected in the WHERE clause. For evaluation_table, we've focused our SELECT statement on the records from March and April 2018, which were previously excluded from the training table.

4. Using the same approach, we can also create the table that will be used to test our machine learning model:

```
CREATE OR REPLACE TABLE `04_nyc_bike_sharing.prediction_
table` AS
SELECT
     tripduration/60 tripduration,
                      starttime,
                      stoptime,
                      start_station_id,
                      start_station_name,
                      start_station_latitude,
                      start_station_longitude,
                      end_station_id,
                      end_station_name,
                      end_station_latitude,
                      end_station_longitude, bikeid,
                      usertype, birth_year, gender,
                      customer_plan
FROM
     `bigquery-public-data.new_york_citibike.citibike_
trips`
WHERE
     EXTRACT (YEAR FROM starttime)=2018
     AND EXTRACT (MONTH FROM starttime)=05
     AND (tripduration>=3*60 AND tripduration<=3*60*60)
     AND birth_year is not NULL
     AND birth_year < 2007;
```

The query will apply the necessary logic but will only take the month of May 2018 into consideration.

Now that we've segmented our dataset and we're clear about which records to use for the training, evaluation, and test phases, let's dive into the ML model's creation.

# Training the linear regression model

Training a BigQuery ML model is not a one-shot operation, but it's a process that can require multiple attempts and recycles to get closer to the final goal of developing an effective asset with good performance, according to the requirements of the business scenario. For our use case, we'll go try to improve the performance of our ML model multiple times. Let's get started:

1. First, let's start training a new machine learning model named `trip_duration_by_stations`:

```
CREATE OR REPLACE MODEL `04_nyc_bike_sharing.trip_
duration_by_stations`
OPTIONS
  (model_type='linear_reg') AS
SELECT
  start_station_name,
  end_station_name,
  tripduration as label
FROM
  `04_nyc_bike_sharing.training_table`;
```

In this statement, we can notice the CREATE OR REPLACE MODEL keyword, which is used to create a new model. This keyword is followed by the identifier of the model, which is represented by concatenating the dataset and ML model name.

After these first lines, we have the OPTIONS keyword, where the type of machine learning model to use is specified. In this case, we're using a linear regression identified by model_type='linear_reg'.

After OPTIONS, we need to specify the set of records that the ML model will be trained on. For this first attempt, we will decide to use only two features: the names of the start and of stop stations of the bike trip.

With the as label keyword, we are instructing BigQuery to use tripduration as the label for our machine learning model. As an alternative, it is possible to include the label among the list of OPTIONS with the INPUT_LABEL_COLS keyword, as shown in the following snippet of code:

```
OPTIONS
  (model_type='linear_reg'
  input_label_cols=['tripduration'])
```

After a few seconds, the BigQuery ML model will be created and available in the navigation menu, under the `04_nyc_bike_sharing` dataset. Select the ML model and click on the **Evaluation** tab, where we will find some performance indicators for our brand-new ML model; that is, `trip_duration_by_stations`.

In this case, we'll focus our attention on **Mean absolute error**. This value represents the average distance between the actual value and the predicted value of the label.

As shown in the following screenshot, it's very close to 7 minutes:

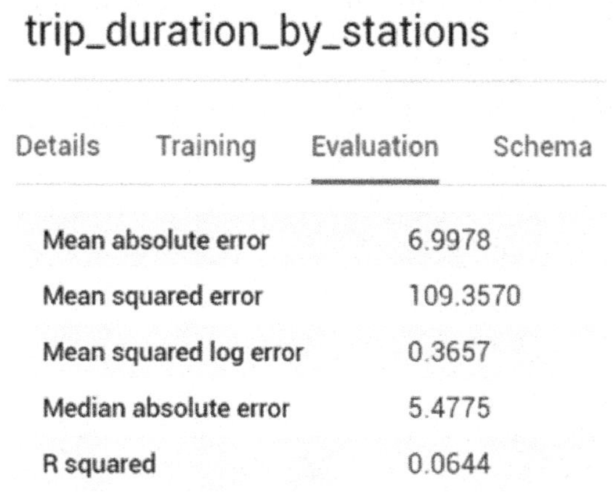

## trip_duration_by_stations

| Details | Training | Evaluation | Schema |
|---------|----------|------------|--------|

| | |
|---|---|
| Mean absolute error | 6.9978 |
| Mean squared error | 109.3570 |
| Mean squared log error | 0.3657 |
| Median absolute error | 5.4775 |
| R squared | 0.0644 |

Figure 4.11 – The Evaluation tab shows some key performance indicators of the ML model

2. Now, let's try to enrich the ML model with other features that can bring additional value:

```
CREATE OR REPLACE MODEL `04_nyc_bike_sharing.trip_
duration_by_stations_and_day`
OPTIONS
  (model_type='linear_reg') AS
SELECT
  start_station_name,
  end_station_name,
    IF (EXTRACT(DAYOFWEEK FROM starttime)=1 OR
        EXTRACT(DAYOFWEEK FROM starttime)=7,
        true, false) is_weekend,
  tripduration as label
FROM
  `04_nyc_bike_sharing.training_table`;
```

In this second model, we've added a new feature called `is_weekend`. This field is a **boolean** value that calculates and extracts the day of the week in which the bike rental happened. It is generated by an `IF` statement that returns `true` if the day is Sunday or Saturday, represented by the values `1` and `7`; otherwise, it's `false`.

If we check the mean absolute error of this new BigQuery ML model, we can notice that we've slightly improved the performance of our model with a value of 6.7784.

3.  Since we've had some improvements from adding more features, let's try including the age of the customer as a new parameter for our ML model:

```
CREATE OR REPLACE MODEL
    `04_nyc_bike_sharing.trip_duration_by_stations_day_age`
OPTIONS
    (model_type='linear_reg') AS
SELECT
    start_station_name,
    end_station_name,
    IF (EXTRACT(DAYOFWEEK FROM starttime)=1 OR
        EXTRACT(DAYOFWEEK FROM starttime)=7,
        true, false) is_weekend,
    EXTRACT(YEAR FROM starttime)-birth_year as age,
    tripduration as label
FROM
    `04_nyc_bike_sharing.training_table`;
```

Compared to the previous model, we've added the new `age` column, which is calculated as the difference between the year of `starttime` and the customer's birth year.

Once we've executed the query statement, we will see that the new `age` feature doesn't improve the performance of our ML model. This is because the mean absolute error is 6.9508. This value is better compared to our first attempt, but worse than the second.

In this section, we created different ML models while trying to use different features in our dataset. Next, we will continue using the `trip_duration_by_stations_and_day` model, which, during the training phase, realized the best performance in terms of mean absolute error.

Now, let's learn how to start the evaluation phase.

# Evaluating the linear regression model

For the evaluation stage of our BigQuery ML model, we'll use the `ML.EVALUATE` function and the table that we've expressly created to host the evaluation records. These are completely separate from the rows that are used during the training phase.

Let's execute the following query to evaluate our ML model on the evaluation table:

```
SELECT
  *
FROM
  ML.EVALUATE(MODEL `04_nyc_bike_sharing.trip_duration_by_
stations_and_day`,
    (
    SELECT
        start_station_name,
        end_station_name,

        IF (EXTRACT(DAYOFWEEK FROM starttime)=1 OR
            EXTRACT(DAYOFWEEK FROM starttime)=7,
            true, false) is_weekend,
        tripduration as label
    FROM
        `04_nyc_bike_sharing.evaluation_table`));
```

The `SELECT` statement extracts all the fields returned by the `ML.EVALUATE` function. The evaluation function is applied to the `04_nyc_bike_sharing.trip_duration_by_stations_and_day` model and on the rows that have been extracted from the `evaluation_table` table.

The most internal `SELECT` extracts the same fields that were used to train the ML model as the features that are applying the same transformations, such as on the `is_weekend` field, which is calculated with the same logic as the training phase.

The results of the query show a mean absolute error very close to 7 minutes, which is similar to the value of 6.7784 that was achieved during the training phase. For this reason, we can say that the ML model maintains its performance on a dataset different from the training one. We can say that the model is not affected by overfitting.

In the following screenshot, you can see the performance indicators that have been extracted by the evaluation query:

Figure 4.12 – The query results of the EVALUATE function show the ML key performance calculated on the evaluation table

Now that we've trained the model and we're also satisfied with the outcomes of the evaluation stage, let's learn how to apply our machine learning model to other records and get predictions.

# Utilizing the linear regression model

To use our BigQuery ML model, we'll use the ML.PREDICT function and the table that we've expressly created to host the records that we haven't used yet.

The following query will predict the label using the data in prediction_table:

```
SELECT
    tripduration as actual_duration,
    predicted_label as predicted_duration,
    ABS(tripduration - predicted_label) difference_in_min
FROM
  ML.PREDICT(MODEL `04_nyc_bike_sharing.trip_duration_by_
stations_and_day`,
    (
    SELECT
          start_station_name,
          end_station_name,
          IF (EXTRACT(DAYOFWEEK FROM starttime)=1 OR
                EXTRACT(DAYOFWEEK FROM starttime)=7,
                true, false) is_weekend,
          tripduration
      FROM
```

```
                    `04_nyc_bike_sharing.prediction_table`
      ))
      order by  difference_in_min asc;
```

The query statement is composed of a `SELECT` keyword, which extracts the actual and the predicted duration of the rental. It calculates the difference in minutes and orders the results from the minimum to the maximum difference of minutes. To calculate the difference, we used the `ABS` function, which extracts the absolute value of a numeric.

The `ML.PREDICT` function is applied to the `SELECT` statement, which extracts the features and the actual duration from `prediction_table`. This last field is only used for comparison with the predicted value and is not used to run the ML model.

In the following screenshot, you can see the results of the query execution:

**Query results**    ⬇ SAVE RESULTS    📊 EXPLORE DATA ▾

Query complete (6.5 sec elapsed, 97.7 MB processed)

Job information    Results    JSON    Execution details

| Row | actual_duration | predicted_duration | difference_in_min |
|-----|-----------------|--------------------|--------------------|
| 1 | 18.6 | 18.599995101018067 | 4.8989819347866614E-6 |
| 2 | 13.116666666666667 | 13.116674835753656 | 8.169086989084917E-6 |
| 3 | 13.916666666666666 | 13.916703420349222 | 3.67536825560677E-5 |
| 4 | 16.85 | 16.84995424610679 | 4.5753893211042396E-5 |
| 5 | 13.866666666666667 | 13.866617554671393 | 4.911199527413146E-5 |
| 6 | 12.183333333333334 | 12.183281020308641 | 5.23130246925518135E-5 |
| 7 | 14.116666666666667 | 14.11660604993267 | 6.0616733996671008E-5 |
| 8 | 12.166666666666666 | 12.166597239696785 | 6.94269698815475E-5 |
| 9 | 10.333333333333334 | 10.333412595877235 | 7.926254390078213E-5 |
| 10 | 12.35 | 12.34991964386063 | 8.035613936918651E-5 |
| 11 | 13.633333333333333 | 13.633251609004219 | 8.172432911379701E-5 |
| 12 | 18.783333333333335 | 18.783416480979213 | 8.314764587780132E-5 |

Figure 4.13 – The query results of the PREDICT function show the actual and the predicted duration.

Now that we've applied our model, let's formulate some final considerations and provide the answers to our managers about the possibility of predicting the trip duration of a bike rental.

# Drawing business conclusions

In this section, we'll formulate some final considerations using the results that we got from applying our ML model.

By enriching the previous query with a parent SELECT COUNT statement, we can identify how many predictions are less than 15 minutes away from the actual value.

Let's execute the following query to calculate how often the trip duration predictions are far from the actual values:

```
SELECT COUNT (*)
FROM (
SELECT
    tripduration as actual_duration,
    predicted_label as predicted_duration,
    ABS(tripduration - predicted_label) difference_in_min
FROM
  ML.PREDICT(MODEL `04_nyc_bike_sharing.trip_duration_by_
stations_and_day`,
    (
    SELECT
          start_station_name,
          end_station_name,
          IF (EXTRACT(DAYOFWEEK FROM starttime)=1 OR
                EXTRACT(DAYOFWEEK FROM starttime)=7,
                true, false) is_weekend,
          tripduration
    FROM
          `04_nyc_bike_sharing.prediction_table`
    ))
    order by difference_in_min asc) where difference_in_
min<=15;
```

The result of the SELECT COUNT query returns a value of 1,548,370 predictions, with a difference between the predicted and the actual value being less than 15 minutes.

Considering that the total size of the prediction_table table is 1,728,078, we can say that in 89.6% of cases, our machine learning model is able to predict the trip duration with a gap that's less than 15 minutes.

For the reasons we expressed previously, we can suggest to management to start with a quarterly fare for the new on-demand and pay-as-you-go pricing model. With this strategy, when a customer picks up a bike from a start station and specifies its destination on the mobile application on a specific day of the week, our model will be able to predict the exact fare of the ride with a mean absolute error of about 7 minutes. The 89.6% the application will provide a good estimation of the price to our customer.

# Summary

In this chapter, we built our first machine learning use case based on a real-life scenario. After a brief introduction to the use case, we discovered what linear regression is and how it can be used to predict numerical values.

Before diving into actually developing the machine learning model, we learned that having a clear understanding of the data and checking its quality is fundamental to getting effective machine learning models. To start from a solid foundation, we leveraged the BigQuery public dataset, which collects information about all the rentals for a bike sharing service in New York City.

For training the model, we used different features to understand which variables are relevant to building our BigQuery ML model.

Then, we chose one machine learning model to carry on to the evaluation stage. In this phase, we used the BigQuery evaluation function to verify that the machine learning model could also effectively work on new rows outside the training dataset.

Finally, we applied our ML model to a third subset of records to predict the duration of each bike rental. We did this by leveraging the start and stop stations chosen by the user and the day of the week that the trip is happening on.

We also calculated that 89% of them have a difference of less than 15 minutes compared to the actual duration of the trip. For this reason, we can conclude that we can provide a good user experience to our customers if the company applies a quarterly fare to our new pay-as-you-go offering.

In the next chapter, we'll discover binary logistic regression and how to use it with BigQuery ML to predict boolean variables.

# Further reading

- **NYC Bike Sharing Public Dataset**: `https://console.cloud.google.com/marketplace/product/city-of-new-york/nyc-citi-bike`

- **BigQuery ML Create Model**: `https://cloud.google.com/bigquery-ml/docs/reference/standard-sql/bigqueryml-syntax-create`

- **BigQuery ML Evaluate Model**: `https://cloud.google.com/bigquery-ml/docs/reference/standard-sql/bigqueryml-syntax-evaluate`

- **BigQuery ML Predict**: `https://cloud.google.com/bigquery-ml/docs/reference/standard-sql/bigqueryml-syntax-predict`

- **BigQuery ML Linear Regression Example**: `https://cloud.google.com/bigquery-ml/docs/bigqueryml-natality`

# 5

# Predicting Boolean Values Using Binary Logistic Regression

Binary logistic regression is one of the most widely used **Machine Learning** (**ML**) algorithms to predict the classification of future events and behaviors. It's used in different industries and contexts. Some variables that can be predicted with this technique are the propensity to buy a product and the probability of getting positive or negative feedback from customers for a specific service.

Most digital native companies offer their services in subscription mode. In streaming video services, telco operators, and pay TVs, the binary logistic regression technique is widely used to predict the probability of churn of a customer. Predicting this kind of information is fundamental to target marketing campaigns and special offers to customers with the highest propensity to buy and increase revenue.

In this chapter, we'll see all the stages necessary to implement a binary logistic regression model leveraging BigQuery ML.

Using the BigQuery ML SQL language, we'll go through the following topics:

- Introducing the business scenario
- Discovering binary logistic regression
- Exploring and understanding the dataset
- Training the binary logistic regression model
- Evaluating the binary logistic regression model
- Using the binary logistic regression model
- Drawing business conclusions

# Technical requirements

This chapter requires access to a web browser and the possibility to leverage the following:

- A GCP account to access Google Cloud Console
- A GCP project to host the BigQuery datasets

Now that we're ready with the technical requirements, let's dive into the analysis and development of our BigQuery ML binary logistic regression model.

Check out the following video to see the Code in Action: `https://bit.ly/2QXCGHM`

# Introducing the business scenario

In this section, we'll introduce the business scenario that will be tackled with binary logistic regression.

Let's take an example wherein you are a taxi driver who is passionate about ML. You're currently working in Chicago and your goal is to provide an additional tool to all your colleagues to understand the probability of getting a tip from your customers.

Getting a tip from a customer is very important for taxi drivers to increase their income. Predicting the probability of getting a tip can be useful to, for example, know when to reserve a particularly gentle treatment for a specific subset of customers.

In the following photo, you can see a taxi in Chicago:

Figure 5.1 – Taxi in Chicago

The city of Chicago has collected information about most of the taxi trips that have occurred since 2013. This dataset is available in the BigQuery public datasets marketplace (`https://console.cloud.google.com/marketplace/details/city-of-chicago-public-data/chicago-taxi-trips`) and can be easily accessed and used.

Your goal is to leverage the available information about taxi trips, such as the payment type, the miles traveled, the fare, and the name of the taxi company, to predict whether a taxi driver will receive a tip at the end of the taxi ride.

Now that we've explained and understood the business scenario, let's take a look at the ML technique that we can use to predict whether a specific event will happen or not.

# Discovering binary logistic regression

In this section, we'll learn what **binary logistic regression** is and we'll understand the use cases that can be tackled with this ML algorithm.

**Logistic regression** is a classification ML technique that can be used to predict a categorical variable. We can apply **binary logistic regression** when the variable to predict is binary and can assume only two values, such as true or false, yes or no, or 1 or 0.

In order to predict one of the two labels, this ML algorithm calculates the probability of two different outcomes and allows us to choose a probability threshold to get the final classification of the binary variable.

Since this is an algorithm based on a regression technique, the prediction of the label is based on a set of independent variables called features that are used to predict the dependent variable, called a label.

This ML technique can be used to answer relevant business questions across different industries, such as the following:

- Will this customer buy my product?
- Is my customer satisfied with my service?
- Will my customer unsubscribe from my service in the next months?
- Will this student pass the next exam?
- Will this person develop diabetes in the next year?

In our business scenario, the possibility of getting a tip at the end of a taxi ride can be predicted by leveraging binary logistic regression. In fact, we're interested in predicting whether a certain event will happen or not. If the taxi driver will get a tip, the binary categorical variable will be valued with 1, otherwise 0.

Training a binary logistic regression model means trying to find the values of the coefficients that can be used in the equation between the input variables, called features, and the binary output variable, called the label.

After the training, we'll leverage a **confusion matrix** to evaluate the performance of our binary logistic regression model. In this matrix, the rows represent the predicted value of the label while the columns are used to store the actual values.

The following figure represents a confusion matrix that is used to evaluate the performances of the binary logistic regression:

| | | Actual Value | |
|---|---|---|---|
| | | **Positive** | **Negative** |
| **Predicted Value** | **Positive** | True Positive | False Positive |
| | **Negative** | False Negative | True Negative |

Figure 5.2 – Confusion matrix

This matrix allows us to visualize the performance of an ML algorithm, comparing the right predictions with the wrong ones.

From the numbers that will be presented in the confusion matrix, we can extract a fundamental performance indicator for logistic regression models: the **Area Under the Curve (AUC)** and the **Receiver Operating Characteristic (ROC)**. The **ROC** is a curve that helps us in measuring the performance of a classification scenario with various thresholds. Basically, it tells us the capability of our ML model in predicting the right class.

The **ROC** curve is a graph plotted using the following two parameters:

- **False positive rate** on the abscissa axis. This parameter is calculated as the ratio between the number of **false positives** and the sum of **false positives** and **true negatives**.

- **True positive rate** on the ordinate axis. This parameter is also called the **recall** of the model. It is calculated as the ratio between **true positives** and the sum of **true positives** and **false negatives**.

If the **area under the curve**, called the **AUC**, is high and close to 1, the model is more likely to be able to predict the right label.

We've learned about the basics of binary logistic regression; now it's time to take a look at the dataset that we'll use to build our ML model.

# Exploring and understanding the dataset

As we learned in *Chapter 4, Predicting Numerical Values with Linear Regression*, before diving into the ML implementation, it's necessary to analyze the data available for our use case. We need to begin by having a clear understanding of the data that can be used for our business scenario.

## Understanding the data

To start exploring the data, we need to do the following:

1. Log in to Google Cloud Console and access the **BigQuery** user interface from the navigation menu.

2. Create a new dataset in the project that we created in *Chapter 2, Setting Up Your GCP and BigQuery Environment*. For this use case, we'll create the `05_chicago_taxi` dataset with the default options.

3.  Open the `bigquery-public-data` GCP project that hosts all the BigQuery public datasets and browse the items until you find the `chicago_taxi_trips` dataset. In this public dataset, we can see only one BigQuery table: `taxi_trips`. This table contains all the information about the taxi rides that happened in the city of Chicago and we'll use it to train and test our ML model:

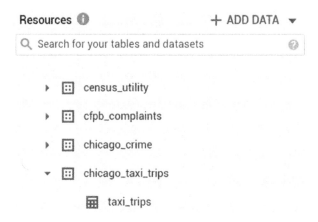

Figure 5.3 – The chicago_taxi_trips dataset contains only one table: taxi_trips

4.  Let's click on the table named **taxi_trips** in the BigQuery navigation menu to access the schema of the table.

    Each field is well described and also the names of the columns seem self-explanatory.

    The table contains the `tips` column, represented with the numeric `FLOAT` format. Apparently, this might seem like a problem because our ML model is only able to predict Boolean values. This situation can easily be overcome by transforming the numeric value into a binary value by applying the following rule: if the value of `tips` is greater than 0, the label is 1, otherwise it's 0.

    We can leverage all the other columns in the table as **features** of our ML model. The duration of the taxi ride could be a good feature because during longer rides, the taxi driver has more time to familiarize themselves with the customer than during short trips of just some minutes. The pick-up and drop-off locations can impact the tip because, as we can imagine, some areas are more profitable than others. For example, an area of the city with a lot of businesses and offices of large companies can increase the probability of getting a tip.

The payment type used to pay for the taxi ride is another important factor in our analysis. When you need to pay a taxi driver with electronic payment, it's usually easier to give a tip simply by pressing a button on the **Point of Sale (POS)** device.

Furthermore, the name of the taxi company could be another important feature to consider. Some taxi companies can offer a better experience to customers in terms of services, professionalism of the drivers, and comfort of the cars. All these ingredients can influence a customer in giving a tip to the taxi driver.

From a schema perspective, this table includes a lot of useful information that can be used to develop our binary logistic regression model. Let's proceed with our analysis, deepening our understanding of the data.

5. As a next step, let's take a look at how many records we have in the table and whether they're enough for our purposes. In the **Details** tab, we can notice that the table contains more than 194 million records. We can be confident in building our ML model with this amount of data:

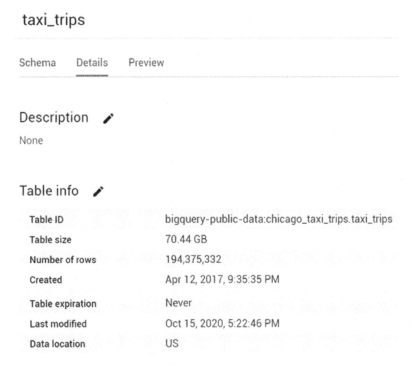

## taxi_trips

Schema    Details    Preview

### Description ✏

None

### Table info ✏

| | |
|---|---|
| Table ID | bigquery-public-data:chicago_taxi_trips.taxi_trips |
| Table size | 70.44 GB |
| Number of rows | 194,375,332 |
| Created | Apr 12, 2017, 9:35:35 PM |
| Table expiration | Never |
| Last modified | Oct 15, 2020, 5:22:46 PM |
| Data location | US |

Figure 5.4 – The Details tab on the taxi_trips table shows the number of records and the table size in terms of GB

6.  Now, let's take a look at the actual data in the `taxi_trips` table:

```
SELECT *
FROM
    `bigquery-public-data.chicago_taxi_trips.taxi_trips`
LIMIT 10;
```

The query shows all the fields of the table filtering on the first 10 rows. The `LIMIT` `10` clause is used to limit the number of records in the result set and returns a random selection of rows from the table.

7.  After getting a preview of the table content, we can analyze the time frame of our dataset:

```
SELECT MIN(trip_start_timestamp),  MAX(trip_start_
timestamp)
FROM
    `bigquery-public-data.chicago_taxi_trips.taxi_trips`;
```

The query extracts the minimum and maximum values of the `trip_start_` `timestamp` field to have a clear understanding of the period over which the data is collected.

In the following screenshot, you can view the result of the query execution:

Figure 5.5 – The query returns the minimum and maximum values of the trip_start_timestamp field

At the time of writing this book, the minimum value is represented by 1 January 2013, while the maximum value is 1 October 2020.

8.  Then, we can apply a data quality check on the `tips` field on which our label will be based. In fact, if the `tips` column is greater than 0, we can assume that the taxi driver got a tip from the customer:

```
SELECT COUNT(*)
FROM
    `bigquery-public-data.chicago_taxi_trips.taxi_trips`
WHERE
        tips IS NULL;
```

In the following screenshot, you can see the result of the query:

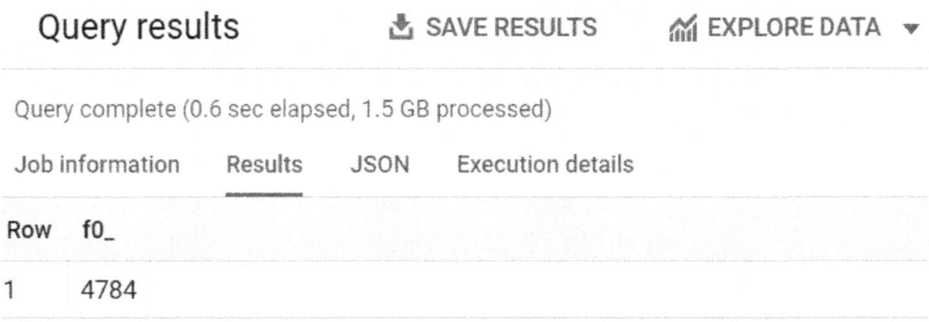

Figure 5.6 – The query returns the 4,784 records with the tips field empty

Executing the `SELECT COUNT(*)` query, we can notice that there are 4,784 records where the `tips` field is empty. We'll take into consideration this aspect during the creation of the ML model, filtering these rows.

In this section, we've analyzed the dataset that we can leverage in order to build our ML model, so now let's start segmenting it into three different sets: training, evaluation, and classification.

## Segmenting the dataset

Before implementing our binary logistic regression model, let's segment our dataset according to the main stages of the ML development: training, evaluation, and use:

1.  To understand how the data is distributed across the years and months, we can use the following query statement:

```
SELECT      EXTRACT (YEAR FROM trip_start_timestamp) year,
            EXTRACT (MONTH FROM trip_start_timestamp)
  month,
```

```
           COUNT(*) total
FROM
           `bigquery-public-data.chicago_taxi_trips.taxi_
trips`
WHERE
           tips IS NOT NULL AND
           trip_seconds IS NOT NULL AND
           trip_miles IS NOT NULL AND
           fare IS NOT NULL AND
           tolls IS NOT NULL AND
           pickup_location IS NOT NULL AND
           dropoff_location IS NOT NULL AND
           pickup_latitude IS NOT NULL AND
           pickup_longitude IS NOT NULL AND
           dropoff_latitude IS NOT NULL AND
           dropoff_longitude IS NOT NULL AND
           company IS NOT NULL AND
           trip_miles > 1 AND
           trip_seconds > 180
GROUP BY
           year, month
ORDER BY
           year, month ASC;
```

The SELECT statement extracts the information about the year and month when the taxi rides occurred and for each month counts the total number of rides. This aggregation is possible by the GROUP BY clause at the end of the query.

The query extracts the records from the taxi_trips table but applies some important filters. All the records with an empty tips field are excluded as well as all the rows with the potential features equal to NULL.

In order to exclude outliers and possible incorrect measurements, we've decided to keep only the taxi rides with a duration greater than 3 minutes and longer than a mile.

Thanks to the ORDER BY clause, the results are ascendingly ordered:

## Query results          ⬇ SAVE RESULTS          📊 EXPLORE DATA ▾

Query complete (1.6 sec elapsed, 28.9 GB processed)

Job information          Results     JSON      Execution details

| 77 | 2019 | 5  | 810569 |
| 78 | 2019 | 6  | 788532 |
| 79 | 2019 | 7  | 680325 |
| 80 | 2019 | 8  | 694797 |
| 81 | 2019 | 9  | 696366 |
| 82 | 2019 | 10 | 744058 |
| 83 | 2019 | 11 | 626830 |
| 84 | 2019 | 12 | 623870 |
| 85 | 2020 | 1  | 522424 |
| 86 | 2020 | 2  | 546626 |
| 87 | 2020 | 3  | 271362 |
| 88 | 2020 | 4  | 28252 |
| 89 | 2020 | 5  | 37673 |
| 90 | 2020 | 6  | 54740 |
| 91 | 2020 | 7  | 68334 |
| 92 | 2020 | 8  | 74976 |
| 93 | 2020 | 9  | 86214 |
| 94 | 2020 | 10 | 4 |

Figure 5.7 – The query returns the distribution of the records in the taxi_trips table

Focusing on the most recent months, we can immediately notice a drop in the numbers in April 2020. This sudden decrease is probably caused by the restrictions introduced to manage the COVID-19 pandemic. To avoid any impact of this event on our analysis, let's focus our implementation only on the year 2019. We'll split our dataset using a time frame that starts from January 2019 up to October 2019.

2.  Let's create a table that contains the rows that will be used to train our BigQuery ML model. For this use case, we'll select only the taxi rides that occurred from January 2019 until August 2019 inclusive:

```
CREATE OR REPLACE TABLE `05_chicago_taxi.training_table`
AS
      SELECT *
      FROM
              `bigquery-public-data.chicago_taxi_trips.taxi_
      trips`
      WHERE
              tips IS NOT NULL AND
              trip_seconds IS NOT NULL AND
              trip_miles IS NOT NULL AND
              fare IS NOT NULL AND
              tolls IS NOT NULL AND
              pickup_location IS NOT NULL AND
              dropoff_location IS NOT NULL AND
              pickup_latitude IS NOT NULL AND
              pickup_longitude IS NOT NULL AND
              dropoff_latitude IS NOT NULL AND
              dropoff_longitude IS NOT NULL AND
              company IS NOT NULL AND
              trip_miles > 1 AND
              trip_seconds > 180 AND
              EXTRACT (YEAR FROM trip_start_timestamp) =
      2019 AND
              (EXTRACT (MONTH FROM trip_start_timestamp) >=1
      AND EXTRACT (MONTH FROM trip_start_timestamp)<=8);
```

As we can notice from the CREATE TABLE statement, the query filters all the rows with empty features and labels that could cause issues during the implementation of the ML model.

3.  After that, we create another table dedicated to the records that will be used to evaluate our ML model:

```
CREATE OR REPLACE TABLE `05_chicago_taxi.evaluation_
table` AS
      SELECT *
```

```
        FROM
                `bigquery-public-data.chicago_taxi_trips.taxi_
trips`
        WHERE
                tips IS NOT NULL AND
                trip_seconds IS NOT NULL AND
                trip_miles IS NOT NULL AND
                fare IS NOT NULL AND
                tolls IS NOT NULL AND
                pickup_location IS NOT NULL AND
                dropoff_location IS NOT NULL AND
                pickup_latitude IS NOT NULL AND
                pickup_longitude IS NOT NULL AND
                dropoff_latitude IS NOT NULL AND
                dropoff_longitude IS NOT NULL AND
                company IS NOT NULL AND
                trip_miles > 1 AND
                trip_seconds > 180 AND
                EXTRACT (YEAR FROM trip_start_timestamp) =
2019 AND
                EXTRACT (MONTH FROM trip_start_timestamp) =
09;
```

The only difference, compared to the table that contains the training data, is in the month that we've selected to create this table. In this case, we've chosen to include the records related to the month of September of 2019.

4.  The last preparatory step is based on the creation of the table that we'll use to test our binary logistic regression model. Let's create `classification_table` as specified in the following SQL statement:

```
CREATE OR REPLACE TABLE `05_chicago_taxi.classification_
table` AS
    SELECT *
    FROM
            `bigquery-public-data.chicago_taxi_trips.taxi_
trips`
        WHERE
                tips IS NOT NULL AND
```

```
            trip_seconds IS NOT NULL AND
            trip_miles IS NOT NULL AND
            fare IS NOT NULL AND
            tolls IS NOT NULL AND
            pickup_location IS NOT NULL AND
            dropoff_location IS NOT NULL AND
            pickup_latitude IS NOT NULL AND
            pickup_longitude IS NOT NULL AND
            dropoff_latitude IS NOT NULL AND
            dropoff_longitude IS NOT NULL AND
            company IS NOT NULL AND
            trip_miles > 1 AND
            trip_seconds > 180 AND
            EXTRACT (YEAR FROM trip_start_timestamp) =
2019 AND
            EXTRACT (MONTH FROM trip_start_timestamp) =
10;
```

Thanks to the selection and the filters that we've applied in this query, our set will contain only the records related to October 2019. We can also notice that all the other filters remain unchanged and uniform across the three datasets: training, evaluation, and classification.

Now that we've divided our dataset into three parts. Let's start the actual training of the binary logistic regression ML model.

# Training the binary logistic regression model

As we already did in *Chapter 4, Predicting Numerical Values with Linear Regression*, we'll adopt an incremental approach in trying to improve the performance of our ML model at each attempt:

1.  Let's start training our first ML model, `binary_classification_version_1`:

    ```
    CREATE OR REPLACE MODEL `05_chicago_taxi.binary_
    classification_version_1`
    OPTIONS
        (model_type='logistic_reg', labels = ['will_get_tip'])
    AS
        SELECT
    ```

```
      trip_seconds,
      IF(tips>0,1,0) AS will_get_tip
FROM  `05_chicago_taxi.training_table`;
```

In this BigQuery ML statement, we can see the CREATE OR REPLACE MODEL keywords used to start the training of the model. These keywords are followed by the identifier of the ML model. After the identifier, we can notice the OPTIONS clause. As our options, we've chosen to train the model with a logistic_reg algorithm and to use the will_get_tip field as the target label.

The SELECT statement points out that the will_get_tip label is valued with 1 if the value of the tips field is greater than 0, otherwise with 0. In the SELECT statement, we've also included the only feature that we're using for our first attempt: trip_seconds. This feature represents the duration expressed in seconds of the taxi ride.

Finally, the SELECT statement is based on the table that we've created to perform the training of the model: 05_chicago_taxi.training_table.

2.   At the end of the training, we can access the ML model from the BigQuery navigation menu to have a look at the performance of the model. Selecting the **Evaluation** tab, we can see the **ROC AUC** value. In this case, we can see we haven't achieved great results because it is not close to 1; it's **0.5696**:

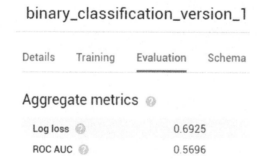

Figure 5.8 – The Evaluation tab shows the ROC AUC value related to the trained ML model

In the same tab, we can also see the ROC curve:

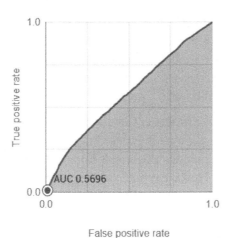

Figure 5.9 – In the Evaluation tab, it is also possible to graphically analyze the ROC curve
and see the blue area under the ROC curve

As we can see from the preceding diagram, the ROC curve, which expresses the rate between the true positive and the false positive, is not close to 1. The blue area under the curve is about 50% of the entire square.

As shown in the following screenshot, we can also leverage the confusion matrix in the same tab to experiment with the outcome of the ML model according to different thresholds:

Score threshold                                             Confusion matrix

| Positive class threshold | ●  0.5118 |
| Positive class | 1 |
| Negative class | 0 |
| Precision | 0.5534 |
| Recall | 0.0111 |
| Accuracy | 0.4828 |
| F1 score | 0.0218 |

| Actual labels | Predicted labels 1 | 0 |
| --- | --- | --- |
| 1 | 1.11% | 98.89% |
| 0 | 0.97% | 99.03% |

Use this slider above to see which score threshold works best
for your model.

Figure 5.10 – In the Evaluation tab, it is also possible to see the confusion matrix of the classification model

3. Let's try to improve our ML model by adding features that can be useful to predict the probability of getting a tip. We'll introduce the fare of the taxi ride, any tolls paid during the ride, and the name of the taxi company as new features:

```
CREATE OR REPLACE MODEL `05_chicago_taxi.binary_
classification_version_2`
OPTIONS
   (model_type='logistic_reg', labels = ['will_get_tip'])
AS
     SELECT
          trip_seconds,
          fare,
          tolls,
          company,
          IF(tips>0,1,0) AS will_get_tip
     FROM  `05_chicago_taxi.training_table`;
```

The CREATE OR REPLACE MODEL part is similar to the previous one but includes the new features previously mentioned. Despite adding the new fields, the improvement in terms of **ROC AUC** is not significant. In fact, with this attempt, we have achieved a value of **0.5902**.

4. It's time to introduce a feature that can be extremely helpful for the development of our ML model. The next ML model, binary_classification_version_3, will introduce the payment type used by the customer to pay the taxi driver:

```
CREATE OR REPLACE MODEL `05_chicago_taxi.binary_
classification_version_3`
OPTIONS
   (model_type='logistic_reg', labels = ['will_get_tip'])
AS
     SELECT
          trip_seconds,
          fare,
          tolls,
          company,
          payment_type,
          IF(tips>0,1,0) AS will_get_tip
     FROM  `05_chicago_taxi.training_table`;
```

After the training of this ML model, we can immediately notice a huge increase in the value of **ROC AUC**. Adding the payment method as a feature to our model, we have achieved a value of **0.9809**. This is very close to 1 and represents a significant improvement in the performance of our binary logistic regression model.

5. The result that we've achieved with the `binary_classification_version_3` ML model in the preceding code block is already a great result. Let's see whether it's possible to further improve our classification model by leveraging the information about the pick-up and drop-off locations of the taxi trip:

```
CREATE OR REPLACE MODEL `05_chicago_taxi.binary_
classification_version_4`
OPTIONS
    (model_type='logistic_reg', labels = ['will_get_tip'])
AS
    SELECT
        trip_seconds,
        fare,
        tolls,
        company,
        payment_type,
        pickup_location,
        dropoff_location,
        IF(tips>0,1,0) AS will_get_tip
    FROM `05_chicago_taxi.training_table`;
```

The query is very similar to the other training statements but introduces two more features: `pickup_location` and `dropoff_location`. The two fields represent the area where the taxi ride started and ended.

After the training of the ML model, we can immediately appreciate that we've further improved the performances of our classification model. This is clearly visible from the **ROC AUC** value, which is **0.9827**.

Looking at the **Confusion matrix**, we can choose the best threshold that gives us the right balance between true positive and true negative predictions.

The threshold value influences the ratio between the True Positive Rate and the False Positive Rate. Finding the best threshold means to find a value that maximize the True Positive Rate and minimize the False Positive Rate.

In the following screenshot, you can see the confusion matrix and the **Positive class threshold** slider:

**Score threshold**

| | |
|---|---|
| Positive class threshold ⑦ | ———●— 0.8886 |
| Positive class | 1 |
| Negative class | 0 |
| Precision | 0.9551 |
| Recall | 0.9818 |
| Accuracy ⑦ | 0.9668 |
| F1 score ⑦ | 0.9682 |

Use this slider above to see which score threshold works best for your model.

**Confusion matrix**

| Actual labels | Predicted labels 1 | 0 |
|---|---|---|
| 1 | 98.18% | 1.82% |
| 0 | 4.92% | 95.08% |

Figure 5.11 – The confusion matrix shows excellent performances in terms of predicted labels versus the actual ones

All the other key performance indicators, such as the precision, recall, and accuracy, are very high and close to the maximum of 1.

From a graphical perspective, we can appreciate the excellent quality of our ML model. In fact, the blue area under the ROC curve is very close to 1 and covers almost the entire area of the square. The following screenshot shows the ROC curve of the last ML model and shows that our ML model has achieved an excellent result:

**ROC curve**

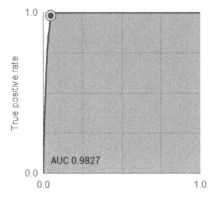

Figure 5.12 – The area under the ROC curve is very close to 1 and to filling in the entire square

In this section, we've trained some binary logistic regression ML models leveraging the features available in our dataset. To proceed with the evaluation stage, we choose to pick up the `binary_classification_version_4` model, which showed the best performance. Now, let's see how to start the evaluation phase.

# Evaluating the binary logistic regression model

To evaluate our BigQuery ML model, we'll use the `ML.EVALUATE` function and the table that we've expressly created as the evaluation dataset.

The following query will tell us whether the model is suffering from overfitting or is also able to perform well on new data:

```
SELECT
  roc_auc,
  CASE
    WHEN roc_auc > .9 THEN 'EXCELLENT'
    WHEN roc_auc > .8 THEN 'VERY GOOD'
    WHEN roc_auc > .7 THEN 'GOOD'
    WHEN roc_auc > .6 THEN 'FINE'
    WHEN roc_auc > .5 THEN 'NEEDS IMPROVEMENTS'
  ELSE
  'POOR'
END
  AS model_quality
FROM
  ML.EVALUATE(MODEL `05_chicago_taxi.binary_classification_version_5`,
    (
    SELECT
        trip_seconds,
        fare,
        tolls,
        company,
        payment_type,
        pickup_location,
        dropoff_location,
```

```
          IF(tips>0,1,0) AS will_get_tip
    FROM `05_chicago_taxi.evaluation_table`));
```

The SELECT statement extracts the roc_auc value returned by the ML.EVALUATE function and also provides a clear description of the quality of the model, starting from 'POOR' and going up to the 'EXCELLENT' grade, passing through some intermediate stages such as 'NEEDS IMPROVEMENTS' and 'GOOD'.

Executing the query, we can see that the score is very high, and the result is EXCELLENT:

| Query results | | ⬇ SAVE RESULTS | 📈 EXPLORE DATA ▾ |
|---|---|---|---|

Query complete (2.1 sec elapsed, 91.6 MB processed)

| Job information | **Results** | JSON | Execution details |
|---|---|---|---|

| Row | roc_auc | model_quality |
|---|---|---|
| 1 | 0.9834195804195804 | EXCELLENT |

Figure 5.13 – The evaluation stage returns an EXCELLENT quality result of our BigQuery ML model

Now that we've evaluated our ML model, let's see how we can apply it to other records to get the predictions.

# Using the binary logistic regression model

In this section, we'll use the ML model to predict the probability of getting a tip from our customers.

To test our BigQuery ML model, we'll use the ML.PREDICT function on the classification_table table:

```
SELECT predicted_will_get_tip, predicted_will_get_tip_probs,
will_get_tip actual
FROM
  ML.PREDICT(MODEL`05_chicago_taxi.binary_classification_
version_5`,
    (
    SELECT
        trip_seconds,
        fare,
        tolls,
```

```
          company,
          payment_type,
          pickup_location,
          dropoff_location,
          IF(tips>0,1,0) AS will_get_tip
    FROM `05_chicago_taxi.classification_table`));
```

The query is composed of a SELECT statement that extracts the actual and predicted values of the will_get_tip field. If not specified, ML.PREDICT will use the value 0.5 as the default threshold.

The output of the query shows the following columns:

- The predicted label in the first column

- The calculated probabilities for each label in the second and third columns

- The actual value extracted from classification_table as the last column

In the following screenshot, you can see the result of the query execution:

**Query results**          SAVE RESULTS          EXPLORE DATA  ▾

Query complete (6.2 sec elapsed, 97.9 MB processed)

Job information    Results    JSON    Execution details

| Row | predicted_will_get_tip | predicted_will_get_tip_probs.label | predicted_will_get_tip_probs.prob | actual |
|-----|------------------------|-----------------------------------|----------------------------------|--------|
| 1 | 0 | 1 | 0.00244179190577581 | 0 |
|   |   | 0 | 0.9975582080942242 |   |
| 2 | 0 | 1 | 0.002320533104078744 | 0 |
|   |   | 0 | 0.9976794668959212 |   |
| 3 | 0 | 1 | 0.002337188720775286 | 0 |
|   |   | 0 | 0.9976628112792247 |   |
| 4 | 0 | 1 | 0.0023279906166238044 | 0 |
|   |   | 0 | 0.9976720093833762 |   |
| 5 | 0 | 1 | 0.0023265590871903693 | 0 |

Figure 5.14 – The output of the query shows the predicted label compared with the actual one

Now that we've tested our BigQuery ML model, let's make some final considerations about the possibility of predicting whether a customer will give a tip to the taxi driver according to the information that we have about the taxi ride.

# Drawing business conclusions

In this section, we'll use our ML model, and we'll understand how many times the BigQuery ML model is able to predict the actual outcome.

Using the default threshold of 0.5, let's see how many times the ML model is able to correctly identify when a driver will get a tip:

```
SELECT COUNT(*)
FROM (
      SELECT predicted_will_get_tip, predicted_will_get_tip_
probs, will_get_tip actual_tip
      FROM
        ML.PREDICT(MODEL`05_chicago_taxi.binary_classification_
version_5`,
            (
              SELECT
                trip_seconds,
                fare,
                tolls,
                company,
                payment_type,
                pickup_location,
                dropoff_location,
                IF(tips>0,1,0) AS will_get_tip
              FROM `05_chicago_taxi.classification_table`)))
WHERE
        predicted_will_get_tip = actual_tip;
```

To calculate this value, we've introduced the WHERE clause, filtering only the rows where the predicted value is equal to the actual one.

SELECT COUNT returns a value of 727,462 predictions corresponding with the predicted value being equal to the actual one.

On a total of 744,058 rows, we can say that our model with a standard threshold of 0.5 predicts the right outcome in 97.76% of cases.

Since we've created a very effective binary logistic regression model leveraging BigQuery ML, we're now confident with providing insights and suggestions to our taxi drivers. Knowing in advance the probability of getting a tip, they can behave differently according to the probability of getting a tip from the customer they're serving.

## Summary

In this chapter, we implemented a binary logistic regression model. We introduced the business scenario based on the data collected by the city of Chicago about taxi services. After that, we learned how the binary logistic regression technique can be used to predict binary values.

In order to build an effective model, we performed a detailed analysis of the data, and then segmented the dataset according to our needs into three tables: one to host training data, the second for evaluation, and the last one to apply our classification model.

During the training phase of the BigQuery ML model, we constantly improved the performances of the ML model based on the confusion matrix and the ROC AUC value.

After that, we evaluated the best ML model on a new set of records to verify the absence of overfitting and gain more confidence in the good quality of our binary logistic regression model.

Finally, we applied our ML model to the last subset of records to predict the probability of getting a tip or not from the customer at the end of each taxi ride. We discovered that our ML model is able to correctly predict the customer's behavior in more than 97% of cases.

In the next chapter, we'll go through multiclass logistic regression and we'll learn how to apply this algorithm to classify trees into different species according to their characteristics.

# Further resources

- **Chicago Taxi Trips public dataset**: `https://console.cloud.google.com/marketplace/details/city-of-chicago-public-data/chicago-taxi-trips`

- **Chicago Open Data**: `https://data.cityofchicago.org/`

- **BigQuery ML CREATE MODEL**: `https://cloud.google.com/bigquery-ml/docs/reference/standard-sql/bigqueryml-syntax-create`

- **BigQuery ML EVALUATE MODEL**: `https://cloud.google.com/bigquery-ml/docs/reference/standard-sql/bigqueryml-syntax-evaluate`

- **BigQuery ML PREDICT**: `https://cloud.google.com/bigquery-ml/docs/reference/standard-sql/bigqueryml-syntax-predict`

- **BigQuery ML binary logistic regression example**: `https://cloud.google.com/bigquery-ml/docs/logistic-regression-prediction`

# 6
# Classifying Trees with Multiclass Logistic Regression

Multiclass logistic regression is the **Machine Learning** (**ML**) algorithm used to classify events, entities, and behaviors into a fixed number of categories. It can be used across different industries and business scenarios when it's necessary to predict the classification of an entity into multiple groups. A typical classification use case is represented by the desire to segment the customer base of a company according to their profitability and preferences in order to target the right customers with the most effective marketing campaigns.

This kind of technique is an extension of the binary logistic regression that allows us to overcome the limits of two possible labels and opens the applicability to other contexts where we can find multiple categories to identify.

In this chapter, we'll see all the stages necessary to implement, evaluate, and test a multiclass logistic regression model leveraging BigQuery ML.

In this chapter, we'll go through the following topics:

- Introducing the business scenario
- Discovering multiclass logistic regression
- Exploring and understanding the dataset
- Training the multiclass logistic regression model
- Evaluating the multiclass logistic regression model
- Using the multiclass logistic regression model
- Drawing business conclusions

# Technical requirements

This chapter requires you to access a web browser and to have the possibility to leverage the following:

- A GCP account to access the Google Cloud Console
- A GCP project to host the BigQuery datasets

Now that we're ready with the technical requirements, let's dive into the analysis and development of our BigQuery ML logistic regression model.

Check out the following video to see the Code in Action: `https://bit.ly/3h4w7xG`

# Introducing the business scenario

For this business scenario, we can imagine being a ML expert in New York City. Among all the activities that the city should perform, a census of the trees and verifying their condition is one of the most time-consuming.

The trees are spread across different areas of New York City and the process of collecting information about each tree is performed manually by volunteers or New York City employees. After the collection of the information, the data is stored in a database and made publicly available through a BigQuery public dataset for further analyses (`https://console.cloud.google.com/marketplace/details/city-of-new-york/nyc-tree-census`).

In the following figure, we can see a picture from Central Park, one of the areas with more trees in New York City:

Figure 6.1 – Trees in Central Park, New York City

In order to support and accelerate the job of the people in charge of classifying the trees and assessing their condition, one of your managers may ask you to build a ML model.

The goal of the ML model would be to automatically classify the trees into different species according to their characteristics, such as their position, size, and health status.

For this use case, we can focus our attention only on the five species of trees most present in the city.

Now that we've briefly explained and understood the business scenario, let's take a look at the ML technique that we can use to classify objects or events into multiple classes.

# Discovering multiclass logistic regression

In this section, we'll learn the basics of multiclass logistic regression and when this technique can be applied.

**Multiclass logistic regression** is a classification technique that can be used to categorize events, objects, customers, or other entities into multiple classes. Different from binary logistic regression, this ML algorithm can be used to classify output values into more than two discrete classes.

In order to predict one of the multiple labels, this ML algorithm calculates the probability of each outcome and selects the label with the highest probability.

Being a regression algorithm, the prediction of the label is based on a set of independent variables called features that are used to predict the dependent variable, called a label.

This ML technique can be used to answer business questions, such as the following:

- Is the comment of my customer *neutral*, *positive*, or *negative*?

- Does my customer belong to the *Gold*, *Silver*, or *Bronze* level?

- Is the probability of churn for a specific customer *high*, *medium*, or *low*?

- Does the image recognition algorithm identify a *cat*, a *dog*, a *mouse*, or a *cow*?

In our business scenario, since there are a limited number of species of trees and we'll focus only on five species, we can leverage multiclass logistic regression. Specifically, we're interested in classifying a tree into one of the five species according to its characteristics in terms of size, position, and health status.

Training a multiclass logistic regression model means trying to find the values of the coefficients that can be used in the equation between the input variables, called features, and the output variable, called a label.

After the training, we'll leverage a **Confusion Matrix** to evaluate the performances of our multiclass logistic regression model. In multiclass logistic regression, multiple rows and multiple columns compose the confusion matrix.

To evaluate the performances of our ML model, we'll again use the **Area Under the Curve (AUC) Receiver Operating Characteristic (ROC)**.

Now that we've learned the basics of multiclass logistic regression, it's time to take a look at the dataset that we'll use to build our ML model.

# Exploring and understanding the dataset

As we've already done in the previous use cases, before diving into the development of the ML model, it's necessary to analyze the data that can be used to solve our use case.

We'll start with the analysis of the table structure to have a clear understanding of the data that can be used for our business scenario.

## Understanding the data

In this section, we'll look take a look at the data to understand its structure and how it can be used to build our ML model.

To start exploring the data, we need to do the following:

1.  Log in to the Google Cloud Console and access the **BigQuery** user interface from the navigation menu.

2.  Create a new dataset under the project that we created in *Chapter 2*, *Setting Up Your GCP and BigQuery Environment*. For this use case, we'll create the dataset 06_nyc_ trees with the default options.

3.  Open the GCP project **bigquery-public-data**, which hosts all the BigQuery public datasets, and browse the datasets until we find new_york_trees.

4.  As we can see in the following screenshot, the BigQuery public dataset contains multiple tables to host the data collected every 10 years:

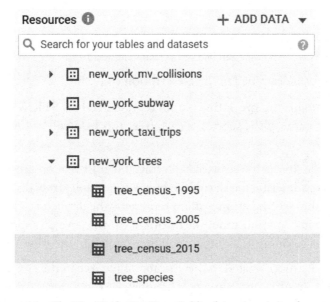

Figure 6.2 – The New York City Trees Public dataset contains the census
of the trees collected every 10 years

5.  We'll use the most recent one: `tree_census_2015`. This table contains all the information about the trees planted in New York City and registered in 2015.

6.  Let's click on the table name `tree_census_2015` in the BigQuery navigation menu to access the schema of the table:

**tree_census_2015**    🔍 QUERY TABLE   📋 COPY TABLE   🗑 DELETE TABLE   ⬆ EXPORT ▾

Schema    Details    Preview

| Field name | Type | Mode | Policy tags ⓘ | Description |
|---|---|---|---|---|
| tree_id | INTEGER | REQUIRED | | Unique identification number for each tree point |
| block_id | INTEGER | NULLABLE | | Identifier linking each tree to the block in the blockface table/shapefile that it is mapped on. |
| created_at | DATE | NULLABLE | | The date tree points were collected in the census software |
| tree_dbh | INTEGER | NULLABLE | | Diameter of the tree, measured at approximately 54" / 137cm above the ground. |
| stump_diam | INTEGER | NULLABLE | | Diameter of stump measured through the center, rounded to the nearest inch. |
| curb_loc | STRING | NULLABLE | | Location of tree bed in relationship to the curb; trees are either along the curb (OnCurb) or offset from the curb (OffsetFromCurb) |
| status | STRING | NULLABLE | | Indicates whether the tree is alive, standing dead, or a stump. |
| health | STRING | NULLABLE | | Indicates the user's perception of tree health. |
| spc_latin | STRING | NULLABLE | | Scientific name for species, e.g. "Acer rubrum" |
| spc_common | STRING | NULLABLE | | Common name for species, e.g. "red maple" |
| steward | STRING | NULLABLE | | Indicates the number of unique signs of stewardship observed for this tree. Not recorded for stumps or dead trees. |
| guards | STRING | NULLABLE | | Indicates whether a guard is present, and if the user felt it was a helpful or harmful guard. Not recorded for dead |

Figure 6.3 – The structure of the tree_census_2015 table lists all the fields
that can be used as labels and features

7.  Each field is well described in the **Description** column.

The table contains the **spc_latin** column represented by a **STRING** that indicates the scientific name of the species of each tree. This field will be the label of our ML model.

In order to classify each tree, we can leverage the information present in other fields. Some columns describe the size of the tree. For example, **tree_dbh** measures the diameter of the tree and **stump_diam** represents the diameter of the stump. We can also leverage information about the **health** of the tree. We can imagine that some species are more robust than others and more suited to the New York City weather.

Other fields are more related to the position of the tree in the city and to the context where it lives. In order to train our ML model, we can use the zip area where the tree resides: **zip_city**. Some other examples are the **boroname** column, which contains the name of the borough where the tree was planted, and **nta_name**, which represents the neighborhood the tree falls into.

We can also assume that some species are more intrusive than others – the **sidewalk** field indicates whether a sidewalk adjacent to the tree was damaged, cracked, or lifted by the roots of the tree.

From a schema perspective, this table includes a lot of useful information that can be used to develop our classification model. Let's proceed with our analysis, diving more into the data.

In this section, we've analyzed the metadata of the **tree_census_2015** table, now it's time to look at the actual data and start querying it.

## Checking the data quality

As we've already understood from the previous use cases, the quality of data is fundamental to build effective ML models. In this section, we'll apply some data quality checks in order to identify the right records to use:

1.  First of all, we'll check if the table `tree_census_2015` contains records with `spc_latin` equals to NULL. This is fundamental because the field `spc_latin` will be used as label of our machine learning model:

```
SELECT   COUNT(*) total
FROM     `bigquery-public-data.new_york_trees.tree_
census_2015`
WHERE
         spc_latin is NULL;
```

The code block will COUNT all the records in the table `bigquery-public-data.new_york_trees.tree_census_2015` where the field `spc_latin` is empty.

In the following screenshot, you can see the results of the query where we got a value higher than thirty one thousand:

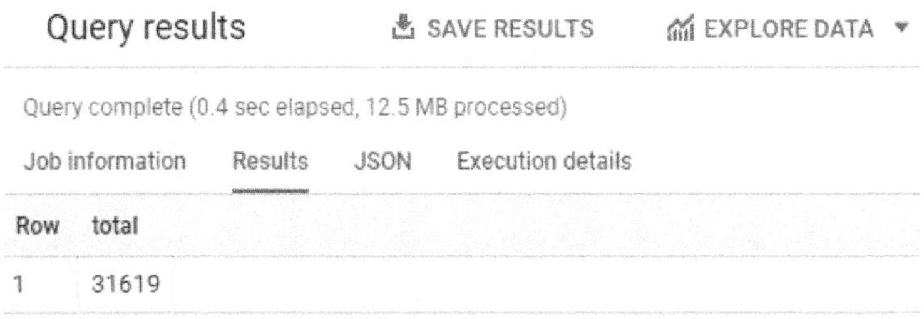

Figure 6.4 – The result of the query shows that some rows contain empty labels

For this reason, in the next queries we'll exclude the records where the field `spc_latin` is empty.

2.  Focusing only on the rows where the field `spc_latin` is `NOT NULL`, we can check the presence of empty values on all the other fields that are potential features of our ML model:

```
SELECT   COUNT(*)
FROM     `bigquery-public-data.new_york_trees.tree_
census_2015`
WHERE
         spc_latin is NOT NULL
         AND (
             zip_city is NULL OR
             tree_dbh is NULL OR
             boroname is NULL OR
             nta_name is NULL OR
             nta_name is NULL OR
             health is NULL OR
             sidewalk is NULL) ;
```

Also, in this case, the result of the query is not zero. In fact, we can easily identify three records that present `NULL` values in the `health` and `sidewalk` fields.

We'll filter these records in the following stages of the ML model life cycle.

Now that we've applied some quality checks to our dataset and we've understood which records should be filtered, let's focus on segmenting our dataset to focus the creation of our BigQuery ML model only on the five most frequent species of trees.

## Segmenting the dataset

In this section, we'll prepare the tables that we'll use to train, evaluate, and test our ML model.

For our purposes, we'll extract the five most frequent species that appear in the dataset. After that, we'll create the BigQuery tables that will be used to train, evaluate, and test our ML model:

1. First of all, we'll identify only the five most frequent species in the `tree_census_2015` table with the following query:

```sql
SELECT    spc_latin,
          COUNT(*) total
FROM      `bigquery-public-data.new_york_trees.tree_
census_2015`
WHERE
          spc_latin is NOT NULL
          AND zip_city is NOT NULL
          AND tree_dbh is NOT NULL
          AND boroname is NOT NULL
          AND nta_name is NOT NULL
          AND health is NOT NULL
          AND sidewalk is NOT NULL
GROUP BY
          spc_latin
ORDER BY
          total desc
LIMIT 5;
```

The SQL statement counts the number of occurrences of each species in the `tree_census_2015` table using the `GROUP BY spc_latin` clause and the `COUNT(*)` operator.

The query orders the records in descending mode according to the value of the field `total` field, which contains the result of the `COUNT`. Finally, the result set of the query is limited to the first five records of the result set with the `LIMIT 5` clause at the end of the query.

The SQL statement is based on the BigQuery public table `tree_census_2015` properly filtered with the data quality checks that we identified in the previous, *Checking the data quality* section.

In the following screenshot, we can see the results of the query and the most common species of tree in our dataset:

## Query results          📥 SAVE RESULTS        📈 EXPLORE DATA ▼

Query complete (1.6 sec elapsed, 55.3 MB processed)

Job information    Results    JSON    Execution details

| Row | spc_latin | total |
|-----|-----------|-------|
| 1 | Platanus x acerifolia | 87014 |
| 2 | Gleditsia triacanthos var. inermis | 64262 |
| 3 | Pyrus calleryana | 58931 |
| 4 | Quercus palustris | 53185 |
| 5 | Acer platanoides | 34189 |

Figure 6.5 – The result of the query shows the most common trees in New York City

From the query result, we can easily read the Latin name of the trees ordered from the most to the least common.

2. Since we'll use this subset of five species in the next SQL queries, we can add a CREATE TABLE statement at the beginning of our SELECT statement in order to materialize the results in the top5_species table:

```
CREATE OR REPLACE TABLE `06_nyc_trees.top5_species` AS
    SELECT    spc_latin,
        COUNT(*) total
    FROM    `bigquery-public-data.new_york_trees.tree_
census_2015`
    WHERE
            spc_latin is NOT NULL
            AND zip_city is NOT NULL
            AND tree_dbh is NOT NULL
            AND boroname is NOT NULL
            AND nta_name is NOT NULL
            AND health is NOT NULL
            AND sidewalk is NOT NULL
    GROUP BY
```

```
                    spc_latin
        ORDER BY
                    total desc
        LIMIT 5;
```

By executing the query, we'll get the creation of a new table that contains only two fields and five records. spc_latin represents the species of the tree, while total counts the number of occurrences of each species in the original dataset.

3.  Now, we can leverage the top5_species table to filter only the species on which we're focusing and create the training table:

```
CREATE OR REPLACE TABLE `06_nyc_trees.training_table` AS
SELECT  *
FROM    `bigquery-public-data.new_york_trees.tree_
census_2015`
WHERE
            zip_city is NOT NULL
            AND tree_dbh is NOT NULL
            AND boroname is NOT NULL
            AND nta_name is NOT NULL
            AND health is NOT NULL
            AND sidewalk is NOT NULL
            AND spc_latin in
            (SELECT spc_latin from  `06_nyc_trees.top5_
    species`)
            AND MOD(tree_id,11)<=8;
```

The query creates a table with all the columns available in the original dataset through the SELECT * statement. It applies all the filters necessary to get not empty values for the spc_latin label and all the other potential features.

With the usage of the IN clause, training_table will contain only the records related to the most five frequent species in the dataset.

The last line of the query, with the clause MOD(tree_id,11)<=8, allows us to only pick up 80% of the records from the entire set of records. MOD stands for modulo and returns the remainder of the division of tree_id by 11.

4.  With a similar approach, we can create the table that will be used for the evaluation of our ML model:

```
CREATE OR REPLACE TABLE `06_nyc_trees.evaluation_table`
AS
SELECT  *
FROM    `bigquery-public-data.new_york_trees.tree_
census_2015`
WHERE
        zip_city is NOT NULL
        AND tree_dbh is NOT NULL
        AND boroname is NOT NULL
        AND nta_name is NOT NULL
        AND health is NOT NULL
        AND sidewalk is NOT NULL
        AND spc_latin in
        (SELECT spc_latin from `06_nyc_trees.top5_
species`)
        AND MOD(tree_id,11)=9;
```

For the evaluation_table, we will pick up only 10% of the records with the filter MOD(tree_id,11)=9.

5.  Finally, we'll execute the following SQL statement in order to create the table that will be used to apply our multiclass classification model:

```
CREATE OR REPLACE TABLE `06_nyc_trees.classification_
table` AS
SELECT  *
FROM    `bigquery-public-data.new_york_trees.tree_
census_2015`
WHERE
        zip_city is NOT NULL
        AND tree_dbh is NOT NULL
        AND boroname is NOT NULL
        AND nta_name is NOT NULL
        AND health is NOT NULL
        AND sidewalk is NOT NULL
        AND spc_latin in
```

```
        (SELECT spc_latin from `06_nyc_trees.top5_
species`)
        AND MOD(tree_id,11)=10;
```

classification_table is very similar to the previous segments of the dataset, but thanks to the MOD function will contain the remaining 10% percent of the dataset.

In this section, we've analyzed the new_york_trees dataset, which contains information about the trees in New York City. We applied some data quality checks to exclude empty values. Then, we segmented the data, focusing on the five most common species that appear in the table. Now that we've completed the preparatory steps, it's time to move on and start the training of our BigQuery ML model.

# Training the multiclass logistic regression model

Now that we've clearly understood the structure of the data and we've segmented it into multiple tables to support the different stages of the ML model life cycle, let's focus on the training of our multiclass logistic regression model. We'll execute the SQL queries to create our multiclass logistic regression models:

1.  Let's start creating the first version of our ML model:

```
CREATE OR REPLACE MODEL `06_nyc_trees.classification_
model_version_1`
OPTIONS
  ( model_type='LOGISTIC_REG',
    auto_class_weights=TRUE
  ) AS
SELECT
  zip_city,
  tree_dbh,
  spc_latin as label
FROM
  `06_nyc_trees.training_table` ;
```

The query used to create the classification_model_version_1 model is based only on two features: the zip area and the diameter of the tree.

The SQL statement starts with the keywords CREATE OR REPLACE MODEL, which are used to run the training, followed by the OPTIONS clause. Among the options, we can specify the model type equals LOGISTIC_REG and auto_class_weights=TRUE. This option can be particularly useful when we're in front of unbalanced training datasets with some labels that appear more frequently than others. In our case, the occurrences of the most common species are more than double the occurrences of the fifth one. For this reason, we've applied this kind of adjustment.

> **Important note**
>
> The BigQuery ML syntax does not distinguish between binary logistic regression and multiclass logistic regression. In both cases, the BigQuery ML model type is LOGISTIC_REG. The difference is caused by the number of distinct values that appear in the column label of the training dataset. If the label presents only two values, BigQuery ML will train a binary logistic regression. If the label contains more than two distinct values, the model will be trained as a multiclass logistic regression.

2.  After the execution of the training, we can access the information of our first ML model by clicking on **classification_model_version_1** from the navigation menu and selecting the **Evaluation** tab.

    The following screenshot presents the key performance indicators of our first attempt:

## classification_model_version_1

Details    Training    Evaluation    Schema

### Aggregate metrics

| | |
|---|---|
| Threshold | 0.0000 |
| Precision | 0.4298 |
| Recall | 0.4358 |
| Accuracy | 0.4690 |
| F1 score | 0.4110 |
| Log loss | 1.3608 |
| ROC AUC | 0.7383 |

Figure 6.6 – The Evaluation tab shows the performance metrics related to the selected BigQuery ML model

To have an idea of the effectiveness of our ML model, we can look at the **ROC AUC** value of **0.7383**.

By scrolling down with the mouse in the **Evaluation** tab, we can take a look at the confusion matrix of our multiclass logistic regression model.

In the following figure, the confusion matrix shows the percentage of predicted and actual labels on the training dataset:

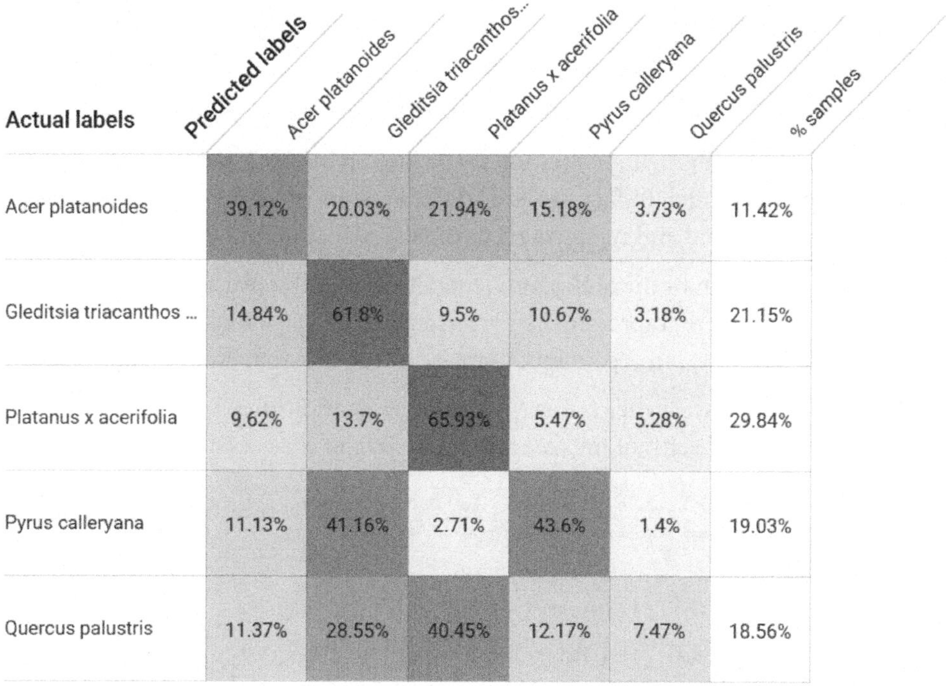

| Actual labels \ Predicted labels | Acer platanoides | Gleditsia triacanthos... | Platanus x acerifolia | Pyrus calleryana | Quercus palustris | % samples |
|---|---|---|---|---|---|---|
| Acer platanoides | 39.12% | 20.03% | 21.94% | 15.18% | 3.73% | 11.42% |
| Gleditsia triacanthos ... | 14.84% | 61.8% | 9.5% | 10.67% | 3.18% | 21.15% |
| Platanus x acerifolia | 9.62% | 13.7% | 65.93% | 5.47% | 5.28% | 29.84% |
| Pyrus calleryana | 11.13% | 41.16% | 2.71% | 43.6% | 1.4% | 19.03% |
| Quercus palustris | 11.37% | 28.55% | 40.45% | 12.17% | 7.47% | 18.56% |

Figure 6.7 – The Evaluation tab shows the confusion matrix related to the selected BigQuery ML model

Looking at the confusion matrix, we can visually notice that our ML model works quite well for some species but performs very poorly for others. For example, when the actual label is **Quercus palustris**, in 40% of the cases the ML model suggests a different species: **Platanus x acerifolia**.

3. Let's try to improve our model by adding new features with the following BigQuery ML SQL statement:

```
CREATE OR REPLACE MODEL `06_nyc_trees.classification_
model_version_2`
OPTIONS
  ( model_type='LOGISTIC_REG',
```

```
       auto_class_weights=TRUE
  ) AS
SELECT
  zip_city,
  tree_dbh,
  boroname,
  nta_name,
  spc_latin as label
FROM
  `06_nyc_trees.training_table` ;
```

In comparison with the first attempt, we've included additional features in the training of our model. In fact, we've added the name of the borough contained in the boroname field and nta_name to the list of features.

After the execution of the SQL statement, let's access the **Evaluation** tab of the new model to see if we're improving its performance. Taking a look at the **ROC AUC** value of **0.7667**, we can see a slight increase in the performance of our model.

4.  As a last attempt, we'll enrich our ML model with additional features. The new fields are related to the health of the tree and to the size of the roots:

```
CREATE OR REPLACE MODEL `06_nyc_trees.classification_
model_version_3`
OPTIONS
  ( model_type='LOGISTIC_REG',
    auto_class_weights=TRUE
  ) AS
SELECT
  zip_city,
  tree_dbh,
  boroname,
  nta_name,
  health,
  sidewalk,
  spc_latin as label
FROM
  `06_nyc_trees.training_table`;
```

Compared to the previous ML model, in `classification_model_version_3` we've included the fields `health`, which describes the health status of our tree, and `sidewalk`, used to specify whether the roots of the tree are damaging the adjacent pavements.

5.  Looking at the performance of our last ML model in the **Evaluation** tab of the BigQuery user interface, we can notice that we've achieved another increase in terms of **ROC AUC** value: `0.7696`.

> **Tip**
>
> Although the usage of more features can increase the ROC AUC value of a BigQuery ML classification model, we need to take into consideration the balance between the performance improvement and the resources spent to achieve it. In real-life scenarios, especially when the volumes are really high, we need to select only the features that can have the highest impact on the performance of our BigQuery ML model.

In this section, we've created different ML models trying to use different features in our dataset. In the next sections, we'll use the model with the highest ROC AUC value: `classification_model_version_3`.

Next, let's evaluate the performance of our ML model leveraging the evaluation dataset.

# Evaluating the multiclass logistic regression model

In this section, we'll execute queries to check the performance of the multiclass logistic regression model.

For the evaluation phase of our BigQuery ML model, we'll use the `ML.EVALUATE` function and the `evaluation_table` table, expressly created to host the evaluation records.

As we can see, the evaluation is performed on the same fields that were used during the training phase of the model but are extracted from the `evaluation_table` table that was created completely disjoint from the training dataset.

The external `SELECT` statement extracts the `roc_auc` value returned by the `ML.EVALUATE` function. It also provides a meaningful description of the quality of the model that starts from `'POOR'` and goes up to the `'EXCELLENT'` grade, passing through some intermediate stages such as `'NEEDS IMPROVEMENTS'` and `'GOOD'`.

Let's execute the following query to extract the key performance indicator of our ML model:

```
SELECT
  roc_auc,
  CASE
    WHEN roc_auc > .9 THEN 'EXCELLENT'
    WHEN roc_auc > .8 THEN 'VERY GOOD'
    WHEN roc_auc > .7 THEN 'GOOD'
    WHEN roc_auc > .6 THEN 'FINE'
    WHEN roc_auc > .5 THEN 'NEEDS IMPROVEMENTS'
  ELSE
    'POOR'
END
  AS model_quality
FROM
  ML.EVALUATE(MODEL `06_nyc_trees.classification_model_
version_3`,
    (
    SELECT
        zip_city,
        tree_dbh,
        boroname,
        nta_name,
        health,
        sidewalk,
        spc_latin as label
      FROM `06_nyc_trees.evaluation_table`));
```

From the following screenshot, we can see the results of the query – the **roc_auc** value achieved more than 0.77. The result of our BigQuery ML model can be considered **GOOD**:

**Query results**      ⬇ SAVE RESULTS      🖾 EXPLORE DATA ▼

Query complete (1.5 sec elapsed, 2.4 MB processed)

| Job information | **Results** | JSON | Execution details |
| --- | --- | --- | --- |

| Row | roc_auc | model_quality |
| --- | --- | --- |
| 1 | 0.7724747252747253 | GOOD |

Figure 6.8 – The query extracts the ROC AUC value of the BigQuery ML model
and a short description of the model quality

Now that we've verified that the ML model maintains its performance on the disjoint evaluation dataset too, we can start using it to classify the trees in our `classification_table` table.

# Using the multiclass logistic regression model

In this section, we'll test our ML model and analyze the results.

To use our BigQuery ML model, we'll use the `ML.PREDICT` function and the `classification_table` table, which hosts the records, to test our model, as seen in the following code block:

```
SELECT
  tree_id,
  actual_label,
  predicted_label_probs,
  predicted_label
FROM
  ML.PREDICT (MODEL `06_nyc_trees.classification_model_
version_3`,
    (
    SELECT
        tree_id,
        zip_city,
        tree_dbh,
        boroname,
        nta_name,
        health,
```

```
        sidewalk,
        spc_latin as actual_label
    FROM
        `06_nyc_trees.classification_table`
    ));
```

The query statement is composed of the `SELECT` keyword, which extracts the `tree_id`, the actual value of the species in the field, `actual_label`, and the predicted fields `predicted_label_probs` and `predicted_label`.

The `ML.PREDICT` function is applied to the `SELECT` statement, which extracts the features and the actual species from the `classification_table`. The `actual_label` field will be used only as a benchmark for our predictions and not during the prediction phase.

In the following screenshot, we can see the structure of a record gotten from the execution of the previous query:

**Query results**    ⬇ SAVE RESULTS    📊 EXPLORE DATA ▾

Query complete (2.2 sec elapsed, 2.6 MB processed)

Job information    Results    JSON    Execution details

| Row | tree_id | actual_label | predicted_label_probs.label | predicted_label_probs.prob | predicted_label |
|---|---|---|---|---|---|
| 1 | 857 | Quercus palustris | Quercus palustris | 0.45149611446110655 | Quercus palustris |
| | | | Platanus x acerifolia | 0.22775251527543908 | |
| | | | Gleditsia triacanthos var. inermis | 0.1409445466034549 | |
| | | | Pyrus calleryana | 0.10671717228619303 | |
| | | | Acer platanoides | 0.07308965137380646 | |

Figure 6.9 – A record of the output dataset generated by the classification model

In this case, **tree_id** is equal to **857**, the tree is a **Quercus palustris**, and is correctly classified by the BigQuery ML model because **predicted_label** is exactly the same. **predicted_label_probs** indicates confidence of 45% for the highest classification label. All the other possible species are characterized by lower probabilities.

Now that we've applied our model, let's formulate some final considerations about our classification use case.

# Drawing business conclusions

Using the results that we got from the previous section, *Using the multiclass logistic regression model*, we'll draw some conclusions about the effectiveness of our ML model.

Enriching the previous query with a parent SELECT COUNT statement, we can count how many predictions are right compared to the total number of records.

Let's execute the following query to calculate how often our BigQuery ML model is able to correctly classify the trees in the classification_table table:

```
SELECT COUNT(*)
FROM (
    SELECT
        tree_id,
        actual_label,
        predicted_label_probs,
        predicted_label
    FROM
        ML.PREDICT (MODEL `06_nyc_trees.classification_model_
version_3`,
        (
        SELECT
            tree_id,
            zip_city,
            tree_dbh,
            boroname,
            nta_name,
            health,
            sidewalk,
            spc_latin as actual_label
        FROM
            `06_nyc_trees.classification_table`
        )
    )
)
WHERE
        actual_label = predicted_label;
```

The result of the SELECT COUNT query returns a value of 13,323 predictions with a correctly predicted label.

Considering that the total size of the `classification_table` table is 27,182, we can declare that in 49% of cases, our ML model is able to predict the right species of tree based on its characteristics and its position.

This could seem like a bad result, but we need to consider that multiclass logistic regression is more complex than a binary one because there are multiple options that could deceive the results of our model.

## Summary

In this chapter, we've built our first multiclass classification model. After a brief introduction to the use case, we discovered what multiclass logistic regression is and how it can be used to classify events, behaviors, and objects according to their features into more than two categories.

Before diving into the development of the ML model, we analyzed the schema of the dataset related to the trees in New York City and applied some data quality checks necessary to build an effective ML model.

During the training stage, we trained three different ML models using different features to gradually improve the performance of the BigQuery ML model.

Then, we chose the third ML model and we evaluated it against the evaluation dataset. In this phase, we noticed that the ML model was able to maintain its performance on new records also and was ready to pass to the next phase.

In the last step, we used our ML model to classify the trees in New York City into five different categories and leveraged their characteristics, such as size, health status, and position in the city.

We also calculated that our classification model is able to classify the right species of tree in 49% of cases.

In the next chapter, we'll introduce unsupervised ML and the K-Means clustering technique.

# Further resources

- **NYC Trees Census Public Dataset**: `https://console.cloud.google.com/marketplace/product/city-of-new-york/nyc-tree-census`

- **BigQuery ML Create Model**: `https://cloud.google.com/bigquery-ml/docs/reference/standard-sql/bigqueryml-syntax-create`

- **BigQuery ML Evaluate Model**: `https://cloud.google.com/bigquery-ml/docs/reference/standard-sql/bigqueryml-syntax-evaluate`

- **BigQuery ML Predict**: `https://cloud.google.com/bigquery-ml/docs/reference/standard-sql/bigqueryml-syntax-predict`

- **BigQuery ML Multiclass Logistic Example**: `https://cloud.google.com/bigquery-ml/docs/logistic-regression-prediction`

# Section 3: Advanced Models with BigQuery ML

In this section, additional and advanced machine learning models are explained and presented with real hands-on examples using BigQuery ML.

This section comprises the following chapters:

# 7

# Clustering Using the K-Means Algorithm

In this chapter, we'll introduce unsupervised machine learning, and you'll learn how to use BigQuery ML to build K-Means algorithms to cluster similar data into multiple categories.

Unsupervised machine learning is particularly useful when we have datasets without any labels, and we need to infer the structure of the data without any initial knowledge.

In different industries, it can be very valuable to identify similar events, objects, and people according to a specific set of features. K-Means clustering is typically used to identify similar customers, documents, products, events, or items according to a specific set of characteristics.

In this chapter, we'll focus our attention on the K-Means clustering algorithm, which is widely used to reveal similarities in structured and unstructured data. We'll go through all the steps required to build a K-Means clustering model, leveraging BigQuery ML.

With an incremental approach, we'll go through the following topics:

- Introducing the business scenario
- Discovering K-Means clustering
- Exploring and understanding the dataset
- Training a K-Means clustering model
- Evaluating a K-Means clustering model
- Using a K-Means clustering model
- Drawing business conclusions

# Technical requirements

This chapter requires you to have access to a web browser and to be able to leverage the following:

- A **Google Cloud Platform** (**GCP**) account to access the **GCP** console
- A GCP project to host the BigQuery datasets

Now that we're ready with the technical requirements, let's dive into the analysis and development of our BigQuery ML clustering model.

Check out the following video to see the Code in Action: `https://bit.ly/2Rx2Uk5`

# Introducing the business scenario

Imagine that you are a business analyst who works for large taxi companies in Chicago. These taxi companies make thousands of trips every day to satisfy the public transport needs of the entire city. The work and the behavior of the taxi drivers are fundamental in generating revenues for companies and delivering an effective service for all customers, every day.

For our business scenario, let's imagine that all the taxi companies want to give an additional reward to drivers who perform the best. The goal of the companies is to segment the drivers into three distinct categories, according to generated revenue and driving speed. The three groups can be described as follows:

- The **Top Drivers** are the employees with the best revenue and efficiency throughout the year. This group will receive a huge additional reward.

- The **Good Drivers** are drivers who performed well but aren't excelling. This group will not receive any reward.

- The **Neutral Drivers** are drivers with neutral or negative results in terms of revenue and efficiency.

The parameters to identify the clusters are not known *a priori* because they can change according to different factors, such as profitability, speed, and traffic conditions. Some years are more profitable than others, and it can happen that the driving speed could be impacted by particular traffic conditions.

As a business analyst, your job is to find the best algorithm to cluster the Chicago taxi drivers according to the described categories in order to classify the drivers into three clusters, according to their performance.

Now that we've explained and understood the problem statement, let's take a look at the machine learning technique that we can use to predict a numerical value such as the duration of a trip.

# Discovering K-Means clustering

In this section, we'll understand what **unsupervised learning** is and we'll learn the basics of the **K-Means** clustering technique.

**K-Means** is an **unsupervised learning** algorithm that solves clustering problems. This technique is used to classify data into a set of classes. The letter $k$ represents the number of clusters that are fixed *a priori*. For our business scenario, we'll use three different clusters.

> **Important note**
>
> While supervised learning is based on a prior knowledge of what the output values of labels should be in a training dataset, unsupervised learning does not leverage labeled datasets. Its goal is to infer the structure of data within a training dataset, without any prior knowledge of it.

Each cluster of data is characterized by a **centroid**. The centroid represents the midpoint of the cluster and is identified during the training stage and according to the features of the model.

After the training of the K-Means clustering model, each entity can be associated with the nearest centroid and included in one of the *k* clusters.

In the following diagram, you can take a look at the graphical representation of a simple clustering model based on two features and a value of *k* equals to 3:

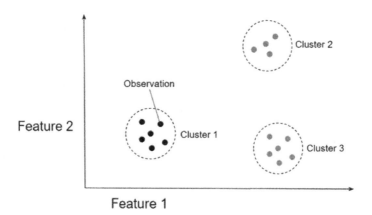

Figure 7.1 – Graphical representation of K-Means clustering

In the preceding Cartesian diagram, you can see some observations represented by dots. The diagram is composed of two axes that correspond to the features used to train the K-Means clustering machine learning model.

According to the values of the two features, some observations are closer than others. Assuming that we need to cluster the observations into three different clusters, the K-Means model is trained to find the three areas that divide the observations into different classes.

We'll not go through all the details of the K-Means clustering algorithm in this book, but we can mention some examples of use cases where this kind of algorithm is applicable. In real life, we can find a lot of scenarios that can be addressed with a clustering model, such as the following:

- **Customer segmentation**: Finding similar customers in the customer base of a company to improve the effectiveness of marketing campaigns and promotions

- **Employee segmentation**: Identifying employees with the best performance

- **Document classification**: Clustering documents into multiple categories according to tags, topics, authors, and publishing dates

In our business scenario, we'll train a K-Means clustering model based on three different clusters: **top**, **good**, and **neutral** drivers. To achieve our goal, we'll use information regarding the revenues generated by each taxi driver and the driving speed, calculated as the ratio between miles driven and the time spent on each ride.

We've learned the basics of K-Means clustering, so now it's time to take a look at the dataset that we'll use to build our machine learning model.

# Exploring and understanding the dataset

Before diving into the machine learning implementation, we'll start analyzing the dataset that will be used to train our machine learning model.

For this use case, we'll use the BigQuery public dataset we've already used in *Chapter 5, Predicting Boolean Values Using Binary Logistic Regression*. This dataset contains information on taxi rides collected by the *City of Chicago*, which can be found at the following link: `https://console.cloud.google.com/marketplace/details/city-of-chicago-public-data/chicago-taxi-trips`.

Let's start by getting a clear understanding of the information that we have in our dataset to build our K-Means clustering model.

## Understanding the data

In this section, we'll explore the structure of the data we'll use to develop our BigQuery ML model.

To start exploring the data, we need to do the following:

1.  Log in to GCP and access the **BigQuery** user interface from the navigation menu.

2.  Create a new dataset under the project that we created in *Chapter 2, Setting Up Your GCP and BigQuery Environment*. For this use case, we'll create a `07_chicago_taxi_drivers` dataset with default options.

3.  Open the `bigquery-public-data` GCP project that hosts all the BigQuery public datasets and browse the items until we find the `chicago_taxi_trips` dataset. In this public dataset, we can see only one BigQuery table: `taxi_trips`. This table contains all the information about taxi rides happening in the city of Chicago, and we'll use it to train and test our K-Means clustering model.

We've already used the same data in *Chapter 5, Predicting Boolean Values Using Binary Logistic Regression*. For this reason, we already know the overall schema of the `taxi_trips` table and its fields.

In the following screenshot, you can see the full list of fields belonging to the `taxi_trips` table:

**taxi_trips**

| | | | |
|---|---|---|---|
| unique_key | STRING | REQUIRED | Unique identifier for the trip. |
| taxi_id | STRING | REQUIRED | A unique identifier for the taxi. |
| trip_start_timestamp | TIMESTAMP | NULLABLE | When the trip started, rounded to the nearest 15 minutes. |
| trip_end_timestamp | TIMESTAMP | NULLABLE | When the trip ended, rounded to the nearest 15 minutes. |
| trip_seconds | INTEGER | NULLABLE | Time of the trip in seconds. |
| trip_miles | FLOAT | NULLABLE | Distance of the trip in miles. |
| pickup_census_tract | INTEGER | NULLABLE | The Census Tract where the trip began. For privacy, this Census Tract is not shown for some trips. |
| dropoff_census_tract | INTEGER | NULLABLE | The Census Tract where the trip ended. For privacy, this Census Tract is not shown for some trips. |
| pickup_community_area | INTEGER | NULLABLE | The Community Area where the trip began. |
| dropoff_community_area | INTEGER | NULLABLE | The Community Area where the trip ended. |
| fare | FLOAT | NULLABLE | The fare for the trip. |
| tips | FLOAT | NULLABLE | The tip for the trip. Cash tips generally will not be recorded. |
| tolls | FLOAT | NULLABLE | The tolls for the trip. |
| extras | FLOAT | NULLABLE | Extra charges for the trip. |
| trip_total | FLOAT | NULLABLE | Total cost of the trip, the total of the fare, tips, tolls, and extras. |
| payment_type | STRING | NULLABLE | Type of payment for the trip. |
| company | STRING | NULLABLE | The taxi company. |
| pickup_latitude | FLOAT | NULLABLE | The latitude of the center of the pickup census tract or the community area if the census tract has been hidden for privacy. |
| pickup_longitude | FLOAT | NULLABLE | The longitude of the center of the pickup census tract or the community area if the census tract has been hidden for privacy. |
| pickup_location | STRING | NULLABLE | The location of the center of the pickup census tract or the community area if the census tract has been hidden for privacy. |
| dropoff_latitude | FLOAT | NULLABLE | The latitude of the center of the dropoff census tract or the community area if the census tract has been hidden for privacy. |
| dropoff_longitude | FLOAT | NULLABLE | The longitude of the center of the dropoff census tract or the community area if the census tract has been hidden for privacy. |
| dropoff_location | STRING | NULLABLE | The location of the center of the dropoff census tract or the community area if the census tract has been hidden for privacy. |

Figure 7.2 – The list of fields belonging to the taxi_trips table

For this use case, we focus our attention on the following fields that will be used in the creation of our machine learning model:

- `trip_miles`: Contains the number of miles traveled by the taxi driver during a specific ride.

- `trip_seconds`: Represents the duration of each taxi ride, expressed in seconds.

- `fare`: This is the fee paid by the customer to the taxi driver and represents the income of the driver.

- `tips`: This column contains the value of the tip that the taxi driver received from the customer.

We deliberately ignore other columns related to the cost of the taxi ride, such as `tolls` and `extras`, because these values are not directly impacted by the taxi driver's activity.

In this section, we've selected the table and columns that will be used to train our machine learning model. Now, it's time to look at the data so that we can understand how to use it.

## Checking the data quality

In this section, we'll apply some data quality checks before developing our machine learning model.

The quality of data is fundamental to building effective K-Means clustering models. Since the goal is to cluster observations into multiple categories, outliers in the data can create unbalanced clusters, based on incorrect values in the data.

Let's start analyzing the dataset that will be used to build our machine learning model, as follows:

1.  In order to identify the time frame of our dataset, let's extract the minimum and maximum value of the `trip_start_timestamp` field, like this:

    ```
    SELECT MAX(trip_start_timestamp),
           MIN(trip_start_timestamp)
    FROM
    `bigquery-public-data.chicago_taxi_trips.taxi_trips`;
    ```

    On executing this **Structured Query Language (SQL)** statement, we can notice that the data ranges from 2013 to 2020.

    The result of the query is presented in the following screenshot:

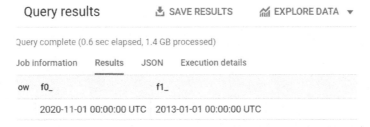

Figure 7.3 – The result of the query shows the time frame of the dataset

To address our business scenario, we can focus our attention on the taxi rides that occurred in 2020.

2.  In the second step, we'll inspect the maximum values of the speed (expressed in miles per hour) and of a taxi driver's income. Let's execute the following query:

```
SELECT MAX (speed_mph), MAX (tot_income)
FROM (
        SELECT taxi_id,
               AVG(trip_miles/(trip_seconds/60/60)) AS
speed_mph,
               SUM (fare+tips) AS tot_income
        FROM `bigquery-public-data.chicago_taxi_trips.taxi_
trips`
        WHERE
               EXTRACT(YEAR from trip_start_timestamp) =
2020
               AND trip_seconds > 0
               AND trip_miles >0
               AND fare > 0
        GROUP BY taxi_id);
```

The internal SELECT statement calculates the average speed, dividing the value of the trip_miles field and the duration of the ride expressed in hours (trip_seconds/60/60). The calculated value is stored in the speed_mph column. It also creates the tot_income field, which sums up the fare and tips values for each taxi_id field. With the EXTRACT(YEAR from trip_start_timestamp) = 2020 filter, we're selecting only the taxi rides that occurred in 2020. Adding filters on the trip_seconds, trip_miles, and fare fields, we're also excluding all the empty and NULL values that can occur in the dataset. The most external SELECT statement identifies the maximum values of the average speed and of the income, using the MAX (speed_mph), MAX (tot_income) keywords.

The result of the query is presented in the following screenshot:

## Query results    📥 SAVE RESULTS    📊 EXPLORE DATA ▼

Query complete (0.9 sec elapsed, 30.8 GB processed)

| Job information | **Results** | JSON | Execution details |
|---|---|---|---|

| Row | f0_ | f1_ |
|---|---|---|
| 1 | 666.9212213809619 | 1064713.44 |

Figure 7.4 – The result of the query shows outliers in terms of speed and income

From the results, it's quite clear that the dataset contains some outliers that are not compatible with the actual use case. In fact, the maximum average speed is about 667 miles per hour, and the maximum income for a taxi driver is more than 1 million **US dollars** (**USD**).

The query that we've just executed points out that there are some unrealistic values in our dataset that need to be filtered out in the next steps.

Now that we've performed some quality checks on our dataset, let's focus on creating our training datasets.

## Creating the training datasets

For K-Means clustering, we only need to create a dataset that will be used to train and test the machine learning model.

Let's start creating our datasets that will be used to train two different K-Means clustering models, as follows:

1. First of all, let's create a table that contains only the speed_mph field as an input feature for our K-Means clustering model, by running the following code:

```
CREATE OR REPLACE TABLE `07_chicago_taxi_drivers.taxi_
miles_per_minute` AS
SELECT *
FROM (
              SELECT taxi_id,
                     AVG(trip_miles/(trip_
seconds/60/60)) AS speed_mph
              FROM `bigquery-public-data.chicago_taxi_
trips.taxi_trips`
```

```
                        WHERE
                            EXTRACT(YEAR from trip_start_
timestamp) = 2020
                            AND trip_seconds > 0
                            AND trip_miles >0
                        GROUP BY taxi_id
        )
WHERE
        speed_mph BETWEEN 0 AND 50;
```

The query creates the `taxi_miles_per_minute` table in the `07_chicago_taxi_drivers` dataset.

The table contains two different fields: the identifier of the taxi in the `taxi_id` column, and the average speed (expressed in miles per hour) in the `speed_mph` field. The average speed is calculated for each `taxi_id` field present in the `taxi_trips` table, using the `GROUP BY taxi_id` clause. The new table includes only the taxi rides that occurred in 2020.

The last two lines of the query contain the `WHERE` clause that is used to filter out outliers. We're assuming that the maximum realistic average speed is 50 miles per hour.

2. In the second step, we'll create another table to host the additional feature (namely, `tot_income`), as follows:

```
CREATE OR REPLACE TABLE `07_chicago_taxi_drivers.taxi_
speed_and_income` AS
SELECT *
FROM (
        SELECT taxi_id,
                AVG(trip_miles/(trip_seconds/60/60)) AS
speed_mph,
                SUM (fare+tips) AS tot_income
        FROM `bigquery-public-data.chicago_taxi_trips.
taxi_trips`
        WHERE
                EXTRACT(YEAR from trip_start_timestamp) =
2020
                AND trip_seconds > 0
                AND trip_miles >0
```

```
            AND fare > 0
        GROUP BY taxi_id
    )
WHERE
        speed_mph BETWEEN 0 AND 50
        AND tot_income BETWEEN 0 AND 150000;
```

The execution of the query generates a `taxi_speed_and_income` table. This table includes the `speed_mph` field calculated with the same rules of *Step 1*. The table also includes the `tot_income` field. This value is calculated as the SUM of the `fare` and the `tips` for each `taxi_id` field and for the entire duration of 2020.

Compared to the table created in *Step 1*, we've added another filter that limits the annual `tot_income` value to 150,000.

This second table will be used to create another K-Means clustering machine learning model based on the two `speed_mph` and `tot_income` features.

Now that we've created the tables on which our BigQuery ML model will be trained, let's dive into the creation of the machine learning model.

# Training the K-Means clustering model

In this section, we'll create two different K-Means machine learning models. The first model will be created using `taxi_miles_per_minute` as a training dataset, while the second will include also `tot_income` as a feature and will leverage `taxi_speed_and_income`. Let's proceed as follows:

1.  As a first step, let's start training a machine learning model named `clustering_by_speed` by running the following code:

    ```
    CREATE OR REPLACE MODEL `07_chicago_taxi_drivers.
    clustering_by_speed`
    OPTIONS(model_type='kmeans', num_clusters=3, kmeans_init_
    method = 'KMEANS++') AS
      SELECT * EXCEPT (taxi_id)
      FROM `07_chicago_taxi_drivers.taxi_miles_per_minute`;
    ```

    The first lines of the SQL statement are composed of the CREATE OR REPLACE MODEL keywords, followed by the identifier of the `07_chicago_taxi_drivers. clustering_by_speed` machine learning model and the OPTIONS clause.

Now, let's take a look at the options that we've used to train the machine learning model. The selected model type is `'kmeans'`. This option describes the technique that we're using to train the model. The `num_clusters` option is valued at 3 because we're trying to classify observations into three different clusters: *Top*, *Good*, and *Neutral*.

By default, BigQuery ML starts the training of the K-Means clustering algorithm with a random starting point. The quality of the machine learning model also depends on this point, which is randomly chosen by BigQuery. By using the `kmeans_init_method = 'KMEANS++'` option, the point is initialized leveraging the **K-Means++** algorithm. This type of algorithm is able to produce better and repeatable results by selecting the starting points for the training stage. It's always recommended to use 'KMEANS++' as the initialization method.

The training of the model is based on all the columns of the `taxi_miles_per_minute` table except for the `taxi_id` column, which will only be used during the prediction phase.

2.  After the training of the first machine learning model, let's train a second one, which also includes the `tot_income` value of the taxi driver during the year, as illustrated in the following code snippet:

```
CREATE OR REPLACE MODEL `07_chicago_taxi_drivers.
clustering_by_speed_and_income`
OPTIONS(model_type='kmeans', num_clusters=3, standardize_
features = true, kmeans_init_method = 'KMEANS++') AS
    SELECT * EXCEPT (taxi_id)
    FROM `07_chicago_taxi_drivers.taxi_speed_and_income`;
```

This query is very similar to the SQL statement executed for the creation of the previous K-Means clustering model, but we can immediately notice a relevant difference. The `clustering_by_speed_and_income` model is trained using an additional option, `standardize_features = true`. This option is particularly useful when you have numeric features with different orders of magnitude. In this case, the model is using the `speed_mph` field (which goes from 0 to 50) and the `tot_income` field, which can reach a value of 150,000.

Now that we've trained two different machine learning models based on the K-Means clustering algorithm, let's take a look at how we can evaluate them leveraging BigQuery ML SQL syntax and the BigQuery **user interface** (**UI**).

# Evaluating the K-Means clustering model

In this section, we'll learn how to evaluate the performance of our K-Means clustering model.

The evaluation stage of a K-Means clustering model is different from the supervised machine learning models that we've performed in the previous chapters. Let's take a look at the steps we need to take to evaluate our machine learning model, as follows:

1. Let's extract the centroids from the first machine learning model that we trained in the previous section, by running the following code:

```
SELECT *
FROM ML.CENTROIDS
        (MODEL `07_chicago_taxi_drivers.clustering_by_
speed`)
ORDER BY centroid_id;
```

The `ML.CENTROIDS` function returns information about the centroids of the K-Means model. It accepts the model name as input in the round brackets, preceded by the `MODEL` keyword.

> **Important note**
>
> A centroid represents the center of a cluster in a K-Means clustering model. During the training phase of the machine learning model, the centroids are iteratively optimized to minimize the distance between centroids and observations in the training dataset. When the training stage ends, the centroids are stabilized. BigQuery ML stops iterating when the relative loss improvement is less than the value specified for the `MIN_REL_PROGRESS` parameter.

The execution of the query returns three centroids, as shown in the following screenshot:

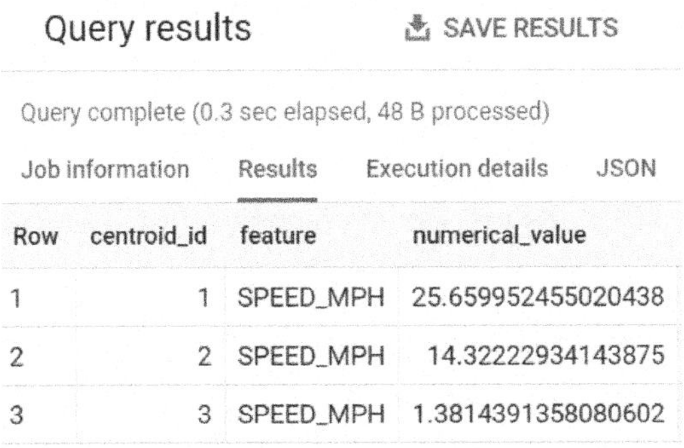


| Row | centroid_id | feature | numerical_value |
|---|---|---|---|
| 1 | 1 | SPEED_MPH | 25.659952455020438 |
| 2 | 2 | SPEED_MPH | 14.32222934143875 |
| 3 | 3 | SPEED_MPH | 1.3814391358080602 |

Figure 7.5 – The result of the query shows the centroids identified by the machine learning model

In this case, each centroid is represented only by the numerical value of the speed_ mph feature that represents the average speed of the taxi driver.

2.  The same information can be achieved leveraging the BigQuery UI. Selecting the clustering_by_speed model from the BigQuery navigation menu and accessing the **Evaluation** tab, we can see the three different centroids, as illustrated in the following screenshot:

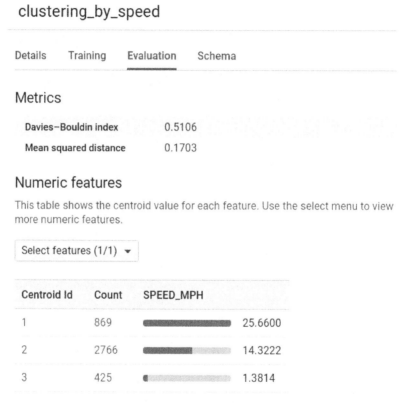

## clustering_by_speed

Details    Training    Evaluation    Schema

## Metrics

| | |
|---|---|
| Davies–Bouldin index | 0.5106 |
| Mean squared distance | 0.1703 |

## Numeric features

This table shows the centroid value for each feature. Use the select menu to view more numeric features.

Select features (1/1) ▼

| Centroid Id | Count | SPEED_MPH | |
|---|---|---|---|
| 1 | 869 | | 25.6600 |
| 2 | 2766 | | 14.3222 |
| 3 | 425 | | 1.3814 |

Figure 7.6 – The Evaluation tab of the clustering_by_speed BigQuery ML model

The centroid with **Centroid Id** equals to 1 belongs to the first cluster and represents the taxi drivers with the best average speed: the *Top Drivers*. From the BigQuery UI, we can also notice that 869 taxi drivers belong to this cluster.

The second centroid includes most of the population, with a speed_mph value of 14.3222. This centroid is the center of the *Good Drivers* cluster.

The last centroid is the center of the cluster with the slowest drivers and includes 425 observations in the *Neutral Drivers* cluster.

3.  If we choose to analyze the `clustering_by_speed_and_income` model from the **Evaluation** tab in the BigQuery UI, we'll see the following information:

### clustering_by_speed_and_income

Details    Training    Evaluation    Schema

## Metrics

| | |
|---|---|
| **Davies–Bouldin index** | 0.9098 |
| **Mean squared distance** | 0.9598 |

## Numeric features

This table shows the centroid value for each feature. Use the select menu to view more numeric features.

Select features (2/2) ▼

| Centroid Id | Count | speed_mph | TOT_INCOME |
|---|---|---|---|
| 1 | 466 | 18.7581 | 34,577.3886 |
| 2 | 417 | 1.5105 | 8,950.8633 |
| 3 | 3174 | 16.7193 | 9,625.2282 |

Figure 7.7 – The Evaluation tab of the clustering_by_speed_and_income BigQuery ML model

Looking at the clusters and centroids identified by this second model, we can immediately notice that the clusters are based on two different features: `speed_mph` and `tot_income`.

The first cluster, with **Centroid Id** equal to 1, includes the best 466 drivers in terms of speed and annual income: *Top Drivers*. The second one contains the 417 *Neutral Drivers* with the poorest performance. The last centroid includes the majority of the drivers and is the *Good Drivers* cluster.

> **Tip**
> The result of training different iterations of K-Means clustering can generate different values, according to the initialization seeds that are used by BigQuery ML. It could happen that the positions of the centroids are different from the values shown in this section.

Now that we've taken a look at the results created by the training of the K-Means clustering models, let's start using them to classify taxi drivers into different clusters.

# Using the K-Means clustering model

In this section, we'll understand how to use our K-Means clustering model on new data.

To use our BigQuery ML model, we'll use the `ML.PREDICT` function on the same table that we've created to train the machine learning model.

In this case, we'll also include the `taxi_id` column, which identifies each taxi driver. The following query will classify each `taxi_id` field to the nearest cluster, according to the values of the `speed_mph` and `tot_income` fields:

```
SELECT
  * EXCEPT(nearest_centroids_distance)
FROM
  ML.PREDICT( MODEL `07_chicago_taxi_drivers.clustering_by_
speed_and_income`,
  (
    SELECT *
    FROM
      `07_chicago_taxi_drivers.taxi_speed_and_income`
  ));
```

The query statement is composed of a `SELECT` keyword that extracts all the columns returned by the `ML.PREDICT` function, except for the `nearest_centroids_distance` field.

The execution of the query generates the result shown in the following screenshot:

Figure 7.8 – The result of the query shows the application of the K-Means clustering model

Each `taxi_id` field is assigned to a specific centroid and to the corresponding cluster. The assignment is visible from the first column, `CENTROID_ID`.

Now that we've applied our model, let's formulate some final considerations and provide a list of taxi drivers that can be rewarded because they're in the *Top Drivers* cluster.

# Drawing business conclusions

In this section, we'll formulate some final considerations using the results that we got from the application of our machine learning model.

Using the query executed in the *Using the K-Means clustering model* section, we can create a table that contains the *Top Drivers* identified by the `clustering_by_speed_and_income` K-Means machine learning model, as follows:

```
CREATE OR REPLACE TABLE `07_chicago_taxi_drivers.top_taxi_
drivers_by_speed_and_income` AS
SELECT
  * EXCEPT(nearest_centroids_distance)
FROM
  ML.PREDICT( MODEL `07_chicago_taxi_drivers.clustering_by_
speed_and_income`,
    (
      SELECT *
      FROM
          `07_chicago_taxi_drivers.taxi_speed_and_income`
    ))
WHERE CENTROID_ID=1;
```

The execution of the query generates a `top_taxi_drivers_by_speed_and_income` table that contains all the drivers classified in the cluster with `CENTROID_ID=1` and corresponding to the *Top Drivers* cluster. Keep in mind that the K-Means clustering algorithm doesn't always return the same segmentations. For this reason, the clause `CENTROID_ID=1` can vary according to the results generated by each training stage.

This result set includes the identifiers of the taxi drivers that should be rewarded for their performances.

# Summary

In this chapter, we've built our unsupervised machine learning model. After a brief introduction of the business scenario, we've discovered what unsupervised machine learning is and used the K-Means clustering algorithm to group similar observations within the same clusters.

Before diving into the development of the machine learning models, we applied some data quality checks to our dataset and selected the fields to use as features of our machine learning models.

During the training stage, we trained two different machine learning models to learn how to create a K-Means clustering model.

Then, we evaluated the two models, leveraging BigQuery ML SQL syntax and the functionalities available in the BigQuery UI.

In the last step, we tested our machine learning model to cluster the taxi drivers available in the dataset according to their features and into the clusters generated by the K-Means model.

Finally, we've also created a list of drivers belonging to the *Top Drivers* cluster that can be rewarded because they can be considered top performers against the average of the other drivers.

In the next chapter, we'll introduce forecasting, using time series data.

# Further resources

- **Chicago Taxi Trips public dataset**: `https://console.cloud.google.com/marketplace/details/city-of-chicago-public-data/chicago-taxi-trips`

- **Chicago Open Data**: `https://data.cityofchicago.org/`

- **BigQuery ML** `CREATE MODEL` **statement**: `https://cloud.google.com/bigquery-ml/docs/reference/standard-sql/bigqueryml-syntax-create`

- **BigQuery** `ML.EVALUATE` **function**: `https://cloud.google.com/bigquery-ml/docs/reference/standard-sql/bigqueryml-syntax-evaluate`

- **BigQuery** `ML.PREDICT` **function**: `https://cloud.google.com/bigquery-ml/docs/reference/standard-sql/bigqueryml-syntax-predict`

- **BigQuery ML K-Means clustering example**: `https://cloud.google.com/bigquery-ml/docs/kmeans-tutorial`

# 8
# Forecasting Using Time Series

Predicting future trends using historical data is one of the most fascinating activities that we can do with machine learning.

Making predictions based on historical data points and time series is particularly interesting and can be very useful in different industries. Forecasting can help us in predicting the future, but also in identifying anomalies in data that don't respect the expected pattern.

In this chapter, we'll focus on time series forecasting by using the ARIMA Plus algorithm. This technique can be used to predict numerical values in different fields, such as the sales of a company, the customers in a restaurant, stock prices, and the electricity consumption of a building.

To understand how we can use BigQuery ML to forecast trends and to effectively present our results, we'll go through the following topics:

- Introducing the business scenario
- Discovering time series forecasting
- Exploring and understanding the dataset
- Training the time series forecasting model
- Evaluating the time series forecasting model

- Using the time series forecasting model
- Presenting the forecast

# Technical requirements

This chapter requires you to access a web browser and to have the possibility to leverage the following:

- A GCP account to access Google Cloud Console
- A GCP project to host the BigQuery datasets

Now, that we're ready with the technical requirements, let's dive into the analysis and development of our BigQuery ML forecasting model.

Check out the following video to see the Code in Action: `https://bit.ly/2QYoQlp`

# Introducing the business scenario

Imagine being a business analyst who works for the state of Iowa. The state monitors the retail distribution of liquors and spirits by collecting data from every shop in the territory. Controlling liquor sales is particularly important for monitoring citizen health and for checking tax income.

In the following screenshot, you can see a picture of typical shelves of liquors and spirits in a shop:

Figure 8.1 – The shelves in a liquor shop

For our business scenario, we can imagine that the state of Iowa wants to predict the number of liters that will be sold in the first 30 days of 2020 leveraging the historical data collected in the previous years.

Your manager may ask you to predict the number of liters that will be sold by all the shops in the state by leveraging the time series data that was already collected in the database.

As a business analyst, your job is to find the best algorithm to forecast the sales volumes and to present the results in a graphical way to the governor's staff.

Now that we've explained and understood the problem statement, let's take a look at the machine learning technique that we can use to forecast the sales, by using historical data.

# Discovering time series forecasting

A **time series** is a sequence of data points mapped at a certain time frequency. For example, it can contain the price of a stock collected at regular intervals, the sales volumes of each day in a specific timeframe, or the temperature measured by an **Internet of Things (IoT)** sensor during the day.

In the following diagram, you can see a time series graph of the data collected by a temperature sensor in the first 15 days of 2020:

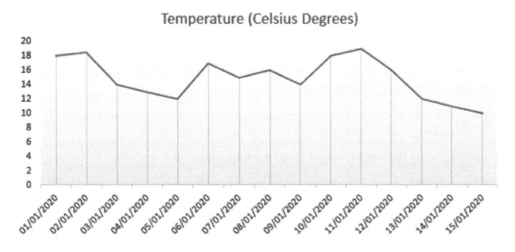

Figure 8.2 – Example of time series generated by a temperature sensor

**Forecasting** using time series analysis comprises the use of machine learning models to predict the future values of a specific measure by leveraging the known past data.

BigQuery ML provides a specific machine learning algorithm to forecast numerical values using time series data. The algorithm is designed and developed to do the following:

- Automatically clean and adjust the training data to overcome the data quality issues, for example, missing or duplicated values and spikes.

- Compensate for variations caused by specific periods, such as holidays.

- Decompose trends using the Seasonal and Trend Decomposition Loess algorithm.

- Extrapolate the seasonality from the data.

- And finally, apply the trend modeling of the **Autoregressive Integrated Moving Average (ARIMA)** model to predict future numerical values using historical ones.

You can use ARIMA models to discover hidden patterns in time series data or to forecast the future values of a specific measure.

In this section, we've learned the basics of time series forecasting. Now let's take a look at the dataset that we'll use to build our BigQuery ML model.

# Exploring and understanding the dataset

Before starting the development of the machine learning model, we'll start looking at the dataset and its structure.

Let's start by getting a clear understanding of the time series data that we have in the BigQuery public dataset to build our forecasting model in the next section.

## Understanding the data

In this section, we'll analyze the structure of the data to identify the fields to use for the machine learning model creation.

To start exploring the data, we need to do the following:

1. Log into our Google Cloud Console and access the **BigQuery** user interface from the navigation menu.

2. Create a new dataset under the project that we created in *Chapter 2, Setting Up Your GCP and BigQuery Environment*. For this use case, we'll create the dataset `08_sales_forecasting` with the default options.

3. Open the GCP project **bigquery-public-data** that hosts the BigQuery public datasets and browse the datasets until we find `iowa_liquor_sales`.

As seen in the following screenshot, the BigQuery public dataset contains only one table that hosts the data collected from the liquor shops in Iowa:

Figure 8.3 – The Iowa liquor sales public dataset contains the sales of all the liquor shops in Iowa

We'll use the table **sales** to build our forecasting model. This table contains all the information about the liquor sold in the state of Iowa since 2012.

4.   Let's click on the table name **sales** in the BigQuery navigation menu to access the schema of the table:

sales                                                                    Q QUERY TABLE      COPY

Schema    Details    Preview

| Field name | Type | Mode | Policy tags | Description |
|---|---|---|---|---|
| invoice_and_item_number | STRING | NULLABLE | | Concatenated invoice and line number associated with the liquor order. This provides a unique identifier for the individual liquor products included in the store order. |
| date | DATE | NULLABLE | | Date of order |
| store_number | STRING | NULLABLE | | Unique number assigned to the store who ordered the liquor. |
| store_name | STRING | NULLABLE | | Name of store who ordered the liquor. |
| address | STRING | NULLABLE | | Address of store who ordered the liquor. |
| city | STRING | NULLABLE | | City where the store who ordered the liquor is located |
| zip_code | STRING | NULLABLE | | Zip code where the store who ordered the liquor is located |
| store_location | STRING | NULLABLE | | Location of store who ordered the liquor. The Address, City, State and Zip Code are geocoded to provide geographic coordinates. Accuracy of geocoding is dependent on how well the address is interpreted and the completeness of the reference data used. |
| county_number | STRING | NULLABLE | | Iowa county number for the county where store who ordered the liquor is located |
| county | STRING | NULLABLE | | County where the store who ordered the liquor is located |
| category | STRING | NULLABLE | | Category code associated with the liquor ordered |
| category_name | STRING | NULLABLE | | Category of the liquor ordered. |
| vendor_number | STRING | NULLABLE | | The vendor number of the company for the brand of liquor ordered |
| vendor_name | STRING | NULLABLE | | The vendor name of the company for the brand of liquor ordered |

Figure 8.4 – The structure of the table lists all the information collected in the table

5.  Each field is well described in the **Description** column.

    The table contains the column **date**, which represents the day of the sale. For our purposes, we'll try to forecast the total number of liters sold on a specific day. For this reason, we can notice the presence of the field **volume_sold_liters**. This numeric field expresses the quantity of liquor sold during each transaction.

In this section, we've analyzed the metadata of the **sales** table and understood which fields are interesting to build our forecasting model on. Next, it's time to look at the actual data and start querying it.

## Checking the data quality

In this section, we'll apply some data quality checks to analyze the completeness of our training dataset.

Let's start analyzing the table that will be used to build our BigQuery ML model:

1.  In order to identify the timeframe of our dataset, let's extract the minimum and maximum value of the date field from the `bigquery-public-data.iowa_liquor_sales.sales` table:

    ```
    SELECT min(date), max(date) FROM `bigquery-public-data.
    iowa_liquor_sales.sales`;
    ```

    By executing this SQL statement, we can notice that the data goes from 2012 to the end of November 2020.

    The result of the query is presented in the following screenshot:

Figure 8.5 – The result of the query shows the timeframe of the dataset

For our purposes, we can focus our attention on the sales that occurred in 2018 and 2019 to forecast the first 30 days of 2020.

2.  In the second step, we'll analyze the number of distinct dates that we can find in the chosen timeframe:

```
SELECT COUNT(DISTINCT date)
FROM
        `bigquery-public-data.iowa_liquor_sales.sales`
WHERE
        EXTRACT (year from date) = 2019
        OR  EXTRACT (year from date) = 2018;
```

The query COUNT and the DISTINCT values available in the field date. With the expression EXTRACT (year from date), the SQL statement considers only the sales that happened in 2018 and 2019.

The result of the query is presented in the following screenshot:

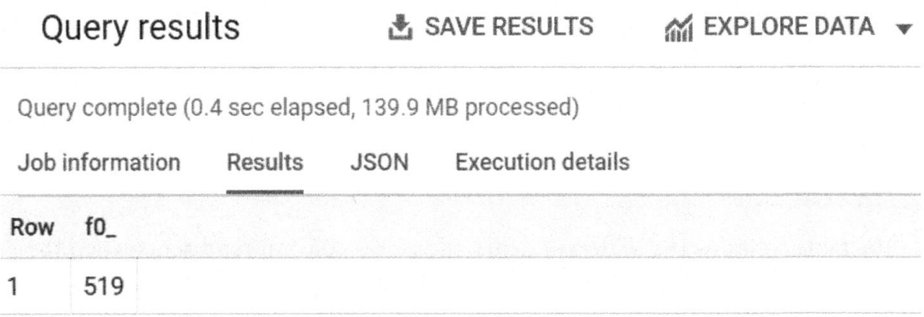

Figure 8.6 – The result of the query shows the distinct dates in the dataset

From the results, it's clear that the dataset doesn't contain the information for each day of the 2 years. This is probably caused by missing values due to public holidays and store closures. This is not a big issue because BigQuery ML will automatically manage the missing values during the training phase.

Now that we've performed some SQL queries to better understand our dataset, let's focus on creating our training dataset.

# Creating the training dataset

In this section, we'll create a table to store the data points that will be used to train the forecasting model in the next section. Before training the model, we'll also use Data Studio to graphically analyze the time series.

To train our model, we'll create a specific table that will host the historical data points of our time series:

1. Let's create a table that contains only two fields. The first one is `date` and the second one is `total_sold_liters`:

```
CREATE OR REPLACE TABLE `08_sales_forecasting.iowa_
liquor_sales` AS
SELECT
        date,
        SUM(volume_sold_liters) total_sold_liters
FROM
        `bigquery-public-data.iowa_liquor_sales.sales`
WHERE
        EXTRACT (year from date) = 2019 OR  EXTRACT (year
from date) = 2018
GROUP BY
        date;
```

The query creates the table `iowa_liquor_sales` in the dataset `08_sales_forecasting`.

The table contains two different fields: the `date` column represents when the transaction happened and the second field is calculated as the SUM of the liquor quantities sold in a day. `total_sold_liters` is an aggregated value calculated on the GROUP BY date clause and for each day of the years 2018 and 2019.

2. The second step will be to graphically analyze the data stored in the table `iowa_liquor_sales`.

As shown in the following screenshot, from the BigQuery navigation menu on the left, let's select the dataset `08_sales_forecasting` and then the table `iowa_liquor_sales`:

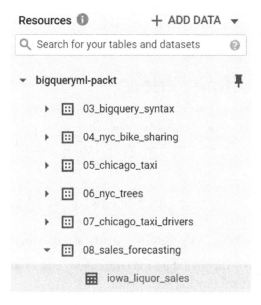

Figure 8.7 – The training table iowa_liquor_sales is visible in the BigQuery navigation menu

3.  After that, let's click on **EXPORT** and then **Explore with Data Studio** as presented in the following screenshot:

Figure 8.8 – From BigQuery, it's possible to open Data Studio

**Data Studio** is a free data visualization tool provided by Google and natively integrated with BigQuery that can be easily used to plot data in reports and diagrams.

4.  In Data Studio, we can select **Time series chart** as the chart type as shown in the following screenshot:

Figure 8.9 – In Data Studio, it's possible to select Time series chart to visualize the data

5.  Then, we can choose the field **date** for **Dimension** and **total_sold_liters** for **Metric**, as is presented in the following screenshot:

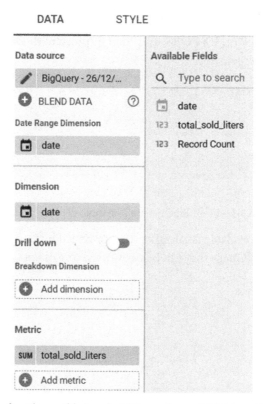

Figure 8.10 – In Data Studio, it's possible to select Dimension and Metric settings to draw the diagram

6.  After that, we can move to the **Style** tab and select **Linear interpolation** in the **Missing Data** combo box:

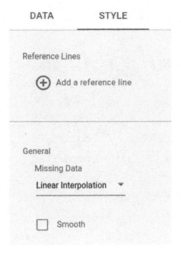

Figure 8.11 – The Linear interpolation option allows to improve the visualization
of the diagram in case of missing values

7.  After these configurations, we can visualize the diagram drawn by Data Studio that represents the trend line of the liquor quantities sold in the selected period:

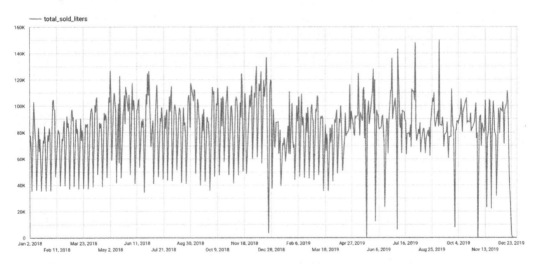

Figure 8.12 – The time series is shown in Data Studio with a blue line on the chart

Now that we've created the table on which our forecasting model will be trained and visualized the data in a diagram, let's dive into the creation of the machine learning model.

# Training the time series forecasting model

In this section, we'll train the BigQuery ML time series forecasting model.

Let's start training the machine learning model `liquor_forecasting`, executing the following SQL statement:

```
CREATE OR REPLACE MODEL `08_sales_forecasting.liquor_
forecasting`
OPTIONS
 (model_type = 'ARIMA',
  time_series_timestamp_col = 'date',
  time_series_data_col = 'total_sold_liters',
  auto_arima = TRUE,
  data_frequency = 'AUTO_FREQUENCY'
) AS
SELECT *
FROM
  `08_sales_forecasting.iowa_liquor_sales`;
```

The SQL statement is composed of the following parts:

- The first lines of the query start with the keywords CREATE OR REPLACE MODEL, followed by the identifier of the machine learning model, `08_sales_ forecasting.liquor_forecasting`, and by OPTIONS.

- Now let's focus on the options that we've used to train our machine learning model. The selected model type is 'ARIMA'. This option describes the algorithm that we're using to train the BigQuery ML forecasting model.

- time_series_timestamp_col = 'date' specifies the column that is used to host the time of the data points in the time series.

- The next option selects the column total_sold_liters as the column that stores the value of each data point and it's represented by the clause time_ series_data_col = 'total_sold_liters'.

- The property auto_arima, set to TRUE, allows BigQuery ML to automatically identify the parameters p, d, and q of the model.

- With the last parameter, 'AUTO_FREQUENCY', BigQuery automatically infers the frequency of the time series. In this case, the frequency is daily. The other options are 'HOURLY', 'DAILY', 'WEEKLY', 'MONTHLY', 'QUARTERLY', and 'YEARLY'.

- The final part of the SQL statement is composed of the SELECT statement applied on the training table iowa_liquor_sales.

Now that we've trained the time series forecasting model based on the ARIMA algorithm, let's take a look at how we can evaluate it with the BigQuery ML syntax and the BigQuery UI.

# Evaluating the time series forecasting model

In this section, we'll evaluate the performance of the machine learning model that we trained in the previous one.

The evaluation stage of a time series model can be performed by using the ML.EVALUATE BigQuery ML function.

Let's execute the following query to extract all the evaluation parameters that characterize the ARIMA model:

```
SELECT *
FROM
  ML.EVALUATE(MODEL `08_sales_forecasting.liquor_forecasting`);
```

The results of the query are visualized in the following screenshot:

**Query results**        ⬓ SAVE RESULTS        ⚞ EXPLORE DATA  ▾

Query complete (0.3 sec elapsed, 0 B processed)

Job information    Results    Execution details    JSON

| Row | non_seasonal_p | non_seasonal_d | non_seasonal_q | has_drift | log_likelihood | AIC | variance | seasonal_periods |
|---|---|---|---|---|---|---|---|---|
| 1 | 2 | 0 | 2 | false | -7243.539564267745 | 14499.07912853549 | 4643261.925923536 | WEEKLY |
| | | | | | | | | YEARLY |
| 2 | 0 | 0 | 5 | false | -7512.837377267166 | 15039.674754534331 | 5.217748599236709E7 | WEEKLY |
| | | | | | | | | YEARLY |
| 3 | 1 | 0 | 4 | false | -7516.227643892098 | 15046.455287784196 | 5.265806696837348E7 | WEEKLY |
| | | | | | | | | YEARLY |
| 4 | 0 | 0 | 4 | false | -7533.462259347871 | 15078.924518695741 | 5.5213926685826115E7 | WEEKLY |
| | | | | | | | | YEARLY |
| 5 | 4 | 0 | 1 | false | -7537.232481577719 | 15088.464963155438 | 2.8862543133593697E7 | WEEKLY |
| | | | | | | | | YEARLY |
| 6 | 5 | 0 | 0 | false | -7540.728707305453 | 15095.457414610906 | 5.648265375520058E7 | WEEKLY |
| | | | | | | | | YEARLY |

Figure 8.13 – The records extracted from the evaluation of the time series forecasting model

Each row defines each non-seasonal ARIMA model classified as an **ARIMA(p,d,q)** model. For each row, we can notice the following:

- The field **non_seasonal_p** represents the parameter **p** of the ARIMA model. The value of the row is the number of autoregressive terms used for the prediction. It indicates the number of observations used to predict the next value of the time series.

- The field **non_seasonal_d** represents the parameter **d** of the ARIMA model. The value of the row indicates how many times it's necessary to apply the difference between one data point and the previous one to mitigate the seasonality of the dataset.

- **non_seasonal_q** represents the parameter **q** of the ARIMA model. It indicates the number of observations to calculate the moving average that is used to predict the next value of the time series.

- **has_drift** shows if a drift constant was applied to the model.

- **log_likelihood** is a parameter that measures the level of fit of a statistical model to a specific dataset.

- **AIC** represents the **Akaike Information Criterion**. This value is used to evaluate the goodness of the model. Lower values of AIC are generally better. For this reason, we can consider the first model the best.

- **variance** measures how far the data points are from the average value of the series.

- The **seasonal_periods** column expresses the seasonal patterns in our data. In this case, BigQuery ML has identified a **WEEKLY** and **YEARLY** pattern in the sales time series.

Now that we've presented the performance indicators of our time series forecasting model, let's try using it to forecast the first 30 days of 2020.

# Using the time series forecasting model

To use our BigQuery ML model, we'll use the `ML.FORECAST` function to specify the parameters for the prediction.

The query will extract all the fields produced by the forecast function that accepts the following parameters:

- The model name, `` `08_sales_forecasting.liquor_forecasting` ``, preceded by the keyword `MODEL`.

- A `STRUCT` that includes the `horizon` of the forecast: `30` days and the `confidence_level` chosen for the prediction – in this case, 80%:

```
SELECT
  *
FROM
  ML.FORECAST(MODEL `08_sales_forecasting.liquor_
forecasting`,
              STRUCT(30 AS horizon, 0.8 AS confidence_
level));
```

The execution of the query generates the records shown in the following screenshot:

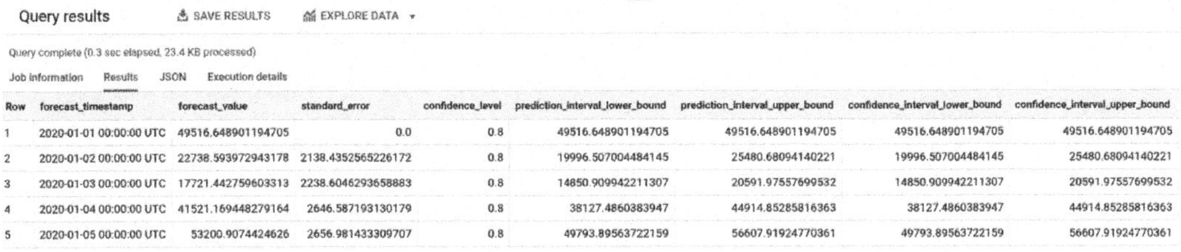

Query results SAVE RESULTS EXPLORE DATA

Query complete (0.3 sec elapsed, 23.4 KB processed)

Job information Results JSON Execution details

| Row | forecast_timestamp | forecast_value | standard_error | confidence_level | prediction_interval_lower_bound | prediction_interval_upper_bound | confidence_interval_lower_bound | confidence_interval_upper_bound |
|---|---|---|---|---|---|---|---|---|
| 1 | 2020-01-01 00:00:00 UTC | 49516.648901194705 | 0.0 | 0.8 | 49516.648901194705 | 49516.648901194705 | 49516.648901194705 | 49516.648901194705 |
| 2 | 2020-01-02 00:00:00 UTC | 22738.593972943178 | 2138.4352565226172 | 0.8 | 19996.507004484145 | 25480.68094140221 | 19996.507004484145 | 25480.68094140221 |
| 3 | 2020-01-03 00:00:00 UTC | 17721.442759603313 | 2238.6046293658883 | 0.8 | 14850.909942211307 | 20591.97557699532 | 14850.909942211307 | 20591.97557699532 |
| 4 | 2020-01-04 00:00:00 UTC | 41521.169448279164 | 2646.587193130179 | 0.8 | 38127.4860383947 | 44914.85285816363 | 38127.4860383947 | 44914.85285816363 |
| 5 | 2020-01-05 00:00:00 UTC | 53200.9074424626 | 2656.981433309707 | 0.8 | 49793.89563722159 | 56607.91924770361 | 49793.89563722159 | 56607.91924770361 |

Figure 8.14 – The results generated by the forecast function

We can notice in *Figure 8.14* that the predictions are chronologically ordered according to the date in the field **forecast_timestamp**. Each row represents a day and its related field **forecast_value** predicted by the BigQuery ML model. Since we've selected a horizon of 30 days, our result set is composed of 30 rows that go from January 1, 2020 to January 30 of the same year. The `confidence_level` value of 0.8 means that 80% of the predicted values should fall into the prediction interval identified by the fields **prediction_interval_lower_bound** and **prediction_interval_upper_bound**.

Now that we've applied our model, let's understand how we can effectively present the results using Data Studio.

# Presenting the forecast

In this section, we'll create a time series diagram with Data Studio in order to graphically present the forecast results.

Using the following query, we can create a table that contains both the historical and forecasted values:

```
CREATE OR REPLACE TABLE `08_sales_forecasting.iowa_liquor_
sales_forecast` AS
SELECT
   history_date AS date,
   history_value,
   NULL AS forecast_value,
   NULL AS prediction_interval_lower_bound,
   NULL AS prediction_interval_upper_bound
FROM
   (
     SELECT
        date AS history_date,
        total_sold_liters AS history_value
     FROM
        `08_sales_forecasting.iowa_liquor_sales`
   )
UNION ALL
SELECT
   CAST(forecast_timestamp AS DATE) AS date,
   NULL AS history_value,
   forecast_value,
   prediction_interval_lower_bound,
   prediction_interval_upper_bound
FROM
   ML.FORECAST(MODEL `08_sales_forecasting.liquor_forecasting`,
               STRUCT(30 AS horizon, 0.8 AS confidence_level));
```

The execution of the SQL statement generates the table `iowa_liquor_sales_forecast`, which is composed of the following:

- All the records are from the training table, `iowa_liquor_sales`, from which we have extracted `history_date` and `history_value` of the time series. We've also added some NULL fields to standardize the schema with the second part of the query separated by UNION ALL.

- All the forecasted records generated by the `ML.FORECAST` function were already applied in the previous section, *Using the time series forecasting model*. It's particularly interesting to notice that we don't extract only `forecast_value`, but also the lower and upper bounds of our predictions represented by the fields `prediction_interval_lower_bound` and `prediction_interval_upper_bound`.

- The presence of the `CAST` function, applied to the column `forecast_timestamp`, is necessary to change the data type from `TIMESTAMP` to `DATE` according to the schema of the training table.

As we've already done in the section *Creating the training dataset*, we can now do the following:

1. Select from the BigQuery navigation menu the `iowa_liquor_sales_forecast` table that we just created.

2. Click on **Export** and then **Explore with Data Studio** to access the reporting tool.

3. From the **chart** panel, choose **Time series chart**.

4. Drag and drop **history_value**, **forecast_value**, **prediction_interval_lower_bound**, and **prediction_interval_upper_bound** into the **Metric** panel as shown in the following screenshot:

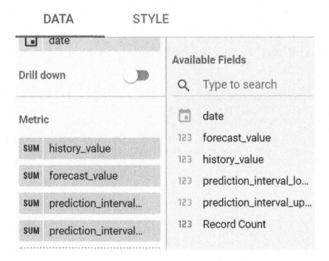

Figure 8.15 – The DATA panel allows us to customize the metrics of the chart

5. Move to the **Style** panel and scroll down until we find the **Missing Data** section. Here, we select **Linear interpolation**.

6.  Then, at the top of the screen, we can apply a filter on the **date** column to focus our chart only on the period that goes from the first of **December 2019** until the thirtieth of **January 2020**:

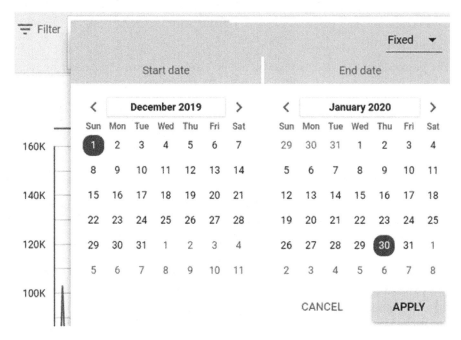

Figure 8.16 – Application of the filter on the date column

7.  Clicking on **APPLY**, the chart will be finally visualized as shown in the following screenshot:

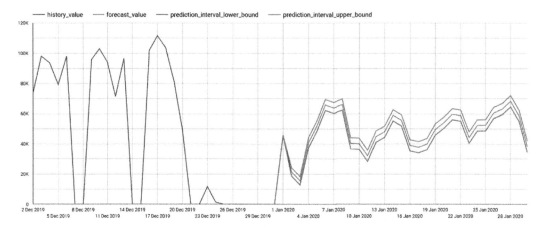

Figure 8.17 – Time series chart in Data Studio

Looking at the legend of the diagram, we can visualize the historical and the forecasted values represented by different colors. We can also notice that the **forecast_value** line is always included in the prediction interval.

# Summary

In this chapter, we've built our time series forecasting machine learning model. After the introduction of the business scenario, we discovered what time series forecasting is, and in particular, the ARIMA algorithm that is used to predict values from historical data points.

Before diving into the development of the BigQuery ML model, we applied some analyses on the data collected by the state of Iowa related to liquor sales in the shops of the territory. For this purpose, we introduced the use of the reporting tool Data Studio, which can be easily accessed by the BigQuery UI and be leveraged to draw a time series chart.

We then created our training table, which includes the time series of historical data, and trained our BigQuery ML model on it. Then, we evaluated the time series forecasting model by leveraging the BigQuery ML SQL syntax.

In the last step, we forecasted the quantity of liquor sold in Iowa with a horizon of 30 days and drew the results in a Data Studio dashboard that could be presented to non-technical people.

In the next chapter, we'll introduce the matrix factorization algorithm to build recommendation engines.

# Further resources

- **Iowa Liquor Retail Sales Public Dataset**: `https://console.cloud.google.com/marketplace/product/iowa-department-of-commerce/iowa-liquor-sales`

- **BigQuery ML Create Model**: `https://cloud.google.com/bigquery-ml/docs/reference/standard-sql/bigqueryml-syntax-create`

- **BigQuery ML Evaluate Model**: `https://cloud.google.com/bigquery-ml/docs/reference/standard-sql/bigqueryml-syntax-evaluate`

- **BigQuery ML Forecast**: `https://cloud.google.com/bigquery-ml/docs/reference/standard-sql/bigqueryml-syntax-forecast`

- **BigQuery ML Time Series Forecasting example**: `https://cloud.google.com/bigquery-ml/docs/arima-single-timeseries-forecasting-tutorial`

# 9

# Suggesting the Right Product by Using Matrix Factorization

Suggesting the right product is one of the most common applications of **Machine Learning (ML)**. Every day, product recommendation systems influence our choices on the internet. Newsletters, e-commerce websites, video streaming companies, and many other services leverage this powerful ML technique to offer us meaningful suggestions about the products that we may buy or like.

In this chapter, with a hands-on and practical approach, we'll execute the main implementation steps to build a new recommendation engine using the matrix factorization algorithm.

With a gradual and incremental approach and by leveraging BigQuery ML, we'll cover the following topics:

- Introducing the business scenario
- Discovering matrix factorization
- Configuring BigQuery Flex Slots
- Exploring and preparing the dataset

- Training the matrix factorization model

- Evaluating the matrix factorization model

- Using the matrix factorization model

- Drawing business conclusions

# Technical requirements

This chapter requires that you have access to a web browser and can leverage the following:

- A GCP account to access the Google Cloud Console.

- A GCP project to host the BigQuery datasets.

- BigQuery Flex slots to train matrix factorization models in BigQuery ML. The training for these kinds of algorithms is only available to flat-rate customers or customers with reservations. If you're using BigQuery with its on-demand pricing, we'll show you how to use BigQuery Flex Slots.

Now that the technical requirements are clear, let's look at our use case about the BigQuery ML matrix factorization model.

# Introducing the business scenario

Imagine being a business analyst that works for the Google Merchandise e-commerce store. The website sells different Google-branded products to different users. Some of the users are registered and have their own identifier, and their clickstream activities are collected in a specific dataset.

> **Important note**
> **Clickstream data** is the digital footprint left by users navigating a specific website. This data typically includes the web pages they visited, the time they spent on each page, the device they used, the origin of the traffic, and other relevant information.

In this scenario, the data is collected by Google using **Google Analytics 360** from the Google Merchandise e-commerce portal. This tool can be integrated with any website and allows us to gather information about the users' behavior on each page of the portal for further analysis and analytics.

The following screenshot is of the Google Merchandise Store, which sells Google-branded gadgets:

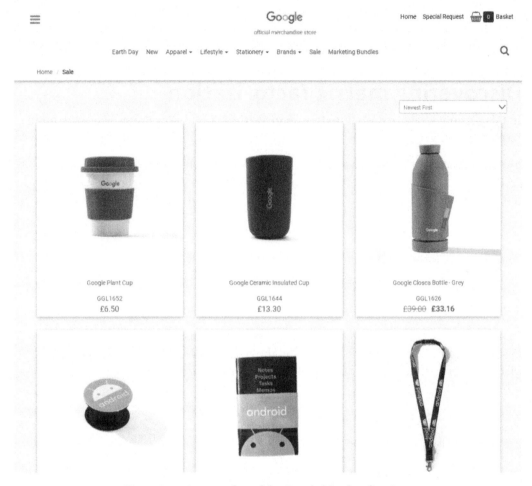

Figure 9.1 – A screenshot of the Google Merchandise Store

For our business scenario, we will imagine that our manager is asking us to build a new recommendation engine that can improve the user experience of their customers, as well as the revenues of their e-commerce sales.

Our goal is to develop a ML model that selects the right product to suggest for each customer who's registered on the website. To achieve this goal, we will use the clickstream data from the Google Merchandise Store that has already been collected and published in a BigQuery public dataset.

As business analysts, our job is to analyze the data, build an effective recommendation engine, and use it on the existing data to provide meaningful information to the marketing team.

Now that we've explained and understood the business scenario, let's take a look at the ML technique that we will use to build a recommendation engine for our e-commerce portal.

# Discovering matrix factorization

In this section, we'll learn what **matrix factorization** is, and how it can be used to build recommendation engines.

**Matrix factorization** represents a class of algorithms usually used to build recommendation engines. These algorithms are built on matrices that represent the interactions between users and items. In these kinds of matrices, the following occurs:

- Each user or customer is represented as a row.
- Each item or product corresponds to a column of the matrix.
- Each cell of the matrix is filled with a numeric value: the **feedback**.

This **feedback** represents a rating that a specific user has given to a specific item.

In the following screenshot, we can see an example of a matrix where the rows are the customers of a video streaming service and the columns are the films offered by the platform. Some of the cells contain a rating that ranges from **1** to **5**:

|  | Shining | Blade Runner | Titanic |
|---|---|---|---|
| User 1 | 3 |  | 1 |
| User 2 |  | 2 | 3 |
| User 3 | 4 |  |  |
| User 4 |  |  | 5 |

Figure 9.2 – Representation of a recommendation matrix

In this example, we can say that **User 1** has expressed an average rating for the film **The Shining**, but disliked **Titanic**. On the other hand, **User 4** assigned the maximum rating to **Titanic**, but didn't rate the other films.

According to different business scenarios, this feedback can be considered explicit or implicit:

- **Explicit feedback** is available when the user voluntarily rates a specific item, such as on a review website.

- If explicit feedback is not available, **implicit feedback** can be calculated and inferred by the developer of the recommendation system. For example, if a customer has bought a product, we can assume they would give positive feedback for that item.

Often, in e-commerce data, feedback is not explicitly given by the users but can be extracted from other information that's collected in the process, such as the number of clicks, the time spent on a specific page, or the quantity of a specific product bought by the user.

Matrix factorization algorithms are widely used in real-life scenarios. Some examples are as follows:

- The suggested books that we see in an online bookshop.

- The recommended TV series that we can see on video streaming services.

- The posts that are highlighted in our social media feeds.

- The products suggested by internet advertising systems.

In this section, we learned about the basics of matrix factorization. Now, let's configure BigQuery Flex Slots.

# Configuring BigQuery Flex Slots

In this chapter, we'll understand how to configure BigQuery **Flex Slots** to train our ML model.

A BigQuery **Slot** is a unit of BigQuery analytics capacity that's used to execute SQL queries and train BigQuery ML models. One BigQuery slot represents the compute capacity of a **Virtual Compute Processing Unit** (**VCPU**).

**Flex Slots** allow us to buy BigQuery analytics capacity for short periods. They are usually used to quickly satisfy sudden demands for resources with a minimum duration of 60 seconds.

Enabling Flex Slots is mandatory to train a matrix factorization model; otherwise, BigQuery will return an error during the training stage.

Let's see how we can enable BigQuery Flex Slots if we're using an on-demand plan:

1.  If you haven't enabled BigQuery Reservations yet, we need to access **Reservations** from the BigQuery menu on the left:

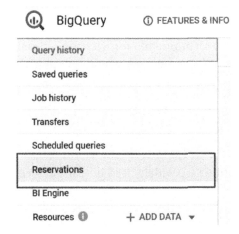

Figure 9.3 – Accessing Reservations from the BigQuery navigation menu

2.  Click on the **BUY SLOTS** button to initialize the buying process for BigQuery Flex Slots:

A BigQuery slot is a unit of computational capacity used to execute SQL, DDL, and DML statements in BigQuery. As an alternative to on-demand, pay-per-query pricing users may choose to take advantage of flat-rate pricing by buying BigQuery slot commitments.

You can take advantage of BigQuery flat-rate by taking the following actions:

1.  Purchase a commitment via 'Buy Slots'.
2.  A 'default' reservation is created for you (optionally, you can create additional reservations).
3.  Assign your GCP projects, folders, or orgs to a reservation.
4.  Note - any projects/folders/orgs not assigned to a reservation will remain on on-demand billing.

Figure 9.4 – Screenshot of the Reservations page

3.  Choose the minimum number of Flex Slots to buy; that is, **100**. Then, click on the **NEXT** button:

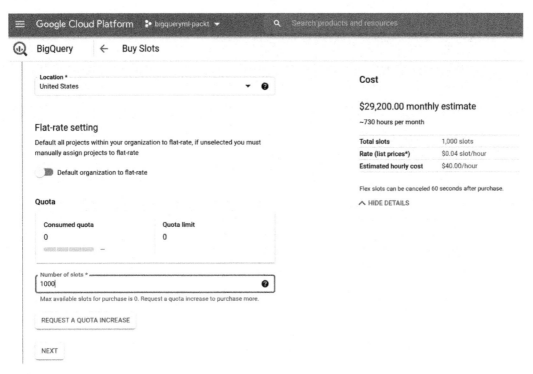

Figure 9.5 – BigQuery Buy Slots process

4.  Confirm your choice by writing **CONFIRM** in the confirmation text box and clicking on the blue **PURCHASE** button:

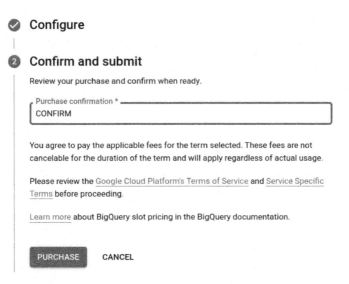

Figure 9.6 – Confirming your BigQuery Slots purchase

5.  Once the purchase has been confirmed, you can switch to the **ASSIGNMENTS** tab to assign the reservation that you've just bought.

6.  On the **ASSIGNMENTS** tab, select your GCP project in the first combo box and the reservation of Flex Slots in the second. After that, click the **CREATE** button to finalize your configuration:

## Create an assignment                                                    ✕

Choose a Google Cloud project, folder, or your entire organization to be assigned the resources of the reservation. When a folder or organization is assigned to a reservation, all child projects are implicitly assigned to that reservation, unless explicitly assigned elsewhere. Please allow a couple minutes for the assignment to take effect in the system.

| Select an organization, folder or proj...     BROWSE |

CREATE     **CANCEL**

Figure 9.7 – Assigning BigQuery slots

7.  When the assignment is complete, we can go back to the BigQuery home page.

> **Important note**
> Warning: Remember to deactivate the reservation of BigQuery slots at the end of this use case. Every BigQuery slot costs $0.04 per hour. Forgetting to disable this reservation will generate unexpected billing for your GCP project.

In this section, we learned how to buy BigQuery Flex Slots so that we can use matrix factorization. Now, we will focus on the data exploration and preparation steps.

# Exploring and preparing the dataset

In this section, we'll analyze the data we'll use to train our BigQuery ML model and apply the data preparation steps.

Let's start by getting a clear understanding of the Google Analytics data that is available in the BigQuery public dataset so that we can build our recommendation system.

# Understanding the data

In this section, we'll import the necessary data and then understand the most relevant fields of the dataset that will be used to train the BigQuery ML model.

Before we start developing the ML model, we'll look at the dataset and its schema. To start exploring the dataset, we need to do the following:

1.  Log into our Google Cloud Console and access the **BigQuery** user interface from the navigation menu.

2.  Create a new dataset under the project that we created in *Chapter 2, Setting Up Your GCP and BigQuery Environment*. For this use case, we'll create the `09_recommendation_engine` dataset with the default options.

3.  After that, we need to open the `bigquery-public-data` GCP project, which hosts the BigQuery public datasets, and browse the datasets until we find `google_analytics_sample`.

4.  The BigQuery public dataset contains multiple tables that host the Google Analytics sample data. Each table presents a different suffix according to the year and the month that it refers to:

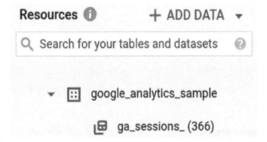

Figure 9.8 – The Google Analytics sample dataset containing the ga_sessions tables

We'll use the **ga_sessions** tables to build our matrix factorization model.

> **Tip**
> The **ga_sessions** table is not well described, but if we need further information about this dataset, we can leverage the examples available in the BigQuery documentation at `https://support.google.com/analytics/answer/4419694?hl=en`.

5.  To simplify the data access process, let's create a single table that unifies all the tables with different suffixes. Let's execute the following SQL statement:

```
CREATE OR REPLACE TABLE `09_recommendation_engine.all_ga_
sessions` AS
SELECT * FROM `bigquery-public-data.google_analytics_
sample.ga_sessions_*`;
```

The query creates a new table called `all_ga_sessions` in our `09_recommendation_engine` dataset. This table stores all the data that comes from the different `ga_sessions` tables into a unique structure. To unify all the records, we've used the wildcard character, `*`.

> **Tip**
> **Wildcards** are useful when a dataset contains multiple tables with similar names and compatible schemas. In this case, we're collecting all the data from the multiple `ga_sessions_*` tables and placing them in our new structure, `all_ga_sessions`.

6.  Now, we can simply query `all_ga_sessions` to get a preview of the schema:

```
SELECT * FROM `09_recommendation_engine.all_ga_sessions`
TABLESAMPLE SYSTEM (10 PERCENT);
```

The results of the query point out that the schema of the table is quite complex and contains multiple nested fields. Fortunately, for our purposes, we will only focus on some of them:

`fullVisitorID` represents the identifier of each registered user that is browsing Google's website.

`productSku` is the product code that identifies a specific product in Google's catalog. Some examples of products are mugs, T-shirts, bags, and socks.

The `action_type` column is the action that a user has performed during a web session. If this field is equal to 6, the row represents a specific product being purchased by a customer.

Now that we've discovered which columns will be used for our ML model, it's time to prepare our training dataset.

# Creating the training dataset

In this section, we'll create the tables that will host the training data of our BigQuery ML model.

To train our model, we'll create a table that will host all the purchases that have been made by the registered customers on the website.

Let's create the `product_purchases` table, which contains three fields:

- The code of each user: `fullVisitorId`

- The identifier of the purchased product: `purchased_product_id`

- The `quantity` field, which specifies the product that's been bought by the customer

Execute the following SQL statement to create the table:

```
CREATE OR REPLACE TABLE `09_recommendation_engine.product_
purchases` AS
SELECT     fullVisitorId,
           hits_product.productSKU AS purchased_product_id,
           COUNT(hits_product.productSKU) AS quantity
FROM
           `09_recommendation_engine.all_ga_sessions`,
           UNNEST(hits) AS hits,
           UNNEST(hits.product) AS hits_product
WHERE fullVisitorId IN (
                    SELECT fullVisitorId
                    FROM
              `09_recommendation_engine.all_ga_sessions`,
                    UNNEST(hits) AS hits
                    WHERE
                 hits.eCommerceAction.action_type = '6'
                    GROUP BY fullVisitorId
                    )
GROUP BY fullVisitorId, purchased_product_id;
```

The most internal query extracts all the customers identified by `fullVisitorId` from the `all_ga_sessions` table that have at least bought a product on the e-commerce portal. To identify these purchases, we've added a `WHERE` clause to `hits.eCommerceAction.action_type = '6'`. To get distinct values of `fullVisitorId`, the query leverages the `GROUP BY fullVisitorId` clause.

In the `FROM` clause of the nested query, we're using the `UNNEST` function to extract the nested fields present in the original table and access them.

> **Important note**
> **UNNEST** is a function that's used to convert an array into a set of multiple rows. It takes an array as input and returns a table with a single row for each item in the array.

In the most external query, we simply extract the three fields that are relevant to our use case: `fullVisitorId`, `purchased_product_id`, and our total `quantity`. This last measure is obtained by using the `SUM` operator on all the transactions being performed by a specific user to buy a specific product.

Now that we've created the table that our recommendation engine will be trained on, let's create the BigQuery ML model.

# Training the matrix factorization model

In this section, we'll train the BigQuery ML matrix factorization model in order to build a recommendation system with the e-commerce data that we've already prepared.

Let's start training the `purchase_recommender` ML model by executing the following SQL statement:

```
CREATE OR REPLACE MODEL `09_recommendation_engine.purchase_
recommender`
OPTIONS(model_type='matrix_factorization',
        user_col='fullVisitorID',
        item_col='purchased_product_id',
        rating_col='quantity',
        feedback_type='implicit'
        )
AS
SELECT fullVisitorID, purchased_product_id, quantity
FROM `09_recommendation_engine.product_purchases`;
```

The first few lines of the query are composed of the CREATE OR REPLACE MODEL keywords, followed by the identifier of the new ML model, `09_recommendation_engine.purchase_recommender`, and OPTIONS.

Now, let's focus on the OPTIONS values that we've used to train our BigQuery ML model:

- The model type is 'matrix_factorization'. This option describes the algorithm that we're using to train our recommendation model.

- The user_col='fullVisitorID' option specifies which column represents the users of the recommendation engine. In our case, we're using the fullVisitorID field, which is assigned to the registered customers of the e-commerce portal.

- With the item_col='purchased_product_id' option, we're using the code of each product that's been purchased by our customers to identify each item in our model.

- Since we don't have an explicit rating for our products, we'll choose feedback_type='implicit' and use the purchased quantity value as the rating for our recommendation engine. In this case, we're assuming that if a user has bought large quantities of a product, they're interested and satisfied with the product.

After about 7 minutes, the matrix factorization model will be trained, and we can move on to the next stage: the evaluation phase.

# Evaluating the matrix factorization model

In this section, we'll evaluate the performances of the matrix factorization model that we trained in the previous section.

The evaluation stage of a matrix factorization model can be performed using the ML.EVALUATE BigQuery ML function or through the BigQuery UI.

Let's execute the following query to extract all the evaluation parameters that characterize the recommendation model that we've just trained:

```
SELECT
  *
FROM
  ML.EVALUATE(MODEL `09_recommendation_engine.recommender`,
    (
    SELECT * FROM `09_recommendation_engine.product_visits`));
```

The result of this query is shown in the following screenshot:

**Query results**         ⬇ SAVE RESULTS      〽 EXPLORE DATA ▾

Query complete (11.1 sec elapsed, 462.3 MB processed)

Job information    Results    JSON    Execution details

| Row | mean_average_precision | mean_squared_error | normalized_discounted_cumulative_gain | average_rank |
|-----|------------------------|--------------------|---------------------------------------|--------------|
| 1 | 0.8508269965973102 | 0.04864193065081121 | 0.98685439363955 | 0.47981128076599766 |

Figure 9.9 – The record that's been extracted from the evaluation of the matrix factorization model

The same information can be accessed by selecting the ML model from the BigQuery navigation menu and then accessing the **Evaluation** tab.

In the following screenshot, you can see the evaluation metrics of the BigQuery ML model:

# purchase_recommender

Details     Training     Evaluation     Schema

## Metrics

| | |
|---|---|
| **Mean average precision** | 0.6278 |
| **Mean squared error** | 0.0979 |
| **Normalized discounted cumulative gain** | 0.2878 |
| **Average rank** | 0.4400 |

Figure 9.10 – The Evaluation tab of the matrix factorization model

Since the value of **Mean squared error** is very low, we can be satisfied with the results that have been achieved by our matrix factorization model.

In this section, we learned how to access the performance indicators of our recommendation model. Now, let's use the recommendation model to find the best products to suggest to our customers.

# Using the matrix factorization model

In this section, we'll test the matrix factorization model to get the recommended products for the users of our website.

To use our BigQuery ML model, we'll use the ML.RECOMMEND function while specifying the parameters for our prediction.

The recommendation engine does not need to take any additional input parameters besides the model itself. If the model has one input column, the model will only return the recommendations for the rows in the input. If no input values are provided, the model will apply the prediction for each combination of users and items in the original dataset.

ML.RECOMMEND returns three columns:

- A column that represents the user. In our implementation, this is identified by the fullVisitorID column.

- A field dedicated to the item that is recommended to a specific user. In our case, this is represented by the purchased_product_id column.

- A third column that represents the predicted rating in the case of an explicit matrix factorization model. If the model is implicit, as in our case, the field stores the predicted confidence of the recommendation.

Let's execute the following query to materialize a table that contains all the recommendations that have been generated by our matrix factorization model:

```
CREATE OR REPLACE TABLE `09_recommendation_engine.product_
recommendations` AS
    SELECT
        DISTINCT fullVisitorID, purchased_product_id, predicted_
quantity_confidence
    FROM
        ML.RECOMMEND(MODEL`09_recommendation_engine.purchase_
recommender`,
        (
        SELECT
            fullVisitorID
        FROM
            `09_recommendation_engine.product_purchases` ));
```

The query creates a new table called `product_recommendations` that stores the `DISTINCT` couples of users and items. In our case, the couples are composed of the `fullVisitorID` and `purchased_product_id` columns.

For each couple, the `ML.RECOMMEND` function also returns a predicted confidence that expresses the probability that a specific user has interest in a product in the e-commerce catalog.

Now that we have the output of our recommendation engine, let's learn how to use this data from a business perspective.

## Drawing business conclusions

Now that we've applied our BigQuery ML model, let's learn how the generated results can be used from a business perspective to improve the effectiveness of our sales strategy.

From the `product_recommendations` table, we can extract relevant information that we can use to improve our marketing campaigns or advertising strategy, and then target the users with higher propensity to buy a specific product.

For example, by executing the following query, we can extract the first `100` users with the highest propensity to buy a specific product from our e-commerce portal:

```
SELECT *
FROM
    `09_recommendation_engine.product_recommendations`
ORDER BY predicted_quantity_confidence DESC
LIMIT 100;
```

Executing this SQL statement returns the following result:

Query results SAVE RESULTS EXPLORE DATA

Query complete (1.1 sec elapsed, 728.8 MB processed)

Job information Results JSON Execution details

| Row | fullVisitorID | purchased_product_id | predicted_quantity_confidence |
|---|---|---|---|
| 1 | 165109760635455356 | GGOEGAAB010515 | 2.201711885341542 |
| 2 | 5526675926038480325 | GGOEGAFJ036214 | 2.064287349370705 |
| 3 | 8740176326132717435 | GGOEGADB057316 | 1.9811156616844734 |
| 4 | 165109760635455356 | GGOEGAAB033815 | 1.9355107333444201 |
| 5 | 6944407004438928008 | GGOEGAAL010616 | 1.8594131694347042 |
| 6 | 6118933348572020566 | GGOEGAAR010716 | 1.8458642578743274 |
| 7 | 3117505679893009709 | GGOEWFKA082999 | 1.8457648537046336 |
| 8 | 3117505679893009709 | GGOEWFKA083199 | 1.8360749834107533 |
| 9 | 3117505679893009709 | GGOEWFKA083299 | 1.8327091431884668 |
| 10 | 6118933348572020566 | GGOEGAAB010515 | 1.8326118557895652 |
| 11 | 5627236441803896511 | GGOEGAAJ080614 | 1.8309599166417336 |
| 12 | 3117505679893009709 | GGOEWFKA083099 | 1.8153957025029692 |
| 13 | 8942866004645538967 | GGOEWEBB082699 | 1.811788361390696 |
| 14 | 165109760635455356 | GGOEGAAL010613 | 1.8067662811268306 |

Figure 9.11 – The customers with the highest propensity to buy a specific product

The list that we've just extracted can be sent to our marketing office to create tailored marketing campaigns. Alternatively, it can be used in our e-commerce portal to recommend the most interesting products for a specific registered customer.

# Summary

In this chapter, we built a recommendation engine based on the matrix factorization algorithm. After we introduced the business scenario, we discovered what matrix factorization is and the difference between explicit and implicit models. Before diving into data exploration, we enabled BigQuery Flex Slots, which are necessary to train this category of ML algorithms.

Then, we applied some analyses and data preparation steps to the sample data collected by Google from the Google Merchandise e-commerce portal. Here, we've focused on the fields that were actually required to build our BigQuery ML model.

Next, we created our training table, which includes the purchases that were made by each user, along with the related quantity for each product.

After that, we trained our matrix factorization model on the data that we'd prepared. When the model was trained, we evaluated its key performance indicators using SQL code and the BigQuery UI.

Finally, we generated some recommendations using our new matrix factorization model and extracted a list of 100 customers that can be targeted with high propensity to buy a set of products.

In the next chapter, we'll introduce the XGBoost algorithm for predicting binary values.

# Further resources

- **Google Analytics 360 public dataset**: `https://console.cloud.google.com/marketplace/product/obfuscated-ga360-data/obfuscated-ga360-data`

- **BigQuery ML create model**: `https://cloud.google.com/bigquery-ml/docs/reference/standard-sql/bigqueryml-syntax-create`

- **BigQuery ML evaluate model**: `https://cloud.google.com/bigquery-ml/docs/reference/standard-sql/bigqueryml-syntax-evaluate`

- **BigQuery ML RECOMMEND**: `https://cloud.google.com/bigquery-ml/docs/reference/standard-sql/bigqueryml-syntax-recommend`

- **BigQuery ML explicit matrix factorization example**: `https://cloud.google.com/bigquery-ml/docs/bigqueryml-mf-explicit-tutorial`

- **BigQuery ML implicit matrix factorization example**: `https://cloud.google.com/bigquery-ml/docs/bigqueryml-mf-implicit-tutorial#implicit-model`

# 10
# Predicting Boolean Values Using XGBoost

**eXtreme Gradient Boosting** (**XGBoost**) is one of the most powerful **machine learning** (**ML**) libraries that data scientists can leverage to solve complex use cases in an efficient and flexible way. It started as a research project, and the first version was released in 2014. The popularity of this ML library grew very quickly, thanks to its capabilities and portability. In fact, it was used in important Kaggle ML contests and is now available for different programming languages and on different operating systems.

This library can be used to tackle different ML problems and is specifically designed for structured data. XGBoost was also recently released for BigQuery ML. Thanks to this technique, BigQuery users are allowed to implement classification and regression ML models using this library.

In this chapter, we'll see all the stages necessary to implement a XGBoost classification model to classify New York City trees into different species according to their characteristics.

Using the BigQuery ML SQL dialect, we'll go through the following topics:

- Introducing the business scenario
- Discovering the XGBoost Boosted Tree classification model
- Exploring and understanding the dataset
- Training the XGBoost classification model
- Evaluating the XGBoost classification model
- Using the XGBoost classification model
- Drawing business conclusions

# Technical requirements

This chapter requires you to have access to a web browser and to be able to leverage the following:

- A **Google Cloud Platform** (**GCP**) account to access the Google Cloud Console
- A GCP project to host the BigQuery datasets

Now that we're ready in terms of the technical requirements, let's dive into the analysis and development of our BigQuery ML XGBoost classification model.

Check out the following video to see the Code in Action: `https://bit.ly/3ujnzH3`

# Introducing the business scenario

In this section, we'll introduce the business scenario that will be tackled with the XGBoost classification algorithm.

The business scenario is very similar to the use case presented and used in *Chapter 6, Classifying Trees with Multiclass Logistic Regression*. In this chapter, we'll use the same dataset but will apply a more advanced ML algorithm.

We can summarize and remember that the goal of the ML model is to automatically classify the trees of New York City into different species according to their characteristics, such as their position, their size, and their health status.

As we've done in *Chapter 9, Suggesting the Right Product by Using Matrix Factorization*, we can focus our attention only on the five most common species of trees present in the city.

Now that we've explained and understood the business scenario, let's take a look at the ML technique that we can use to automatically classify trees according to their features.

# Discovering the XGBoost Boosted Tree classification model

In this section, we'll learn what the **XGBoost Boosted Trees** classification model is, and we'll understand which classification use cases can be tackled with this ML algorithm.

XGBoost is an open source library that provides a portable gradient boosting framework for different languages. The XGBoost library is available for different programming languages such as C++, Java, Python, R, and Scala, and can work on different operating systems. XGBoost is used to deal with supervised learning use cases, where we use labeled training data to predict target variables.

XGBoost's popularity has grown in the ML community over the years because it has often been the choice of many winning teams during ML competitions, such as the *Kaggle - High Energy Physics meets Machine Learning award* in 2016.

The classification capabilities of **XGBoost Boosted Trees** are based on the usage of multiple decision trees that classify data to enable predictions.

In the following diagram, you can see a simple representation of a decision tree that classifies animals:

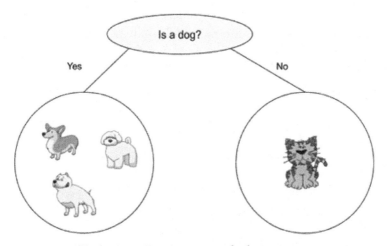

Figure 10.1 – Representation of a decision tree

XGBoost classification models can answer the same questions addressed by multiclass logistic regression, such as the following:

- Is the comment of my customer *neutral*, *positive*, or *negative*?

- Does my customer belong to the *gold*, *silver*, or *bronze* level?

- Is the probability of churn of a specific customer *high*, *medium*, or *low*?

- Does the image recognition algorithm identify a *cat*, a *dog*, a *mouse*, or a *cow*?

In our business scenario, we can classify New York City trees into five different species by leveraging the XGBoost Boosted Tree classification model. In fact, we're interested in predicting the species according to the characteristics of each tree.

During the training phase of a XGBoost algorithm, the ML model tries to find the best values to assign to each tree in order to minimize the final error metric.

After the training, we'll compare the results of this model with the outcomes that we got in *Chapter 6*, *Classifying Trees with Multiclass Logistic Regression*.

Now that we've learned the basics of the XGBoost Boosted Tree algorithm, it's time to take a look at the dataset that we'll use to build our ML model.

# Exploring and understanding the dataset

In this section, we'll analyze and prepare the dataset for our use case. We'll start with some data quality checks, and then we'll segment the data into training, evaluation, and test tables.

Since the dataset has already been used in *Chapter 6*, *Classifying Trees with Multiclass Logistic Regression*, we will not start the analysis from the beginning. Instead, we'll focus on the most relevant queries for our business scenario.

## Checking the data quality

To start our exploration of the data and to carry out data quality checks, we need to do the following:

1. Log in to our Google Cloud Console and access the **BigQuery User Interface (UI)** from the navigation menu.

2. Create a new dataset under the project that we created in *Chapter 2*, *Setting Up Your GCP and BigQuery Environment*. For this use case, we'll create a `10_nyc_trees_xgboost` dataset with the default options.

3.  First of all, let's check if all the records contain a valid value in the spc_latin field by executing the following query:

```
SELECT   COUNT(*)
FROM        `bigquery-public-data.new_york_trees.tree_
census_2015`
WHERE
            spc_latin is NULL;
```

As we can see from the following screenshot, there are **31619** records with a missing value in the spc_latin column. These records will be filtered out during the training stage:

Figure 10.2 – The query result shows that some records should be filtered out

4.  After this first check, we need to verify if any potential feature is characterized by NULL values. Let's run the following **Structured Query Language** (**SQL**) statement:

```
SELECT   COUNT(*)
FROM        `bigquery-public-data.new_york_trees.tree_
census_2015`
WHERE
            spc_latin is NOT NULL
            AND (
                zip_city is NULL OR
                tree_dbh is NULL OR
                boroname is NULL OR
                nta_name is NULL OR
                health is NULL OR
                sidewalk is NULL) ;
```

The query returns a COUNT of three records due to the presence of NULL values in the sidewalk and health fields. Despite the low number, we'll filter out these records in the following queries, to use only meaningful records.

5.  Then, we can extract the most common five tree species from the BigQuery public dataset. Let's execute the following query:

```
SELECT    spc_latin,
          COUNT(*) total
FROM      `bigquery-public-data.new_york_trees.tree_
census_2015`
WHERE
          spc_latin is NOT NULL
          AND zip_city is NOT NULL
          AND tree_dbh is NOT NULL
          AND boroname is NOT NULL
          AND nta_name is NOT NULL
          AND health is NOT NULL
          AND sidewalk is NOT NULL
GROUP BY
          spc_latin
ORDER BY
          total desc
LIMIT 5;
```

The query calculates total as the number of records for each spc_latin field. An ORDER BY clause is used to sort the results from the largest to the smallest values of the total field. Then, a LIMIT 5 clause is used to return only the first five records.

In the following screenshot, you can see the results of the query, which show the five species most frequently present in the dataset:

## Query results    ± SAVE RESULTS    📊 EXPLORE DATA ▾

Query complete (0.5 sec elapsed, 55.3 MB processed)

Job information    Results    JSON    Execution details

| Row | spc_latin | total |
| --- | --- | --- |
| 1 | Platanus x acerifolia | 87014 |
| 2 | Gleditsia triacanthos var. inermis | 64262 |
| 3 | Pyrus calleryana | 58931 |
| 4 | Quercus palustris | 53185 |
| 5 | Acer platanoides | 34189 |

Figure 10.3 – The most frequent tree species in the dataset

6.  In order to materialize these five species into a table, let's execute the following code to create a `10_nyc_trees_xgboost.top5_species` table:

```
CREATE OR REPLACE TABLE `10_nyc_trees_xgboost.top5_species` AS
      SELECT    spc_latin,
         COUNT(*) total
      FROM      `bigquery-public-data.new_york_trees.tree_census_2015`
      WHERE
              spc_latin is NOT NULL
              AND zip_city is NOT NULL
              AND tree_dbh is NOT NULL
              AND boroname is NOT NULL
              AND nta_name is NOT NULL
              AND health is NOT NULL
              AND sidewalk is NOT NULL
      GROUP BY
              spc_latin
      ORDER BY
              total desc
      LIMIT 5;
```

The only difference with the query executed in the previous *Step 5* is represented by the use of CREATE OR REPLACE TABLE keywords that are leveraged to materialize the results of the query into the new table.

In this section, we've analyzed the data quality of the BigQuery public dataset. Now, let's start segmenting it into three different tables for the training, evaluation, and classification stages.

## Segmenting the dataset

Before implementing our XGBoost classification model, let's segment our dataset according to the main stages of the ML development life cycle: training, evaluation, and use. In order to randomly divide the records into three different tables, we'll use a MOD function on the tree_id numerical field. Follow these steps:

1. First of all, let's create a table that will contain the training dataset. To do this, we execute the following SQL statement:

```
CREATE OR REPLACE TABLE `10_nyc_trees_xgboost.training_
table` AS
SELECT   *
FROM     `bigquery-public-data.new_york_trees.tree_
census_2015`
WHERE
         zip_city is NOT NULL
         AND tree_dbh is NOT NULL
         AND boroname is NOT NULL
         AND nta_name is NOT NULL
         AND health is NOT NULL
         AND sidewalk is NOT NULL
         AND spc_latin in
         (SELECT spc_latin from `10_nyc_trees_xgboost.
top5_species`)
         AND MOD(tree_id,11)<=8;
```

The query creates a `10_nyc_trees_xgboost.training_table` table with all the columns available in the original dataset, through a SELECT * statement. It applies all the filters necessary to get not empty values for the spc_latin label and for all the other features.

Using an IN clause, training_table will contain only the records related to the most five common species that we've identified in the dataset.

The last line of the query, with the MOD(tree_id,11)<=8 clause, allows us to pick up only 80% of the records from the entire dataset. MOD stands for *modulo* and returns the remainder of the division of tree_id by 11. With the less than or equal operator (<=), we're approximately extracting 80% of the entire dataset.

2. With a similar approach, we can create a `10_nyc_trees_xgboost. evaluation_table` table that will be used for the evaluation of our ML model. Let's execute the following CREATE TABLE statement:

```
CREATE OR REPLACE TABLE `10_nyc_trees_xgboost.evaluation_
table` AS

SELECT   *

FROM      `bigquery-public-data.new_york_trees.tree_
census_2015`

WHERE
          zip_city is NOT NULL

          AND tree_dbh is NOT NULL

          AND boroname is NOT NULL

          AND nta_name is NOT NULL

          AND health is NOT NULL

          AND sidewalk is NOT NULL

          AND spc_latin in

          (SELECT spc_latin from `06_nyc_trees.top5_
species`)

          AND MOD(tree_id,11)=9;
```

In contrast to when we created the training table, for the evaluation_table table we're picking up only 10% of the records from the entire dataset, by applying a MOD(tree_id,11)=9 filter.

3.   Finally, we'll execute the following SQL statement in order to create a `10_nyc_trees_xgboost.classification_table` table that will be used to apply our XGBoost classification model:

```
CREATE OR REPLACE TABLE `10_nyc_trees_xgboost.
classification_table` AS

SELECT   *

FROM      `bigquery-public-data.new_york_trees.tree_
census_2015`

WHERE
          zip_city is NOT NULL
          AND tree_dbh is NOT NULL
          AND boroname is NOT NULL
          AND nta_name is NOT NULL
          AND health is NOT NULL
          AND sidewalk is NOT NULL
          AND spc_latin in
          (SELECT spc_latin from `10_nyc_trees_xgboost.
top5_species`)
          AND MOD(tree_id,11)=10;
```

This new table is very similar to the previous ones, but thanks to the MOD function will contain the remaining 10% of the dataset.

In this section, we've analyzed the dataset that contains information about trees in New York City, applied some data quality checks to exclude empty values, and segmented the dataset, focusing on the five most common species. Now that we've completed the preparatory steps, it's time to move on and start the training of our BigQuery ML model.

# Training the XGBoost classification model

Now that we've segmented the dataset into multiple tables to support the different stages of the ML model life cycle, let's focus on the training of our XGBoost classification model. Follow these steps:

1.   Let's start with training our first ML model, xgboost_classification_model_version_1, as follows:

```
CREATE OR REPLACE MODEL `10_nyc_trees_xgboost.xgboost_
classification_model_version_1`
OPTIONS
```

```
( MODEL_TYPE='BOOSTED_TREE_CLASSIFIER',
  BOOSTER_TYPE = 'GBTREE',
  NUM_PARALLEL_TREE = 1,
  MAX_ITERATIONS = 50,
  TREE_METHOD = 'HIST',
  EARLY_STOP = FALSE,
  AUTO_CLASS_WEIGHTS=TRUE
) AS
SELECT
  zip_city,
  tree_dbh,
  spc_latin as label
FROM
  `10_nyc_trees_xgboost.training_table` ;
```

In this BigQuery ML statement, we can see `CREATE OR REPLACE MODEL` keywords used to start the training of the model. These keywords are followed by the identifier of the ML model.

After the identifier, we can notice an `OPTIONS` clause. For the `MODEL_TYPE`, we've chosen a `BOOSTED_TREE_CLASSIFIER` option, which allows us to build a XGBoost classification model. The `BOOSTER_TYPE = 'GBTREE'` clause is considered a default option to train XGBoost boosted tree models.

In order to limit the complexity of training and the resource consumption, we've chosen to train only one tree in parallel with a `NUM_PARALLEL_TREE = 1` clause, and to stop the training after 50 iterations using `MAX_ITERATIONS`.

A `HIST` parameter is suggested for large datasets in the XGBoost documentation, and an `EARLY_STOP = FALSE` clause is used to prevent the training phase being stopped after the first iteration.

The last option, `AUTO_CLASS_WEIGHTS=TRUE`, is used to balance the weights— in the case of an unbalanced dataset—with some tree species that can occur more frequently than others.

This first version of the model tries to predict the species of each tree, leveraging only the `zip_city` code where the tree is planted and the diameter of the tree, `tree_dbh`.

2.  At the end of the training, we can access the ML model from the BigQuery navigation menu to have a look at the performance of the model. Selecting the **Evaluation** tab, we can see the **ROC AUC** value. In this case, the value is **0.7775**, as we can see in the following screenshot:

# xgboost_classification_model_version_1

Details    Training    Evaluation    Schema

## Aggregate metrics ⊚

| | |
|---|---|
| Threshold ⊚ | 0.0000 |
| Precision ⊚ | 0.4574 |
| Recall ⊚ | 0.4605 |
| Accuracy ⊚ | 0.4721 |
| F1 score ⊚ | 0.4490 |
| Log loss ⊚ | 1.2664 |
| ROC AUC ⊚ | 0.7775 |

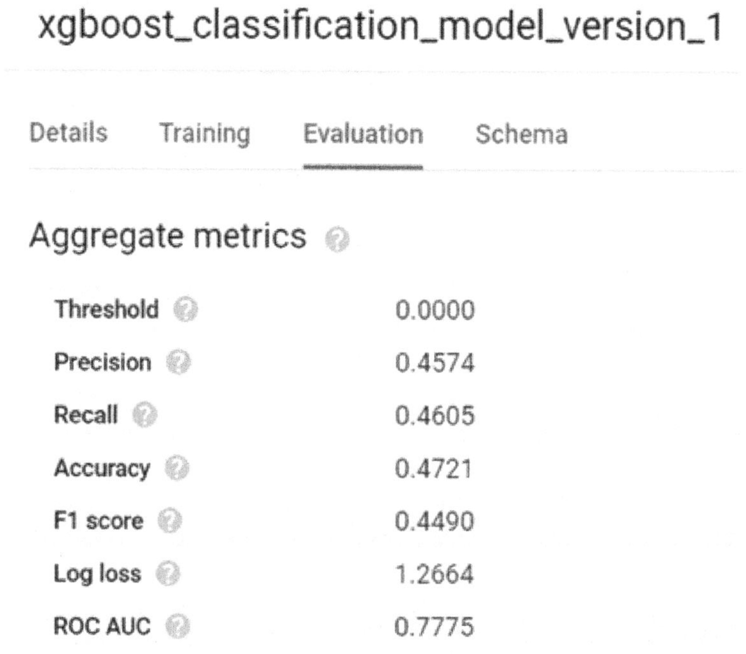

Figure 10.4 – The Evaluation metrics of the XGBoost classification model

In the same **Evaluation** tab, we can also visualize the confusion matrix, which shows how many times the predicted value is equal to the actual one, as illustrated in the following screenshot:

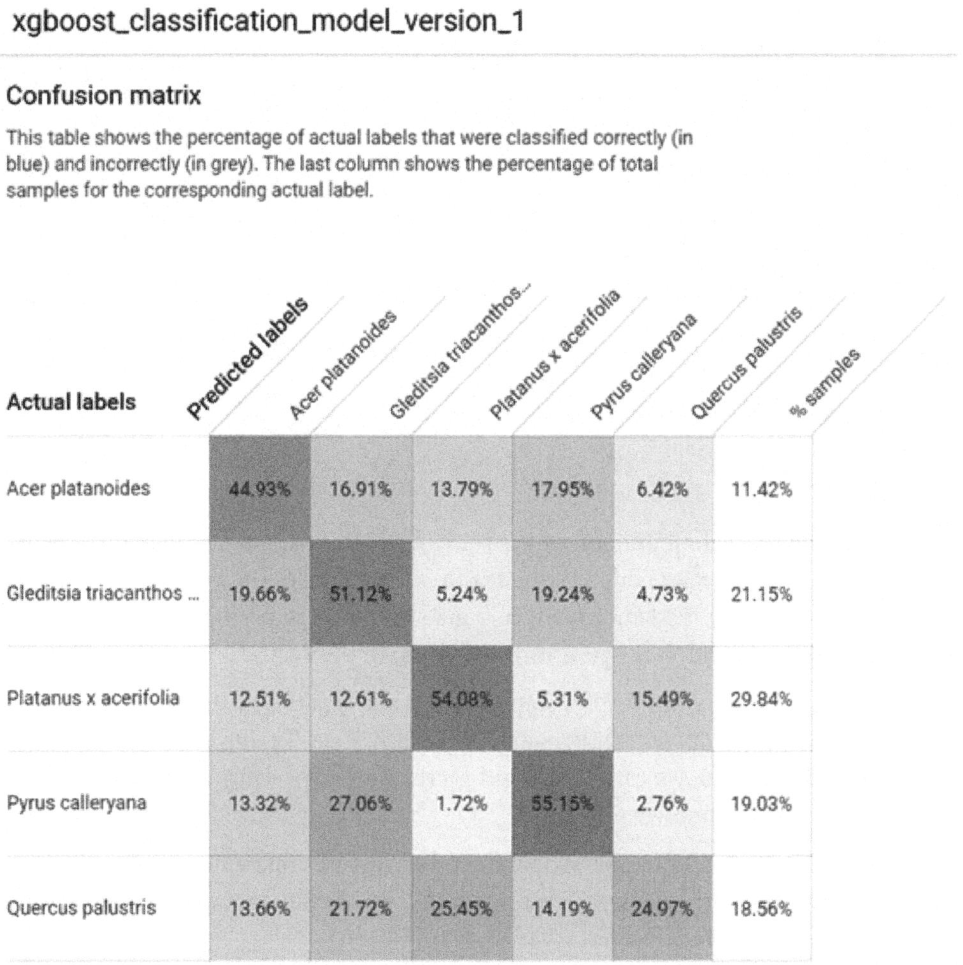

## xgboost_classification_model_version_1

### Confusion matrix

This table shows the percentage of actual labels that were classified correctly (in blue) and incorrectly (in grey). The last column shows the percentage of total samples for the corresponding actual label.

| Actual labels / Predicted labels | Acer platanoides | Gleditsia triacanthos... | Platanus x acerifolia | Pyrus calleryana | Quercus palustris | % samples |
|---|---|---|---|---|---|---|
| Acer platanoides | 44.93% | 16.91% | 13.79% | 17.95% | 6.42% | 11.42% |
| Gleditsia triacanthos ... | 19.66% | 51.12% | 5.24% | 19.24% | 4.73% | 21.15% |
| Platanus x acerifolia | 12.51% | 12.61% | 54.08% | 5.31% | 15.49% | 29.84% |
| Pyrus calleryana | 13.32% | 27.06% | 1.72% | 55.15% | 2.76% | 19.03% |
| Quercus palustris | 13.66% | 21.72% | 25.45% | 14.19% | 24.97% | 18.56% |

Figure 10.5 – The Evaluation tab shows the confusion matrix for the XGBoost classification model

3. Let's try to improve our ML model by adding features that can be useful to classify the trees into different species. Let's train the second version of our BigQuery ML model by running the following code:

```
CREATE OR REPLACE MODEL `10_nyc_trees_xgboost.xgboost_
classification_model_version_2`
OPTIONS
  ( MODEL_TYPE='BOOSTED_TREE_CLASSIFIER',
    BOOSTER_TYPE = 'GBTREE',
    NUM_PARALLEL_TREE = 1,
```

```
      MAX_ITERATIONS = 50,
      TREE_METHOD = 'HIST',
      EARLY_STOP = FALSE,
      AUTO_CLASS_WEIGHTS=TRUE
   ) AS
SELECT
   zip_city,
   tree_dbh,
   boroname,
   nta_name,
   spc_latin as label
FROM
   `10_nyc_trees_xgboost.training_table` ;
```

Compared to the first attempt of the previous *Step 1*, we've included additional features. In fact, we've added to the features the name of the borough contained in the `boroname` field and the `nta_name` field, which provides more specific information related to the position of the tree in the city.

After the execution of the SQL statement, let's access the **Evaluation** tab of the new model to see if we're improving its performance. Taking a look at the **ROC AUC** value of **0.80**, we can see a slight increase in the performance of our model compared to the first version.

4.  Then, we'll try to add to our ML model other features related to the health of the tree and also to the intrusiveness of its roots, which can damage adjacent sidewalks, as follows:

```
CREATE OR REPLACE MODEL `10_nyc_trees_xgboost.xgboost_
classification_model_version_3`
OPTIONS
  ( MODEL_TYPE='BOOSTED_TREE_CLASSIFIER',
    BOOSTER_TYPE = 'GBTREE',
    NUM_PARALLEL_TREE = 5,
    MAX_ITERATIONS = 50,
    TREE_METHOD = 'HIST',
    EARLY_STOP = FALSE,
    AUTO_CLASS_WEIGHTS=TRUE
  ) AS
```

```
SELECT
    zip_city,
    tree_dbh,
    boroname,
    nta_name,
    health,
    sidewalk,
    spc_latin as label
FROM
    `10_nyc_trees_xgboost.training_table`;
```

Compared to the previous ML model, the `xgboost_classification_model_version_3` model includes a `health` field, which describes the health status of our tree, and a `sidewalk` field, which is used to specify if the roots of tree are damaging adjacent sidewalks.

5. Looking at the performances of our last ML model in the **Evaluation** tab of the BigQuery UI, we can notice that we've achieved another increase in terms of the **ROC AUC**, with a value of **0.8121**.

In this section, we've created different ML models by trying to use different features in our dataset. In the next steps, we'll use the model with the highest **ROC AUC** value: `xgboost_classification_model_version_3`.

Now, let's start the evaluation stage of the XGBoost classification model on the evaluation dataset.

# Evaluating the XGBoost classification model

To evaluate our BigQuery ML model, we'll use a `ML.EVALUATE` function and the table that we've expressly created as an evaluation dataset.

The following query will tell us if the model is suffering from overfitting or is able to also perform well on new data:

```
SELECT
    roc_auc,
    CASE
        WHEN roc_auc > .9 THEN 'EXCELLENT'
        WHEN roc_auc > .8 THEN 'VERY GOOD'
        WHEN roc_auc > .7 THEN 'GOOD'
```

```
      WHEN roc_auc > .6 THEN 'FINE'
      WHEN roc_auc > .5 THEN 'NEEDS IMPROVEMENTS'
   ELSE
   'POOR'
END
   AS model_quality
FROM
   ML.EVALUATE(MODEL `10_nyc_trees_xgboost.xgboost_
classification_model_version_3`,
      (
    SELECT
        zip_city,
        tree_dbh,
        boroname,
        nta_name,
        health,
        sidewalk,
        spc_latin as label
      FROM `10_nyc_trees_xgboost.evaluation_table`));
```

The SELECT statement extracts the roc_auc value returned by the ML.EVALUATE function and also provides a clear description of the quality of the model that starts from 'POOR' and can achieve an 'EXCELLENT' grade, passing through some intermediate stages such as 'NEEDS IMPROVEMENTS' and 'GOOD'.

Executing the query, we can see that the score is **VERY GOOD**, as illustrated in the following screenshot:

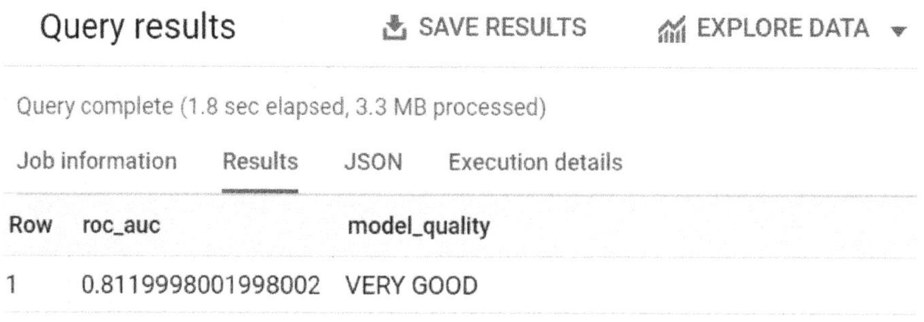

## Query results          ⬇ SAVE RESULTS       📊 EXPLORE DATA  ▼

Query complete (1.8 sec elapsed, 3.3 MB processed)

Job information     Results     JSON     Execution details

| Row | roc_auc | model_quality |
| --- | --- | --- |
| 1 | 0.8119998001998002 | VERY GOOD |

Figure 10.6 – The evaluation stage returns VERY GOOD for the quality of our BigQuery ML model

Now that we've evaluated our ML model, let's see how we can apply it to other records to get a classification of the trees.

## Using the XGBoost classification model

In this section, we'll use the ML model to classify the trees into five different species according to their characteristics.

To test our BigQuery ML model, we'll use a `ML.PREDICT` function on the `classification_table` table, as follows:

```
SELECT
  tree_id,
  actual_label,
  predicted_label_probs,
  predicted_label
FROM
  ML.PREDICT (MODEL `10_nyc_trees_xgboost.xgboost_
classification_model_version_3`,
    (
    SELECT
        tree_id,
        zip_city,
        tree_dbh,
        boroname,
        nta_name,
        health,
        sidewalk,
        spc_latin as actual_label
    FROM
        `10_nyc_trees_xgboost.classification_table`
    )
  );
```

The query is composed of a SELECT statement that extracts the tree_id value, the actual species of the tree, the probability of each predicted species, and the predicted species.

In the following screenshot, you can see the result of the query execution:

**Query results**    📥 SAVE RESULTS    📊 EXPLORE DATA ▼

Query complete (2.0 sec elapsed, 3.5 MB processed)

Job information    Results    JSON    Execution details

|   |        |                 | Acer platanoides                       | 0.7906047105789185   |                  |
|---|--------|-----------------|----------------------------------------|----------------------|------------------|
| 8 | 283502 | Acer platanoides | Quercus palustris                     | 0.06334524601697922  | Acer platanoides |
|   |        |                 | Pyrus calleryana                       | 0.10945531725883484  |                  |
|   |        |                 | Platanus x acerifolia                  | 0.06146503612399101  |                  |
|   |        |                 | Gleditsia triacanthos var. inermis     | 0.14764781296253204  |                  |
|   |        |                 | Acer platanoides                       | 0.618086576461792    |                  |
| 9 | 226929 | Acer platanoides | Quercus palustris                     | 0.051651731133461    | Acer platanoides |
|   |        |                 | Pyrus calleryana                       | 0.1293247640132904   |                  |
|   |        |                 | Platanus x acerifolia                  | 0.052124638110399246 |                  |
|   |        |                 | Gleditsia triacanthos var. inermis     | 0.15599997341632843  |                  |
|   |        |                 | Acer platanoides                       | 0.6108988523483276   |                  |

Figure 10.7 – The output of the query shows the actual and predicted labels with the related probabilities

In the two rows presented in the preceding screenshot, the trees with identifiers **283502** and **226929** are well classified into the **Acer platanoides** species, with a confidence of 61%.

Now that we've tested our BigQuery ML model, let's make some final considerations by comparing the results of the XGBoost classification model with the outcome of the logistic regression used in *Chapter 6*, *Classifying Trees with Multiclass Logistic Regression*.

# Drawing business conclusions

In this section, we'll use our ML model, and we'll understand how many times the BigQuery ML model is able to classify the trees well in the classification_table table.

Let's execute the following query to calculate how many times the predicted species is congruent with the actual one:

```
SELECT COUNT(*)
FROM (
      SELECT
         tree_id,
         actual_label,
         predicted_label_probs,
         predicted_label
      FROM
         ML.PREDICT (MODEL `10_nyc_trees_xgboost.xgboost_
classification_model_version_3`,
            (
            SELECT
               tree_id,
               zip_city,
               tree_dbh,
               boroname,
               nta_name,
               health,
               sidewalk,
               spc_latin as actual_label
            FROM
               `10_nyc_trees_xgboost.classification_table`
            )
         )
)
WHERE
      actual_label = predicted_label;
```

To calculate this value, we've introduced a WHERE clause by filtering only the rows where the predicted value is equal to the actual one.

As we can see in the following screenshot, the SELECT COUNT returns a value of **14277** records:

**Query results**    ⬇ SAVE RESULTS    📊 EXPLORE DATA ▼

Query complete (3.8 sec elapsed, 3.3 MB processed)

Job information    Results    JSON    Execution details

| Row | f0_ |
| --- | --- |
| 1 | 14277 |

Figure 10.8 – The output of the query shows how many times the classification model predicts the right species

Out of a total of 27,182 rows stored in the classification_table table, we can say that our model classifies the trees into the right species in 52.52% of cases.

In the following table, the results of the XGBoost classification model are compared with the results obtained by the multiclass logistic regression, applied in *Chapter 6, Classifying Trees with Multiclass Logistic Regression*:

|  | **XGBoost Classification Model** | **Multiclass Logistic Regression** |
| --- | --- | --- |
| ROC AUC | 0.8121 | 0.7696 |
| Percentage of right predictions | 52.52% | 49% |

Figure 10.9 – Comparison of the XGBoost classification model and multiclass logistic regression

Looking at the preceding table, we can say that to classify the New York City trees into the most common five species, the XGBoost classification model is able to achieve better results when compared to the multiclass logistic regression model.

# Summary

In this chapter, we've implemented a XGBoost classification model. We've remembered the business scenario that was already used in *Chapter 6, Classifying Trees with Multiclass Logistic Regression*, based on the need to automatically classify New York City trees. After that, we've learned the basics of the XGBoost boosted tree classification model.

In order to build an effective model, we performed data quality checks and then segmented the dataset according to our needs into three tables: one to host training data, a second one for the evaluation stage, and a last one to apply our classification model.

During the training phase of the BigQuery ML model, we've constantly improved the performance of the ML model, using ROC AUC as a **key performance indicator** (**KPI**).

After that, we've evaluated the best ML model on a new set of records to avoid any overfitting, becoming more confident about the good quality of our XGBoost classification model.

Finally, we've applied our BigQuery ML model to the last subset of records to classify the trees into species, according to their characteristics. We've discovered that our ML model is able to correctly classify the trees in 52.52% of cases. Then, we've also compared the performance of the XGBoost model with the multiclass logistic regression training we did in *Chapter 6*, *Classifying Trees with Multiclass Logistic Regression* and noticed that XGBoost exceeded the multiclass logistic regression training's performance.

In the next chapter, we'll learn about advanced **deep neural networks** (**DNNs**), leveraging BigQuery SQL syntax.

# Further resources

- **NYC Street Tree Census public dataset**: https://console.cloud.google. com/marketplace/product/city-of-new-york/nyc-tree-census

- **XGBoost home page**: https://xgboost.ai/

- **XGBoost documentation**: https://xgboost.readthedocs.io/en/ latest/index.html

- **BigQuery ML** CREATE MODEL **statement for Boosted Tree models**: https:// cloud.google.com/bigquery-ml/docs/reference/standard-sql/ bigqueryml-syntax-create-boosted-tree

- **BigQuery ML** ML.EVALUATE **function**: https://cloud.google.com/ bigquery-ml/docs/reference/standard-sql/bigqueryml-syntax-evaluate

- **BigQuery ML** ML.PREDICT **function**: https://cloud.google.com/ bigquery-ml/docs/reference/standard-sql/bigqueryml-syntax-predict

# 11
# Implementing Deep Neural Networks

**Deep Neural Networks (DNNs)** are one of the most advanced techniques to implement machine learning algorithms. They're widely used for different use cases and can be considered pervasive in everyday life.

When we interact with a virtual assistant, or we use mobile applications for automatic translation and image recognition, we're leveraging the capabilities of DNNs trained with large datasets of audio and images.

After reading this chapter, you'll be able to develop, evaluate, and test a DNN using BigQuery ML. In this chapter, we'll see all the stages necessary to implement a DNN by using BigQuery ML to predict the duration of rentals related to the New York City bike-sharing service.

Using BigQuery ML, we'll go through the following topics:

- Introducing the business scenario
- Discovering DNNs
- Preparing the dataset

- Training the DNN models

- Evaluating the DNN models

- Using the DNN models

- Drawing business conclusions

# Technical requirements

This chapter requires you to have access to a web browser and to be able to leverage the following:

- A GCP account to access Google Cloud Console

- A GCP project to host the BigQuery datasets

Now that we're ready with the technical requirements, let's dive into the analysis and development of our BigQuery ML DNN models.

Check out the following video to see the Code in Action: `https://bit.ly/33lbq8A`

# Introducing the business scenario

In this section, you'll be introduced to the business scenario that will be handled with the DNNs technique.

The business scenario is very similar to the use case presented and used in *Chapter 4, Predicting Numerical Values with Linear Regression*. In this chapter, we'll use the same dataset related to the New York City bike-sharing service, but we'll apply more advanced machine learning algorithms.

We can remember that the hypothetical goal of the ML model is to predict the trip time of a bike rental. The predicted value could be used to provide a better experience to the customers of the bike-sharing service through the new mobile application. Leveraging the predicted ride duration, the customer will get a clear indication of the time it will take to reach a specific destination and also an estimation of the ride cost.

Now that we've explained and understood the business scenario, let's take a look at the machine learning technique that we can use to automatically classify trees according to their features.

# Discovering DNNs

In this section, we'll learn what **DNNs** are, and we'll understand which regression and classification use cases can be managed with advanced machine learning algorithms.

**Artificial Neural Networks (ANNs)** are artificial systems that try to reproduce the human brain. They're inspired by biological neural networks and are composed of neurons and synapses that connect the neurons. Each neuron of the artificial network is a component that applies a specific mathematical activation function to the input and returns an output that is passed through a synapse to the next neuron. In ANNs, the neurons are usually organized in layers between the input and the output.

Different from linear models, ANNs are designed to model non-linear relationships between the input and the output variables.

**DNNs** are ANNs composed of multiple layers between the input and the output, usually two or more. Each layer of neurons is called a **hidden layer** and its function is to accept a series of input signals and return to the next layer a series of output signals.

In the following diagram, we can see that a DNN is composed of three input variables, two hidden layers, and an output variable:

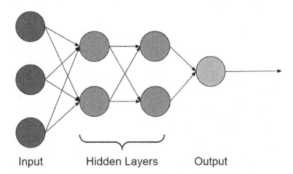

Figure 11.1 – Diagram of a DNN

Each neuron in the network applies a specific function to the input signal and returns the output of the function as the output of the neuron. Training a DNN is an activity focused on finding the right weights of each synapse between each neuron in the network.

Although, to achieve the potential of DNNs we need important hardware resources, the machine learning models implemented with this technique can achieve optimal results in important tasks that are typical of the human brain. Some examples are as follows:

- **Speech recognition**: The ability to process an audio file to identify the words of a speech, making them readable. This capability is widely used in the virtual assistants of our smartphones or in contact center applications.

- **Image and face recognition**: The possibility to recognize different entities, animals, or persons in pictures and videos. This technique is particularly useful to automatically extract insights from images and videos avoiding any manual effort.

- **Natural language processing**: Widely used to analyze and retrieve information from free texts and to analyze the sentiment of the messages. For example, these kinds of algorithms are used to automatically identify the policy violations in the social networks or to evaluate the sentiment in the product reviews.

Now that we've discovered what DNNs are, let's focus on how BigQuery ML offers these powerful algorithms.

## DNNs in BigQuery ML

In this section, we'll learn the model type options provided by BigQuery ML to create a DNN model.

BigQuery ML allows you to create two different types of DNNs:

- **DNNClassifier**: This algorithm can be used to classify events, objects, or entities into a finite number of discrete classes.

- **DNNRegressor**: This kind of model is similar to the previous one with the difference that it returns a continuous result. For this reason, it can be used to predict numerical values.

For our business scenario, we'll use **DNNRegressor** because our goal is to predict a continuous value: *the ride time of the bike rental.*

When we've chosen which type of DNN to use according to our use case, the next choice will be focused on the function that each neuron will apply to the input signal. BigQuery ML allows us to choose one of the following functions:

- **Rectified Linear Function** (**ReLU**): This is a linear function that returns the input value itself if it's positive, otherwise zero.

- **ReLU6**: This is similar to the previous function with a capped maximum output value of 6. This is just an arbitrary value that derives from empirical tests of the different functions.

- **Concatenated Rectified Linear Units (CReLU)**: Different from the previous functions, it preserves the negative values.

- **Exponential Linear Unit (ELU)**: This is an exponential function that tends to converge to the result faster and produce outputs with more accuracy.

- **Scaled Exponential Linear Unit (SELU)**: This is an evolution of ELU that adds the self-normalization of the math function.

- **SIGMOID**: This is similar to a step function and always outputs a value between 0 and 1. This function introduces non-linearity into the DNN.

- **TANH**: This is similar to the sigmoid function but returns a value between -1 and 1.

Each function has some pros and cons, and they should be chosen according to the use case and to the training dataset to achieve the best results. For our business scenario, we'll experiment with the training of DNNs using some of these functions and choose the function that produces the best results.

Now that we've learned the basics of DNNs and the main options that BigQuery ML offers through its SQL interface, let's start preparing the data for the creation of our machine learning models.

# Preparing the dataset

Before starting the ML implementation, it's necessary to analyze and prepare the data for our use case. Since the dataset has been already used in *Chapter 4, Predicting Numerical Values with Linear Regression*, we will not start the analysis from the beginning, but we will focus exclusively on the queries relevant for our use case.

To start the preparation of our data, we need to do the following:

1. Log into Google Cloud Console and access the **BigQuery** user interface from the navigation menu.

2. Create a new dataset under the project that we created in *Chapter 2, Setting Up Your GCP and BigQuery Environment*. For this use case, we'll create the dataset `11_nyc_bike_sharing_dnn` with the default options.

3.  Now we're ready to create the table that will contain the training dataset. Let's execute the following SQL statement:

```sql
CREATE OR REPLACE TABLE `11_nyc_bike_sharing_dnn.
training_table` AS
                SELECT
                        tripduration/60 tripduration,
                        start_station_name,
                        end_station_name,
                        IF (EXTRACT(DAYOFWEEK FROM
starttime)=1 OR EXTRACT(DAYOFWEEK FROM starttime)=7,
true, false) is_weekend,
                        EXTRACT(YEAR FROM starttime)-birth_
year as age
                FROM
                        `bigquery-public-data.new_york_
citibike.citibike_trips`
                WHERE
                        (
                        (EXTRACT (YEAR FROM
starttime)=2017 AND
                        (EXTRACT (MONTH FROM
starttime)>=04 OR EXTRACT (MONTH FROM starttime)<=10))
                        OR (EXTRACT (YEAR FROM
starttime)=2018 AND
                        (EXTRACT (MONTH FROM
starttime)>=01 OR EXTRACT (MONTH FROM starttime)<=02))
                        )
                        AND (tripduration>=3*60 AND
tripduration<=3*60*60)
                        AND  birth_year is not NULL
                        AND birth_year < 2007;
```

The result of the query is stored in the new table, `11_nyc_bike_sharing_dnn.training_table`, which we've created to support the following steps of our use case.

The SELECT statement extracts the fields from the table citibike_trips and applies some transformations. tripduration is converted from seconds to minutes. The fields start_station_name and end_station_name are extracted as is. Using starttime, the query calculates whether the rental is happening during the week or at the weekend. Finally, the age of the customer at the time of the ride is calculated using the difference between starttime and birth_year.

As we've already done in the *Chapter 4, Predicting Numerical Values with Linear Regression*, the WHERE clause allows us to consider only the months that we want to use for the training stage. The time frame goes from April 2017 to February 2018 for the training dataset. In the same WHERE clause, we've also applied the filters that come from the data quality checks.

4.   After the creation of the training table, we can create the second table dedicated to the records that will be used to evaluate our machine learning model:

```sql
CREATE OR REPLACE TABLE  `11_nyc_bike_sharing_dnn.
evaluation_table` AS
SELECT
                  tripduration/60 tripduration,
                  start_station_name,
                  end_station_name,
                  IF (EXTRACT(DAYOFWEEK FROM
starttime)=1 OR EXTRACT(DAYOFWEEK FROM starttime)=7,
true, false) is_weekend,
                  EXTRACT(YEAR FROM starttime)-birth_
year as age
          FROM
                  `bigquery-public-data.new_york_
citibike.citibike_trips`
          WHERE
                  (EXTRACT (YEAR FROM starttime)=2018
AND (EXTRACT (MONTH FROM starttime)=03 OR EXTRACT (MONTH
FROM starttime)=04))
                  AND (tripduration>=3*60 AND
tripduration<=3*60*60)
                  AND  birth_year is not NULL
                  AND birth_year < 2007;
```

The query is very similar to the statement used to create the training table. The only difference is related to the period selected in the WHERE clause. For the table `11_nyc_bike_sharing_dnn.evaluation_table`, we've focused our SELECT statement on the records related to the months of March and April of 2018 that were previously excluded from the training table.

5.  Adopting the same approach, we can also create the table that will be used to test our machine learning model:

```
CREATE OR REPLACE TABLE  `11_nyc_bike_sharing_dnn.
prediction_table` AS
            SELECT
                    tripduration/60 tripduration,
                    start_station_name,
                    end_station_name,
                    IF (EXTRACT(DAYOFWEEK FROM
starttime)=1 OR EXTRACT(DAYOFWEEK FROM starttime)=7,
true, false) is_weekend,
                    EXTRACT(YEAR FROM starttime)-birth_
year as age
            FROM
                    `bigquery-public-data.new_york_
citibike.citibike_trips`
            WHERE
                    EXTRACT (YEAR FROM starttime)=2018
                    AND EXTRACT (MONTH FROM starttime)=05
                    AND (tripduration>=3*60 AND
tripduration<=3*60*60)
                    AND  birth_year is not NULL
                    AND birth_year < 2007;
```

The query applies the same logic used to create the training and the evaluation table but takes into consideration only the month of May 2018.

Now that we've segmented our dataset and are clear on which records to use for the training, evaluation, and test phase, let's train our DNN models with BigQuery ML.

# Training the DNN models

Now that we've segmented the dataset into multiple tables to support the different stages of the ML model life cycle, let's train our DNN regression models using different activation functions:

1. First of all, we can start with the training of a DNN model by using the RELU function. Let's execute the following SQL statement to create the machine learning model `11_nyc_bike_sharing_dnn.trip_duration_by_stations_day_age_relu`:

```
CREATE OR REPLACE MODEL `11_nyc_bike_sharing_dnn.trip_duration_by_stations_day_age_relu`

OPTIONS
    (model_type='DNN_REGRESSOR',
        ACTIVATION_FN = 'RELU') AS

SELECT
    start_station_name,
    end_station_name,
    is_weekend,
    age,
    tripduration as label

FROM
    `11_nyc_bike_sharing_dnn.training_table`;
```

In the SQL statement, we can notice the keywords CREATE OR REPLACE MODEL used to create a new model. These keywords are followed by the identifier of the model represented by the concatenation of the dataset and ML model name.

After these first lines, we find the OPTIONS keyword where the type of machine learning model is specified. Since we're trying to predict the continuous field tripduration, we've chosen to use DNN_REGRESSOR as model_type.

The other important option during the training of a DNN is the activation function that will be applied to the neurons of the network. For this first attempt, we're using one of the most common functions: RELU. This choice is specified with the clause ACTIVATION_FN = 'RELU'.

After OPTIONS, we need to specify the set of records on which the ML model will be trained. Since we've already identified the relevant fields in *Chapter 4, Predicting Numerical Values with Linear Regression*, the query uses the fields start_station_name, end_station_name, is_weekend, and age as features of the DNN model.

With the keywords as label, we are instructing BigQuery ML to use tripduration as the label of our machine learning model. As an alternative, it is possible to include the label among the list of OPTIONS with the keyword INPUT_LABEL_COLS.

Since DNNs are advanced and complex models, it can take several minutes before converging to the solution and generating the machine learning model.

2. At the end of the execution of the SQL query, we can select the DNN model trip_duration_by_stations_day_age_relu in the BigQuery navigation menu and click on the **Evaluation** tab. This tab shows important key performance indicators of the model that we've just built. In this case, we'll focus our attention on the **Mean absolute error**. This value represents the average distance between the actual and the predicted value of the label tripduration.

As you can see in the following screenshot, the **Mean absolute error** is very close to 4 minutes:

## trip_duration_by_stations_day_age_relu

| Details | Training | Evaluation | Schema |
|---------|----------|------------|--------|

| Mean absolute error | 4.0784 |
|---------------------|--------|
| Mean squared error | 64.1248 |
| Mean squared log error | 0.1564 |
| Median absolute error | 2.6227 |
| R squared | 0.4462 |

Figure 11.2 – The Evaluation tab shows some key performance indicators of the DNN model

3.  As a second attempt, we can try to change the activation function in the neurons of our neural network to see if the performance of the first model can be further improved. Let's run the following SQL statement using the CRELU activation function:

```
CREATE OR REPLACE MODEL `11_nyc_bike_sharing_dnn.trip_
duration_by_stations_day_age_crelu`
OPTIONS
   (model_type='DNN_REGRESSOR',
        ACTIVATION_FN = 'CRELU') AS
SELECT
   start_station_name,
   end_station_name,
   is_weekend,
   age,
   tripduration as label
FROM
   `11_nyc_bike_sharing_dnn.training_table`;
```

The query to train the DNN `11_nyc_bike_sharing_dnn.trip_ duration_by_stations_day_age_crelu` is very similar to the SQL statement that we used in our first attempt. The only difference is represented by the different activation function specified in OPTIONS. Using the clause ACTIVATION_FN = 'CRELU', we're using the CRELU function in the neurons of the network.

The execution of the training query will take several minutes to complete.

4.  At the end of the execution of the SQL query, we can select the DNN model trip_duration_by_stations_day_age_crelu in the BigQuery navigation menu and visualize the performance in the **Evaluation** tab.

As you can see in the following screenshot, the **Mean absolute error** is almost close to 4 minutes:

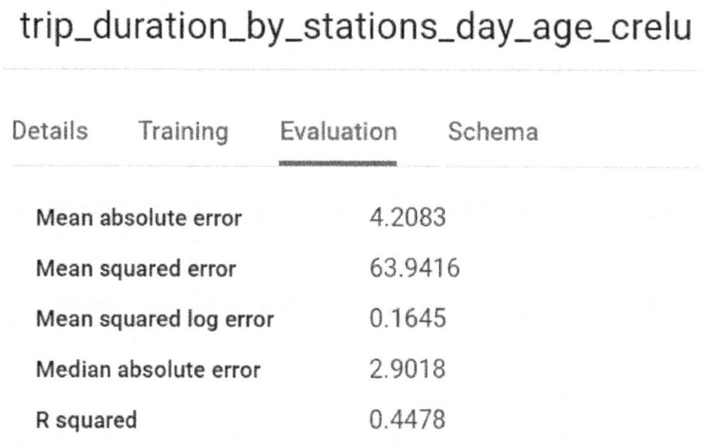

## trip_duration_by_stations_day_age_crelu

Details     Training     Evaluation     Schema

| | |
|---|---|
| Mean absolute error | 4.2083 |
| Mean squared error | 63.9416 |
| Mean squared log error | 0.1645 |
| Median absolute error | 2.9018 |
| R squared | 0.4478 |

Figure 11.3 – The Evaluation tab shows some key performance indicators of the DNN model

Now, let's start the evaluation of the DNNs that we've trained in this section.

# Evaluating the DNN models

To evaluate our BigQuery ML DNNs, we'll use the ML.EVALUATE function and the table that we've expressly created as an evaluation dataset:

1.  First of all, we can start evaluating the model `11_nyc_bike_sharing_dnn. trip_duration_by_stations_day_age_relu`. Let's run the following query:

```
SELECT
    *
FROM
    ML.EVALUATE(MODEL `11_nyc_bike_sharing_dnn.trip_
duration_by_stations_day_age_relu`,
    (
    SELECT
            start_station_name,
            end_station_name,
            is_weekend,
            age,
```

```
              tripduration as label
    FROM
              `11_nyc_bike_sharing_dnn.evaluation_table` ));
```

In the SQL statement, we can notice the keyword ML.EVALUATE is used to evaluate the DNN. The evaluation function is followed by the identifier of the BigQuery ML model: `11_nyc_bike_sharing_dnn.trip_duration_by_stations_day_age_relu`.

The evaluation function is applied on the SELECT statement that extracts all the fields from the table: `11_nyc_bike_sharing_dnn.evaluation_table`.

After some seconds, we can see the results of the evaluation stage as shown in the following screenshot:

Figure 11.4 – The results of the evaluation SQL statement

We can notice that the **mean_absolute_error** value is not so different from the value that we've achieved during the training phase. We can say that our model is not affected by overfitting and works well on the new records of the evaluation dataset.

2. Let's apply the same evaluation logic on the second model, `11_nyc_bike_sharing_dnn.trip_duration_by_stations_day_age_crelu`. To evaluate the performance of this BigQuery ML model, we run the following SQL statement:

```
SELECT
    *
FROM
    ML.EVALUATE(MODEL `11_nyc_bike_sharing_dnn.trip_
duration_by_stations_day_age_crelu`,
        (
        SELECT
                start_station_name,
                end_station_name,
```

```
            is_weekend,
            age,
            tripduration as label
    FROM
            `11_nyc_bike_sharing_dnn.evaluation_table` ) );
```

The only difference between the last query and the previous one is in the name of the DNN that is subject to the evaluation: `11_nyc_bike_sharing_dnn.trip_duration_by_stations_day_age_crelu`.

After some seconds, we'll see the results of the evaluation as presented in the following screenshot:

Query results      ⬇ SAVE RESULTS      📊 EXPLORE DATA ▾

Query complete (15.1 sec elapsed, 123.3 MB processed)

Job information    Results    JSON    Execution details

| Row | mean_absolute_error | mean_squared_error | mean_squared_log_error | median_absolute_error | r2_score | explained_variance |
|-----|---------------------|--------------------|------------------------|-----------------------|----------|--------------------|
| 1 | 4.477826375960933 | 76.0608663891324 | 0.1774726009482601 | 2.9987768173217777 | 0.42402265976280895 | 0.42439958489328344 |

Figure 11.5 – The results of the evaluation SQL statement

Also, in this case, the **mean_absolute_error** value is not far from the value of 4 minutes that we achieved during the training stage. This model is not affected by overfitting and works similar to the previous one.

Now that we've evaluated our BigQuery ML models, let's see how we can use the DNN based on the ReLU activation function to get predictions about the duration of the bike rentals.

# Using the DNN models

In this section, we'll use the DNN model based on the ReLU function and trained to leverage the BigQuery ML capabilities to predict the duration of the bike rides for the New York City bike-sharing company.

To test our DNN, we'll use the `ML.PREDICT` function on the table `prediction_table`. Let's run the following SQL statement:

```
SELECT
    tripduration as actual_duration,
    predicted_label as predicted_duration,
    ABS(tripduration - predicted_label) difference_in_min
FROM
    ML.PREDICT(MODEL `11_nyc_bike_sharing_dnn.trip_duration_by_
stations_day_age_relu`,
    (
    SELECT
        start_station_name,
        end_station_name,
        is_weekend,
        age,
        tripduration
    FROM
            `11_nyc_bike_sharing_dnn.prediction_table`
    ))
    order by  difference_in_min asc;
```

The query statement is composed of a `SELECT` keyword that extracts the actual and the predicted duration of the rental. It calculates the difference in minutes and orders the results from the minimum to the maximum difference of minutes. To calculate the difference, we've used the `ABS` function that extracts the absolute value of a numeric.

The `ML.PREDICT` function is applied to the `SELECT` statement, which extracts the features and the actual duration from `prediction_table`. This last field is used only for comparison with the predicted value and is not used by the DNN to return the prediction.

In the following screenshot, you can see the results of the query execution:

| Query results | 📥 SAVE RESULTS | 📊 EXPLORE DATA ▼ |
|---|---|---|

Query complete (13.2 sec elapsed, 100.5 MB processed)

Job information    Results    JSON    Execution details

| Row | actual_duration | predicted_duration | difference_in_min |
|---|---|---|---|
| 1 | 7.3 | 7.2999958992004395 | 4.100799560369239E-6 |
| 2 | 33.833333333333336 | 33.833343505859375 | 1.0172526039298191E-5 |
| 3 | 6.883333333333334 | 6.883319854736328 | 1.3478597005622817E-5 |
| 4 | 10.316666666666666 | 10.316648483276367 | 1.818339029924232E-5 |
| 5 | 15.466666666666667 | 15.466686248779297 | 1.958211263008991E-5 |
| 6 | 8.433333333333334 | 8.433313369750977 | 1.996358235700768E-5 |
| 7 | 7.7 | 7.7000226974487305 | 2.2697448730291114E-5 |
| 8 | 13.316666666666666 | 13.316642761230469 | 2.390543619767982E-5 |
| 9 | 22.3 | 22.300024032592773 | 2.4032592772726957E-5 |
| 10 | 14.633333333333333 | 14.633358001708984 | 2.4668375651515362E-5 |
| 11 | 9.033333333333333 | 9.033361434936523 | 2.810160319022259E-5 |
| 12 | 9.433333333333334 | 9.4332914352417 | 4.189809163435143E-5 |
| 13 | 20.466666666666665 | 20.46662139892578 | 4.5267740883758734E-5 |

Figure 11.6 – The output of the query shows the actual and the predicted label
with the difference expressed in minutes

Now that we've tested our BigQuery ML model, let's look at some final considerations comparing the results of the DNN based on the CReLU activation function with the results that we achieved using linear regression in *Chapter 4, Predicting Numerical Values with Linear Regression*.

# Drawing business conclusions

In this section, we'll apply our DNN model and understand how many times the BigQuery ML model is able to predict a rental duration close to the actual one.

We'll add a parent SELECT COUNT statement to the previous query to count how many times the difference between the actual duration and the predicted one is less than 15 minutes.

Let's execute the following query to calculate how often the trip duration predictions are far from the actual values:

```
SELECT COUNT (*)
FROM (
SELECT
    tripduration as actual_duration,
    predicted_label as predicted_duration,
    ABS(tripduration - predicted_label) difference_in_min
FROM
    ML.PREDICT(MODEL  `11_nyc_bike_sharing_dnn.trip_duration_by_
stations_day_age_relu`,
    (
    SELECT
            start_station_name,
            end_station_name,
            is_weekend,
            age,
            tripduration
    FROM
            `11_nyc_bike_sharing_dnn.prediction_table`
    ))
    order by  difference_in_min asc) where difference_in_
min<=15 ;
```

The result of the SELECT COUNT query returns a value of 1,640,446 predictions with a difference between the predicted and the actual value of less than 15 minutes.

Considering that the total size of the table prediction_table is 1,728,078, we can say that in 94.92% of the cases our DNN is able to predict the trip duration with a difference less than 15 minutes.

Now we can compare the best results that we've achieved with the DNN with the performance that we've reached using the linear regression model in *Chapter 4, Predicting Numerical Values with Linear Regression*.

## Deep neural networks versus linear models

In the following table, the results of the DNN model based on the `CReLU` activation function are compared to the linear regression model:

|  | DNN | **Linear Logistic Regression** |
|---|---|---|
| Mean Absolute Error | 4.0784 | 6.9978 |
| Percentage Of Predictions With A Gap Of Less Than 15 Minutes | 94.92% | 89.6% |

Figure 11.7 – Comparison between the DNN model and the linear regression model

Looking at the preceding table, we can say that to predict the trip duration of the New York City bike-sharing service, the best results can be achieved using a DNN model. For this reason, we can suggest using a DNN model to suggest the trip duration to the customers of the company. Using the DNN we can decrease the mean absolute error by more than 43%. In some industries, such an improvement could be a great competitive advantage for the company.

# Summary

In this chapter, we've implemented two DNNs. We remembered the business scenario that was already introduced in *Chapter 4, Predicting Numerical Values with Linear Regression*. The use case was based on the need to predict the rental time for the New York City bike-sharing service. After that, we learned the basics of DNNs and the different activation functions that can be used to implement the neurons in a network.

We segmented the BigQuery public dataset into three different tables: one to host training data, the second one for the evaluation stage, and the last one to test our DNN model.

During the training phase of the BigQuery ML model, we tested two different activation functions, `ReLU` and `CReLU`, comparing the mean absolute error to find the best one.

After that, we evaluated our DNN models on a new set of records to prevent any overfitting and get more confident about the good quality of our BigQuery ML models.

Finally, we applied the model, based on the `ReLU` function, to the last subset of records to predict the trip duration of each bike rental. We discovered that our BigQuery ML model is able to predict a trip duration within a range of 15 minutes of the actual one for more than 94% of the rentals.

Finally, we also compared the performance of the DNN model with the linear regression outcomes achieved in *Chapter 4*, *Predicting Numerical Values with Linear Regression*. We noticed that the DNN outperforms linear regression, decreasing the mean absolute error by 43%, and can achieve better results for our business scenario.

In the next chapter, we'll learn how to use BigQuery ML with GCP AI notebooks.

## Further resources

- **NYC Bike-Sharing Public Dataset**: `https://console.cloud.google.com/marketplace/product/city-of-new-york/nyc-citi-bike`

- **BigQuery ML Create Model**: `https://cloud.google.com/bigquery-ml/docs/reference/standard-sql/bigqueryml-syntax-create-dnn-models`

- **BigQuery ML Evaluate Model**: `https://cloud.google.com/bigquery-ml/docs/reference/standard-sql/bigqueryml-syntax-evaluate`

- **BigQuery ML Predict**: `https://cloud.google.com/bigquery-ml/docs/reference/standard-sql/bigqueryml-syntax-predict`

# Section 4: Further Extending Your ML Capabilities with GCP

In this section, all the integrations of BigQuery ML with other GCP components are explained and presented in detail.

This section comprises the following chapters:

# 12
# Using BigQuery ML with AI Notebooks

For data scientists and machine learning engineers, notebooks are a fundamental productivity tool. Notebooks allow us to interact with computing resources because we can use them to write and execute code, visualize the results, and share the outcomes with other data scientists. Data engineers, data scientists, and machine learning engineers make experiments and explore data before deploying code into the production environment. They leverage notebooks because they offer a flexible and agile environment to develop and test in.

In this chapter, we'll learn what **AI Platform Notebooks** is, how to provision a notebook environment, and how to use it to develop a BigQuery ML model.

We'll start by discovering the basics of notebooks and then start getting some hands-on practice with **Google Cloud Platform** (**GCP**).

In this chapter, we'll cover the following topics:

- Discovering AI Platform Notebooks
- Implementing BigQuery ML models within notebooks

# Technical requirements

This chapter requires that you have access to a web browser and can leverage the following:

- A GCP account to access the Google Cloud Console

- A GCP project to host BigQuery datasets

Now that we know about the technical requirements for this chapter, let's learn how to develop a machine learning model using AI Platform Notebooks.

Check out the following video to see the Code in Action: `https://bit.ly/2QVZ1oY`

# Discovering AI Platform Notebooks

In this section, we'll learn what **AI Platform Notebooks** is and the advantages that it can provide.

**AI Platform Notebooks** is a fully managed service that allows data engineers and data scientists to use a JupyterLab development environment. This service allows us to develop, evaluate, test, and deploy machine learning models.

**JupyterLab** is a web tool for data scientists that is developed and maintained by Project Jupyter (`https://jupyter.org/about`). The goal of the project is to develop open source software and standards that offer a unique interface across different programming languages.

Using AI Platform Notebooks with JupyterLab can bring several advantages:

- We can easily set up our pre-configured machine learning environments with the most important and useful ML libraries, such as TensorFlow, Keras, PyTorch, and others.

- We can leverage the scalability of the cloud by increasing the size of the hardware resources according to our requirements. For example, we can improve the performance of our notebook by scaling up the RAM or adding **Graphics Processing Units (GPUs)**.

- We are allowed to access the other Google Cloud services from our notebook without the need to perform any additional configuration. From AI Platform Notebooks, we can easily leverage BigQuery, Dataflow, and Dataproc.

- We can integrate our development environment with code versioning applications such as Git.

- We can easily share our notebooks with colleagues or friends, thus making collaboration faster and increasing productivity.

  In the following screenshot, you can see the web interface of a JupyterLab notebook:

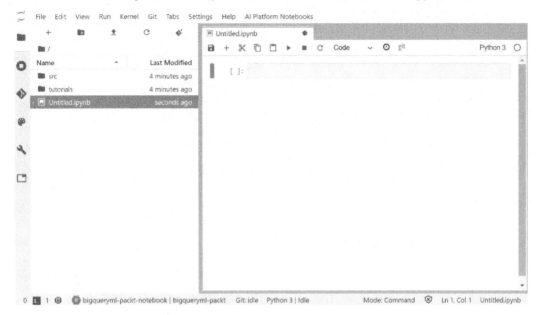

Figure 12.1 –JupyterLab's web interface

A notebook can contain descriptive content, code blocks, and results. It is composed of a sequence of cells that can be executed. There are two types of cells:

- **Code cells**: Contain executable code to run. The result of their execution is visualized immediately after the code.

- **Markdown cells**: Contain HTML code to produce headers, lists, and formatted text. These cells are usually used to describe the code and make the entire notebook readable and easy to understand.

Let's move on to the next section!

## AI Platform Notebooks pricing

In this section, you'll understand how the price of AI Notebooks is calculated and billed to your Google Cloud account.

Since the JupyterLab software is open source, when you use AI Platform Notebooks, you're only charged for the Google Cloud resources that you consume.

To start using AI Platform Notebooks, you'll have to pay for the following:

- **Google Compute Engine** (**GCE**), the virtual machine that's used to deploy your development environment. GCE is charged according to the provisioned number of virtual CPUs, memory, and disk that you have.

- Any other service that can be invoked from the notebook, such as BigQuery.

> **Tip**
> Remember to turn off the GCE that hosts your AI Platform Notebook when you are not using it. If the virtual machine is left active, you will continue to pay for those resources, even if you are not actually using them.

Now that we've learned what AI Platform Notebooks is and why it can be useful when you're developing a machine learning model, in the next section, we'll understand how to configure our first notebook.

# Configuring the first notebook

In this section, we'll set up our first AI Platform notebook, which will be used to train, evaluate, and test the BigQuery ML model.

After logging into the GCP console, we can start configuring our first notebook. Let's get started:

1. First, let's browse the console's navigation menu until we find the **AI Platform (Unified)** item. From the submenu, select **Notebooks**:

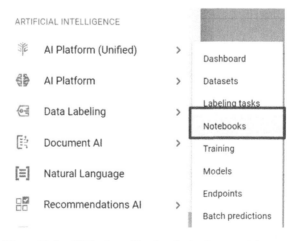

Figure 12.2 – AI Platform Notebooks in the console's menu

2.  If this is the first time that we're accessing this service, we will be asked to enable the API. We can click the blue **ENABLE** button to start using the service:

# Notebooks API

Google

AI Platform Notebooks API is used to manage notebook resources in Google Cloud.

ENABLE    TRY THIS API 🗗

Figure 12.3 – Enabling the Notebooks API

3.  After a few minutes, the service will be enabled and ready to use. We'll be redirected to a web page containing the statistics of the API that we've just enabled:

Figure 12.4 – The statistics of the Notebooks API

4. Selecting the **Notebooks** item from the console's navigation menu once more, we'll access the page dedicated to AI Platform Notebooks. By selecting the blue **CREATE INSTANCE** button, we'll start configuring the notebook:

You don't have any notebook instances in this project yet

CREATE INSTANCE

Figure 12.5 – Creating new instances

5. To create a notebook instance, we need to choose an **Instance name**, **Region**, and **Zone** that we want to use. We also need to choose an **Operating System** and **Environment**:

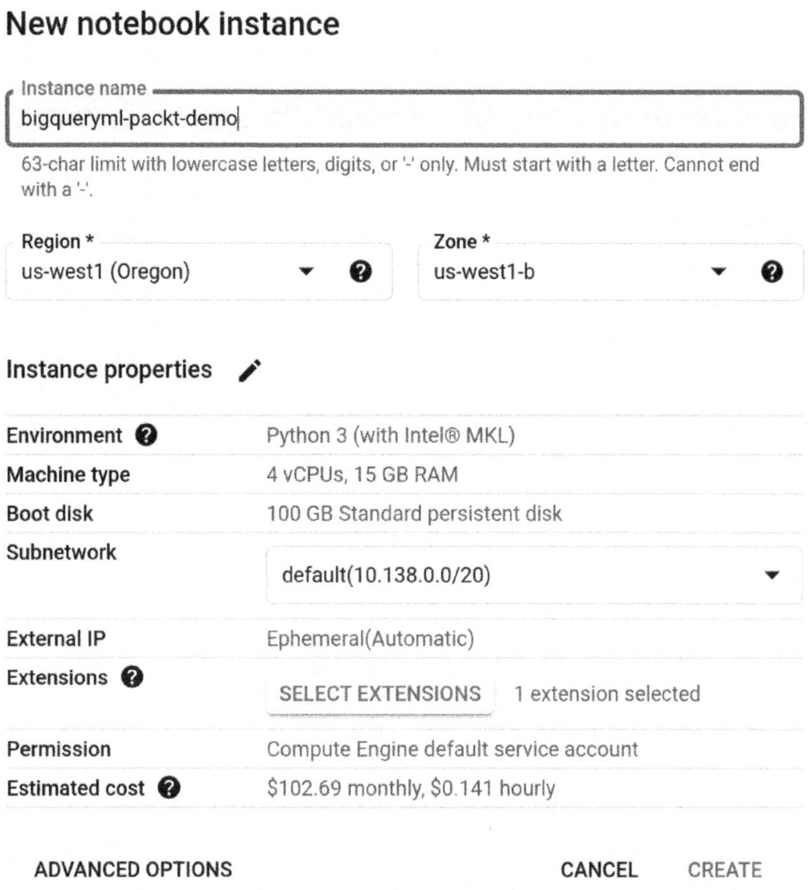

# New notebook instance

Instance name
bigqueryml-packt-demo

63-char limit with lowercase letters, digits, or '-' only. Must start with a letter. Cannot end with a '-'.

Region *
us-west1 (Oregon)           ▼  ❷

Zone *
us-west1-b                  ▼  ❷

## Instance properties  ✏

| | |
|---|---|
| Environment ❷ | Python 3 (with Intel® MKL) |
| Machine type | 4 vCPUs, 15 GB RAM |
| Boot disk | 100 GB Standard persistent disk |
| Subnetwork | default(10.138.0.0/20) ▼ |
| External IP | Ephemeral(Automatic) |
| Extensions ❷ | SELECT EXTENSIONS   1 extension selected |
| Permission | Compute Engine default service account |
| Estimated cost ❷ | $102.69 monthly, $0.141 hourly |

ADVANCED OPTIONS                    CANCEL    CREATE

Figure 12.6 – The available options for creating a notebook instance

For our use case, we will set bigqueryml-packt-notebook for **Instance name**, **us-west1** for **Region**, **use-west1-a** for **Zone**, **Debian 10** for **Operating System**, and **Python 3 (with Intel MKL)** for **Environment**.

6.  Scrolling down the configuration page, select **n1-standard-2** for **Machine type**. After that, we can start creating the instance by clicking the blue **CREATE** button:

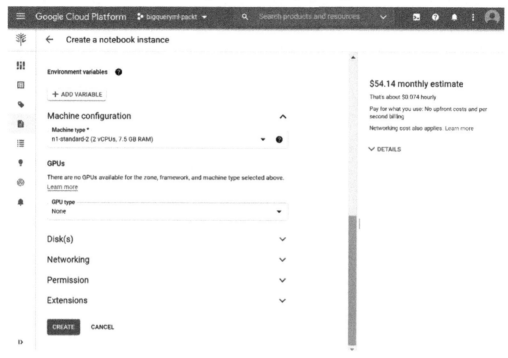

Figure 12.7 – Additional options for creating a notebook instance

7.  After a few minutes, the notebook instance will be ready to use. Upon selecting **OPEN JUPYTERLAB**, the JupyterLab notebook will open a new window containing the development environment:

Figure 12.8 – The list of notebook instances available in the GCP project

8.  In the web interface of the JupyterLab notebook, we can initialize the first notebook file by selecting **Python 3** as the notebook type:

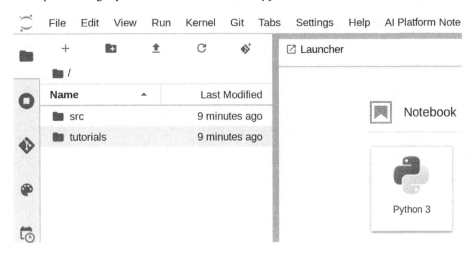

Figure 12.9 – Selecting the runtime engine to use in the notebook

9.  Upon making this selection, a new notebook file will be created and ready for us to develop our BigQuery ML machine learning model:

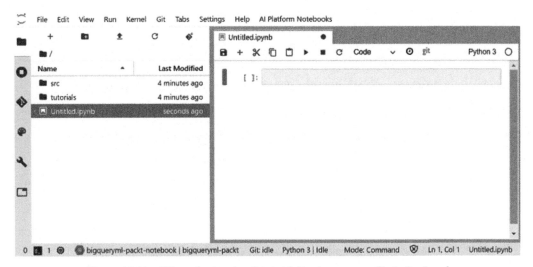

Figure 12.10 – When the notebook is initialized, an empty file is displayed

In this section, we configured our first AI Platform notebook. In the next section, we'll use it to execute some code blocks in order to create, evaluate, and test a BigQuery ML machine learning model.

# Implementing BigQuery ML models within notebooks

In this section, we'll leverage the notebook instance that we configured in the *Configuring the first notebook* section to run BigQuery SQL statements and develop the BigQuery ML machine learning model.

To learn how a notebook can be used, we'll reuse some of the code blocks that we built in *Chapter 4, Predicting Numerical Values with Linear Regression*. It's important to remember that the goal of the use case was to predict the rental time of each ride for the New York City bike sharing service. To achieve this goal, we've trained a simple linear regression machine learning model. In this section, we'll use the same technique; that is, we'll be embedding the code into an AI Platform notebook.

## Compiling the AI notebook

In this section, we'll compile the notebook using **Code** cells to embed the SQL queries and **Markdown** cells to create titles and descriptions. Let's start compiling our notebook by performing the following steps:

1.  First, let's create a title for our notebook. From the cell type drop-down menu, we can select **Markdown** and insert the following code block into the first cell of the notebook:

    ```
    # NYC Bike Sharing Linear Regression
    ```

    In the following screenshot, you can see how the first cell is configured:

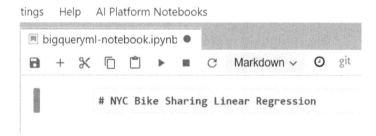

Figure 12.11 – An example of a Markdown cell

The # character preceding the text is used to identify a title at the first level.

2.  By clicking on the + button in the notebook menu, you'll add a new cell. Let's select **Markdown** as the cell type and insert the following text, which describes the notebook:

    ```
    The following steps will show you how to train, evaluate
    and test a linear regression model using BigQuery ML.
    ```

3.  To check whether we've written the previous steps properly, we can use the Run button in the notebook menu. We can run each cell to visualize the result:

Figure 12.12 – The Run button in the notebook menu

In the following screenshot, you can see the outcome of executing the first two steps, which contain the title and a short description:

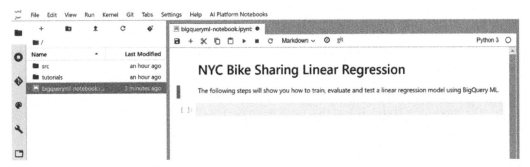

Figure 12.13 – The result of executing the first few cells

4.  Let's add a subtitle to start the data preparation section of the model. We'll add another **Markdown** cell by inserting the following title:

    ```
    ## Data preparation
    ```

The double ## character preceding the text is used to identify a title of the second level. It can be considered a subtitle of the title we wrote in *Step 1*.

5. Now, we're ready to create the `12_notebook` BigQuery dataset, which will be used to host our BigQuery ML models. Let's create a **Code** cell with the following Python code:

```python
from google.cloud import bigquery

# Construct a BigQuery client object.
client = bigquery.Client()

dataset_id = "{}.12_notebook".format(client.project)

# Construct a full Dataset object to send to the API.
dataset = bigquery.Dataset(dataset_id)

# Geographic location where the dataset should reside.
dataset.location = "US"

# Dataset creation
dataset = client.create_dataset(dataset, timeout=30)
print("Created dataset {}.{}".format(client.project,
dataset.dataset_id))
```

The preceding code creates the `12_notebook` dataset in US within the current GCP project. At the end of the cell, the `print` command is used to present a confirmation message, stating that the dataset has been created successfully.

6. Now, we can add a new **Code** cell and write the following SQL statement to create the `12_notebook.training_table` table:

```sql
%%bigquery

### Creation of the training table ###
CREATE OR REPLACE TABLE `12_notebook.training_table` AS
            SELECT
                    tripduration/60 tripduration,
                    starttime,
                    stoptime,
                    start_station_id,
                    start_station_name,
```

```
                    start_station_latitude,
                    start_station_longitude,
                    end_station_id,
                    end_station_name,
                    end_station_latitude,
                    end_station_longitude,
                    bikeid,
                    usertype,
                    birth_year,
                    gender,
                    customer_plan
            FROM
                    `bigquery-public-data.new_york_
citibike.citibike_trips`
            WHERE
                    (
                            (EXTRACT (YEAR FROM
starttime)=2017 AND
                            (EXTRACT (MONTH FROM
starttime)>=04 OR EXTRACT (MONTH FROM starttime)<=10))
                            OR (EXTRACT (YEAR FROM
starttime)=2018 AND
                            (EXTRACT (MONTH FROM
starttime)>=01 OR EXTRACT (MONTH FROM starttime)<=02))
                    )
                    AND (tripduration>=3*60 AND
tripduration<=3*60*60)
                    AND  birth_year is not NULL
                    AND birth_year < 2007;
```

The `%%bigquery` keyword allows us to include code blocks that contain SQL queries. The SQL statement will be run directly on BigQuery through the native integration of the AI Platform notebook and the analytical database.

The business logic to create the table is the same as what we used to create the `04_nyc_bike_sharing.training_table` table in *Chapter 4*, *Predicting Numerical Values with Linear Regression*.

7.  Now, let's include an additional **Code** cell in the notebook to create the evaluation table, as follows:

```
%%bigquery

### Creation of the evaluation table ###
CREATE OR REPLACE TABLE  `12_notebook.evaluation_
table` AS
SELECT
                    tripduration/60 tripduration,
                    starttime,
                    stoptime,
                    start_station_id,
                    start_station_name,
                    start_station_latitude,
                    start_station_longitude,
                    end_station_id,
                    end_station_name,
                    end_station_latitude,
                    end_station_longitude,
                    bikeid,
                    usertype,
                    birth_year,
                    gender,
                    customer_plan
            FROM
                    `bigquery-public-data.new_york_
citibike.citibike_trips`
            WHERE
                    (EXTRACT (YEAR FROM starttime)=2018
AND (EXTRACT (MONTH FROM starttime)=03 OR EXTRACT (MONTH
FROM starttime)=04))
                    AND (tripduration>=3*60 AND
tripduration<=3*60*60)
                    AND  birth_year is not NULL
                    AND birth_year < 2007;
```

The business logic to create the table is the same as what we used to create the `04_nyc_bike_sharing.evaluation_table` table in *Chapter 4, Predicting Numerical Values with Linear Regression*.

8.  Finally, let's add another **Code** cell to create the prediction table with the following SQL statement:

```
%%bigquery


### Creation of the prediction table ###
CREATE OR REPLACE TABLE  `12_notebook.prediction_table`
AS
        SELECT
                tripduration/60 tripduration,
                starttime,
                stoptime,
                start_station_id,
                start_station_name,
                start_station_latitude,
                start_station_longitude,
                end_station_id,
                end_station_name,
                end_station_latitude,
                end_station_longitude,
                bikeid,
                usertype,
                birth_year,
                gender,
                customer_plan
        FROM
                `bigquery-public-data.new_york_
citibike.citibike_trips`
        WHERE
                EXTRACT (YEAR FROM starttime)=2018
                AND EXTRACT (MONTH FROM starttime)=05
                AND (tripduration>=3*60 AND
tripduration<=3*60*60)
```

```
                  AND  birth_year is not NULL
                  AND birth_year < 2007;
```

The business logic to create the table is the same as what we used to create the `` `04_nyc_bike_sharing.prediction_table` `` table in *Chapter 4, Predicting Numerical Values with Linear Regression*.

9. Let's add a subtitle to start the training section of the model. We'll add a **Markdown** cell by inserting the following title:

```
## Training the linear regression
```

10. Now, we're ready to write the BigQuery ML query that will train our machine learning model from the notebook. Let's add a new **Code** cell by including the following SQL statement:

```
%%bigquery

CREATE OR REPLACE MODEL `12_notebook.trip_duration_
notebook`
OPTIONS
   (model_type='linear_reg') AS
SELECT
   start_station_name,
   end_station_name,
   IF (EXTRACT(DAYOFWEEK FROM starttime)=1 OR
EXTRACT(DAYOFWEEK FROM starttime)=7, true, false) is_
weekend,
   EXTRACT(YEAR FROM starttime)-birth_year as age,
   tripduration as label
FROM
   `12_notebook.training_table`;
```

The BigQuery ML code that we used to create the `` `12_notebook.trip_duration_notebook` `` machine learning model contains the same business logic that we used in *Chapter 4, Predicting Numerical Values with Linear Regression*, to train the `` `04_nyc_bike_sharing.trip_duration_by_stations_and_day` `` model.

11. Let's add a subtitle to start the training section of the model. We'll add a **Markdown** cell by inserting the following title:

```
## Evaluating the linear regression
```

12. Now, we're ready to write the BigQuery ML query that will evaluate the machine learning model. Let's add a new **Code** cell by including the following SQL statement:

```
%%bigquery

SELECT
    *
FROM
    ML.EVALUATE(MODEL `12_notebook.linear_regression_
notebook`,
      (
      SELECT
            start_station_name,
            end_station_name,
            IF (EXTRACT(DAYOFWEEK FROM starttime)=1 OR
EXTRACT(DAYOFWEEK FROM starttime)=7, true, false) is_
weekend,
            tripduration as label
      FROM
            `12_notebook.evaluation_table`));
```

The code block that we used to evaluate the `12_notebook.trip_duration_notebook` machine learning model contains the same business logic that we used in *Chapter 4, Predicting Numerical Values with Linear Regression*, to evaluate the `04_nyc_bike_sharing.trip_duration_by_stations_and_day` model.

13. Let's add a subtitle to start the prediction section of the model. We'll add a **Markdown** cell by inserting the following title:

```
## Testing the linear regression
```

14. Now, we can include the BigQuery ML query that we'll use for our ML model. Let's add a new **Code** cell by including the following SQL statement:

```
%%bigquery

SELECT
    tripduration as actual_duration,
    predicted_label as predicted_duration,
    ABS(tripduration - predicted_label) difference_in_min
FROM
    ML.PREDICT(MODEL `12_notebook.linear_regression_
notebook`,
    (
    SELECT
            start_station_name,
            end_station_name,
            IF (EXTRACT(DAYOFWEEK FROM starttime)=1 OR
EXTRACT(DAYOFWEEK FROM starttime)=7, true, false) is_
weekend,
            tripduration
    FROM
            `12_notebook.prediction_table`
    ))
    order by  difference_in_min asc;
```

The code block that we used to test the `12_notebook.trip_duration_notebook` machine learning model contains the same business logic that we used in *Chapter 4*, *Predicting Numerical Values with Linear Regression*, to use the `04_nyc_bike_sharing.trip_duration_by_stations_and_day` model.

15. At the end of the compilation phase, we can save the notebook using the **Save Notebook** button in the main menu or by using the **Save Notebook As...** option.

In this section, we compiled our notebook using code cells and Markdown cells. In the next section, we'll run the code that we've written in the notebook.

# Running the code in the AI notebook

In this section, we'll run the code that we wrote in the *Compiling the AI notebook* section. Let's start by taking a look at the notebook that we've prepared.

In the following screenshot, we can visualize our AI notebook, which alternates between descriptive cells and code cells:

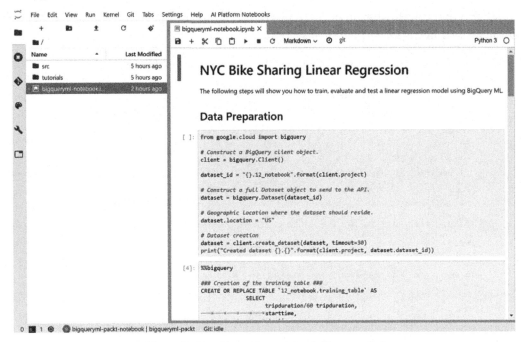

Figure 12.14 – The entire notebook file compiled

To run the entire notebook, we can simply open the **Run** menu at the top of the window and select **Run All Cells**, as shown in the following screenshot:

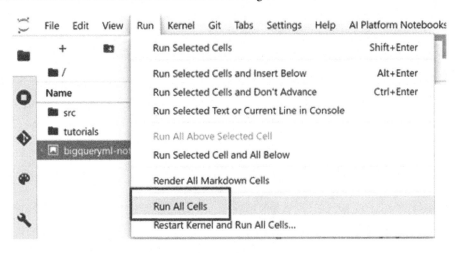

Figure 12.15 – Running all the cells

Upon selecting **Run All Cells**, all the cells in the AI Platform notebook will be executed sequentially.

At the end of the evaluation step, the results of the ML.EVALUATE function will be shown in the *Evaluating the linear regression* section.

The following screenshot shows the values returned by the evaluation stage:

### Evaluating the linear regression

```
[7]: %%bigquery

SELECT
  *
FROM
  ML.EVALUATE(MODEL `12_notebook.linear_regression_notebook`,
    (
    SELECT
          start_station_name,
          end_station_name,
          IF (EXTRACT(DAYOFWEEK FROM starttime)=1 OR EXTRACT(DAYOFWEEK FROM starttime)=7, true, false) is_weekend,
          tripduration as label
    FROM
          `12_notebook.evaluation_table`));
```

| | mean_absolute_error | mean_squared_error | mean_squared_log_error | median_absolute_error | r2_score | explained_variance |
|---|---|---|---|---|---|---|
| **0** | 7.124097 | 119.461055 | 0.377953 | 5.51093 | 0.095371 | 0.095479 |

Figure 12.16 – The values returned by the evaluation function

At the end of the prediction step, the results of the ML.PREDICT function will be shown in the `Testing the linear regression` section.

In the following screenshot, we can visualize the results presented at the end of the notebook:

## Testing the linear regression

```
[8]: %%bigquery

SELECT
    tripduration as actual_duration,
    predicted_label as predicted_duration,
    ABS(tripduration - predicted_label) difference_in_min
FROM
    ML.PREDICT(MODEL `12_notebook.linear_regression_notebook`,
    (
    SELECT
            start_station_name,
            end_station_name,
            IF (EXTRACT(DAYOFWEEK FROM starttime)=1 OR EXTRACT(DAYOFWEEK FROM starttime)=7, true, false) is_weekend,
            tripduration
    FROM
        `12_notebook.prediction_table`
    ))
    order by  difference_in_min asc;
```

[8]:

|  | actual_duration | predicted_duration | difference_in_min |
|---|---|---|---|
| 0 | 16.616667 | 16.616668 | 9.775469e-07 |
| 1 | 15.683333 | 15.683348 | 1.502998e-05 |
| 2 | 12.233333 | 12.233349 | 1.526299e-05 |
| 3 | 12.133333 | 12.133318 | 1.571753e-05 |
| 4 | 12.800000 | 12.800024 | 2.423694e-05 |
| ... | ... | ... | ... |
| 1728073 | 179.316667 | 11.867817 | 1.674489e+02 |
| 1728074 | 179.350000 | 11.151197 | 1.681988e+02 |
| 1728075 | 178.316667 | 9.539430 | 1.687772e+02 |
| 1728076 | 178.916667 | 9.539430 | 1.693772e+02 |

Figure 12.17 – The values returned by the PREDICT function

As you can see, after executing the code block, the notebook presents the results of the predictions immediately after the SQL statement. This characteristic is particularly important if we wish to increase the readability and understanding of the BigQuery ML development steps.

In this section, we learned how to compile an AI notebook and how to run all the cells that contain code blocks or titles and descriptions.

# Summary

In this chapter, we learned what AI notebooks are and why they can be useful in the development of a machine learning model, and we also understood the pricing model. We discovered the relationship between Google AI Platform Notebooks and the open source environment JupyterLab.

First, we provisioned our first notebook instance using the Google Cloud Console web interface. Then, we used this new instance to develop a simple linear regression model, alternating code blocks and descriptive cells in the notebook file in the meantime.

Finally, we executed all the steps in the notebook and visualized the results directly in its web interface.

In the next chapter, we'll learn how to invoke TensorFlow models directly from BigQuery using BigQuery ML.

# Further resources

- **NYC Bike Sharing public dataset**: `https://console.cloud.google.com/marketplace/product/city-of-new-york/nyc-citi-bike`

- **BigQuery ML create model**: `https://cloud.google.com/bigquery-ml/docs/reference/standard-sql/bigqueryml-syntax-create`

- **BigQuery ML evaluate model**: `https://cloud.google.com/bigquery-ml/docs/reference/standard-sql/bigqueryml-syntax-evaluate`

- **BigQuery ML PREDICT**: `https://cloud.google.com/bigquery-ml/docs/reference/standard-sql/bigqueryml-syntax-predict`

- **BigQuery ML linear regression example**: `https://cloud.google.com/bigquery-ml/docs/bigqueryml-natality`

- **Jupyter Notebooks best practices**: `https://cloud.google.com/blog/products/ai-machine-learning/best-practices-that-can-improve-the-life-of-any-developer-using-jupyter-notebooks`

- **Prototyping models in AI Platform**: `https://codelabs.developers.google.com/codelabs/prototyping-caip-notebooks/#0`

# 13
# Running TensorFlow Models with BigQuery ML

TensorFlow is one of the most used and relevant **Machine Learning (ML)** frameworks available. It allows data scientists and ML engineers to develop advanced models, and it also provides great flexibility and a rich set of mathematical functions.

The advanced features that TensorFlow offers provide a huge opportunity for data analysts that want to leverage existing models developed by data scientists and ML engineers.

Furthermore, the interoperability between BigQuery ML and TensorFlow represents a way to fill the gap between business and technical stakeholders within companies. The first group is usually more focused on in-depth knowledge of the data, while the second is technical-oriented and focused on programming skills.

In this chapter, we'll learn what TensorFlow is and how it can be used with BigQuery ML. We'll understand how to export a BigQuery ML model into the TensorFlow format and how to run TensorFlow models using BigQuery ML SQL syntax.

To understand how we can complement BigQuery ML with TensorFlow, we'll cover the following topics:

- Introducing TensorFlow
- Discovering the relationship between BigQuery ML and TensorFlow
- Converting BigQuery ML models into TensorFlow
- Running TensorFlow models with BigQuery ML

# Technical requirements

This chapter requires that you have access a web browser and can leverage the following:

- A GCP account to access the Google Cloud Console
- A GCP project to host BigQuery datasets
- A GCP project to host the Google Cloud storage bucket

Now that we've covered the technical requirements, let's start exploring BigQuery ML for TensorFlow models.

Check out the following video to see the Code in Action: `https://bit.ly/33ngmdf`

# Introducing TensorFlow

In this section, we'll introduce **TensorFlow**, its origins, and what this framework has achieved in the ML community.

**TensorFlow** is an open source library that's used to develop ML models. It's very flexible and can be used to address a wide variety of use cases and business scenarios. Since TensorFlow is based on math functions, its name comes from the mathematical concept of the **Tensor**.

In math, a **Tensor** is an algebraic object that describes a relationship between sets of other algebraic objects. Some examples of tensors are vectors and matrixes.

The TensorFlow library was originally created by Google's engineers and then released under the Apache License in 2015. Now, it is recognized as one of the most popular ML frameworks due to its potential and flexibility. In fact, a TensorFlow model can be executed on local machines, on-premises servers, in the cloud, or at the edge, such as on mobile phones and video surveillance cameras.

> **Important note**
> **Edge computing** is a computing paradigm that brings the computation of
> business logic closer to the location where it is required. When a ML model
> runs at the edge, it is typically executed directly on the sensors or cameras that
> collect the data for the model to function without connecting to other systems.

TensorFlow is widely used by the ML community and is applied to solve different
challenges in the artificial intelligence space, such as the following:

- Airbnb leverages TensorFlow to classify customers pictures, thus improving
  the virtual tours of houses to rent. For more details, you can visit the following
  link: `https://medium.com/airbnb-engineering/categorizing-`
  `listing-photos-at-airbnb-f9483f3ab7e3`.

- Google uses TensorFlow to empower its products, such as Google Search, Gmail,
  and Translate, with artificial intelligence capabilities. For more details, you can
  visit the following link: `https://ai.googleblog.com/search/label/`
  `TensorFlow`.

- PayPal uses TensorFlow to prevent fraud and applies ML to increase the accuracy
  of its fraud detection models. For more details, you can visit the following link:
  `https://medium.com/paypal-engineering`.

- Twitter leverages TensorFlow to identify and show the most relevant tweets to
  its users. For more details, you can visit the following link: `https://blog.`
  `tensorflow.org/2019/03/ranking-tweets-with-tensorflow.html`.

- Other interesting use cases can be found on the TensorFlow case studies web page
  at `https://www.tensorflow.org/about/case-studies?hl=en`.

Compared to what happens with BigQuery ML, advanced programming skills are
required to develop a ML model using TensorFlow. In fact, the high flexibility of the
TensorFlow library is balanced by the need to invest a certain amount of time in code
development to create the model. Now, the suggested programming language to develop
ML models with TensorFlow is Python.

Once the development and training phase of a TensorFlow model is completed, it can be
exported into the **SavedModel** format.

The **SavedModel** format contains the entire TensorFlow model. This format allows us to deploy the model without the need to run the code again in all the compatible environments. A SavedModel is composed of multiple files and folders stored in the same parent folder:

- The SavedModel file stores the TensorFlow logic. This file is called `saved_model.pb`.
- The `variables` directory contains the parameters of the trained model.
- The `assets` folder can contain the external and additional files that are used by the ML model.

When a TensorFlow model is in the SavedModel format, it can be easily loaded and used on the platform where we want to use this model. The platform could be a physical server, a cloud instance, a smartphone, or an **Internet of Things** (**IoT**) device.

In this section, we introduced the basics of TensorFlow. In the next section, we'll discover how BigQuery ML is linked to TensorFlow.

# Discovering the relationship between BigQuery ML and TensorFlow

In this section, we'll understand the relationship between BigQuery ML and TensorFlow. After completing this section, we'll be able to understand when to use BigQuery ML and TensorFlow according to our use case, but also how to get the best out of the two technologies, when they're used together.

## Understanding commonalities and differences

BigQuery ML and TensorFlow have some similar aspects, but there are also some relevant differences to highlight.

In the following table, we have summarized the main similarities and differences of these two frameworks:

| | **BigQuery ML** | **TensorFlow** |
| --- | --- | --- |
| Model Types | Limited to the model types officially supported by BigQuery | Maximum flexibility in terms of model types to implement |
| Format of the data | Structured data | Structured and semi-structured data, images, audio, and videos |
| Programming Language | SQL (BigQuery dialect) | Python |
| Target Personas | Business and data analysts | Data scientists and machine learning engineers |

Figure 13.1 – Comparing BigQuery ML and TensorFlow

First, it is important to underline that TensorFlow offers greater flexibility in terms of the ML models that can be implemented. While BigQuery ML is characterized by a specific list of supported model types (`https://cloud.google.com/bigquery-ml/docs/introduction#supported_models_in`), TensorFlow offers a wider spectrum of ML techniques.

BigQuery ML was designed as an extension of BigQuery and for this reason, it only focuses on structured data, which can be represented in a tabular format. All the BigQuery ML techniques are based on the possibility to train and apply the models to rows stored in BigQuery tables. On the other hand, TensorFlow is open to different formats, including free text, images, audio, and videos.

To train, evaluate, and test BigQuery ML models, the user should know the SQL syntax and have minimal ML experience. Implementing a TensorFlow model, on the other hand, requires good programming skills and good knowledge of ML topics because the framework provides higher flexibility in terms of customization.

Considering the features of these two technologies, it is clear that they are addressed to different stakeholders in the companies. While BigQuery ML can easily be used by business analysts and data analysts that are familiar with data analytics tasks and SQL queries, TensorFlow is designed for advanced programmers, such as experienced data scientists and ML engineers.

Now that we have understood the commonalities and the differences of BigQuery ML and TensorFlow, in the next section, we'll learn how these two frameworks can complement each other.

# Collaborating with BigQuery ML and TensorFlow

In this section, we'll discover how to use BigQuery ML and TensorFlow together to get the maximum value from both technologies.

The following diagram shows the interactions between business analysts and data scientists using BigQuery ML and TensorFlow:

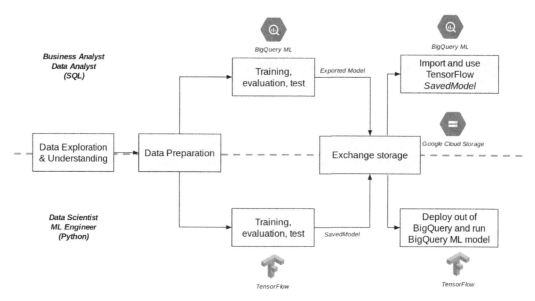

Figure 13.2 – Interactions between BigQuery ML and TensorFlow

As we've described in *Chapter 1, Introduction to Google Cloud and BigQuery*, the first steps of the ML development cycle are exploring the data and completely understanding it.

After this first phase of analysis, the data needs to be cleaned and prepared to train the ML algorithm. This phase is fundamental to creating a valuable ML model and proceeding on to the training stage.

When it's time to actually develop the ML model, depending on our knowledge, background, and previous experience, we have two options:

- If you are a business analyst or data analyst, you will prefer using BigQuery ML for its simplicity and immediacy thanks to the SQL syntax.

- If you're a data scientist or a ML engineer, you will choose to train a TensorFlow model due to its flexibility and because it offers more opportunities for customization.

As shown in the preceding diagram, the upper branch represents the typical workflow of a business or data analyst who leverages BigQuery ML SQL statements to create, evaluate, and use a ML model on data that's already been stored in BigQuery. This branch requires that you have good knowledge of the SQL language, the basics of ML, and the underlying data.

On the other hand, the lower branch of the diagram represents the development process based on a TensorFlow library that's been made by data scientists or ML engineers, who have a great experience in programming and ML algorithms.

Typically, data analysts know the data very well but have little knowledge of the most advanced programming techniques, while data scientists and ML engineers have in-depth coding skills but a limited comprehension of the business data. This situation usually occurs in more established companies due to the employees having different professional backgrounds. This can cause friction between those who know the industry very well and the business processes where other people are more focused on programming.

In order to reduce this gap and mitigate the risk of friction, BigQuery ML allows us to do the following:

- Export the ML models that have been developed with BigQuery ML into the TensorFlow SavedModel format.
- Import TensorFlow ML models in the SavedModel format.

Looking at the preceding diagram, we can see that a business analyst can export BigQuery ML models and deploy them to other environments that are different from BigQuery and compatible with TensorFlow.

On the other hand, a data scientist who has implemented advanced TensorFlow models can save them into a Google Cloud storage bucket, which means they can be imported into BigQuery ML.

This kind of bidirectional interaction between BigQuery ML and the TensorFlow framework allows us to do the following:

- Extend the applicability of a BigQuery ML model that is no longer confined to using data stored in BigQuery.
- Import BigQuery ML advanced TensorFlow models that were not originally supported by the BigQuery ML syntax and use them, through SQL queries, on the data stored in BigQuery.

In this section, we learned how BigQuery ML and TensorFlow can interact and why it's so important to leverage this kind of integration. In the next section, we'll train a BigQuery ML model and export it in TensorFlow format.

# Converting BigQuery ML models into TensorFlow

In this section, we'll train the same deep neural network that we trained in *Chapter 11, Implementing Deep Neural Networks*, and then export this model into the TensorFlow SavedModel format.

## Training the BigQuery ML to export it

Before we start training the model, let's access BigQuery to create the dataset and the tables that will be used for training and prediction:

1. Log into our Google Cloud Console and access the **BigQuery** user interface from the navigation menu.

2. Create a new dataset under the project that we' created in *Chapter 2, Setting Up Your GCP and BigQuery Environment*. For this use case, we'll create a dataset called `13_tensorflow_model` with the default options.

3. Now, we're ready to create the table that will contain the training dataset. Let's execute the following SQL statement:

```
CREATE OR REPLACE TABLE `13_tensorflow_model.training_
table` AS
           SELECT
                  tripduration/60 tripduration,
                  start_station_name,
                  end_station_name,
                  IF (EXTRACT(DAYOFWEEK FROM
starttime)=1 OR EXTRACT(DAYOFWEEK FROM starttime)=7,
true, false) is_weekend,
                  EXTRACT(YEAR FROM starttime)-birth_
year as age
           FROM
                  `bigquery-public-data.new_york_
citibike.citibike_trips`
           WHERE
```

```
                              (
                    (EXTRACT (YEAR FROM
starttime)=2017 AND
                        (EXTRACT (MONTH FROM
starttime)>=04 OR EXTRACT (MONTH FROM starttime)<=10))
                    OR (EXTRACT (YEAR FROM
starttime)=2018 AND
                        (EXTRACT (MONTH FROM
starttime)>=01 OR EXTRACT (MONTH FROM starttime)<=02))
                              )
                    AND (tripduration>=3*60 AND
tripduration<=3*60*60)
                    AND  birth_year is not NULL
                    AND birth_year < 2007;
```

The result of this query is stored in the new `13_tensorflow_model.training_table` table that we created to support the following steps of our use case.

The business logic of this query is the same as what we applied in the *Preparing the dataset* section of *Chapter 11, Implementing Deep Neural Networks*.

4. Now, we will create the table that will be used to test our ML model:

```
CREATE OR REPLACE TABLE  `13_tensorflow_model.prediction_
table` AS
              SELECT
                    tripduration/60 tripduration,
                    start_station_name,
                    end_station_name,
                    IF (EXTRACT(DAYOFWEEK FROM
starttime)=1 OR EXTRACT(DAYOFWEEK FROM starttime)=7,
true, false) is_weekend,
                    EXTRACT(YEAR FROM starttime)-birth_
year as age
                  FROM
                    `bigquery-public-data.new_york_
citibike.citibike_trips`
                  WHERE
                    EXTRACT (YEAR FROM starttime)=2018
                    AND EXTRACT (MONTH FROM starttime)=05
```

```
                                 AND (tripduration>=3*60 AND
      tripduration<=3*60*60)
                                 AND  birth_year is not NULL
                                 AND birth_year < 2007;
```

This query applies the same logic that was used to create the training table but only takes May 2018 into consideration.

5. Now, let's train our ML model, which will be exported into TensorFlow format in the *Exporting the BigQuery ML model* section:

```
CREATE OR REPLACE MODEL `13_tensorflow_model.bigquery_ml_
model_to_export`
OPTIONS
   (model_type='DNN_REGRESSOR',
         ACTIVATION_FN = 'CRELU') AS
SELECT
   start_station_name,
   end_station_name,
   is_weekend,
   age,
   tripduration as label
FROM
   `13_tensorflow_model.training_table`;
```

The business logic that was used to create the `13_tensorflow_model.bigquery_ml_model_to_export` ML model is the same logic we used to train the CRELU deep neural network in the *Training the deep neural network models* section of *Chapter 11*, *Implementing Deep Neural Networks*.

Now that we've trained a ML model, in the next section, we'll learn how to export it into the TensorFlow SavedModel format.

# Exporting the BigQuery ML model

In this section, we'll export a BigQuery ML model into a Google Cloud storage bucket in the TensorFlow SavedModel format. Let's get started:

1.  First, we need to access to the Cloud Shell from the Google Cloud Console:

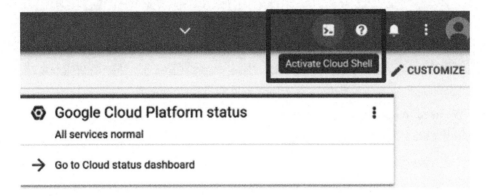

Figure 13.3 – The Activate Cloud Shell button in the Google Cloud Console

> **Important note**
> The **Cloud Shell** is an online Linux-based environment that can be accessed from the web browser of the Google Cloud Console. With the Cloud Shell, you can manage your Google Cloud resources by leveraging its preloaded utilities, such as the **gcloud** command-line tool.

2.  After clicking on the **Cloud Shell** button, a Linux command line will be provisioned and presented at the bottom of the screen. If this is the first time you're using the Google Cloud Shell, the following banner will be presented:

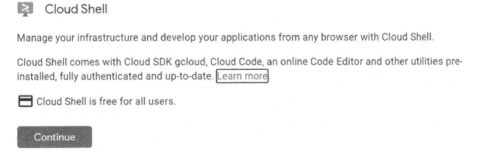

Figure 13.4 – The Cloud Shell information box

After clicking on the blue **Continue** button, the Linux command line will be provisioned, as shown in the following screenshot:

CLOUD SHELL
Terminal    (bigqueryml-packt) ×  +  ▾

```
Welcome to Cloud Shell! Type "help" to get started.
Your Cloud Platform project in this session is set to bigqueryml-packt.
Use "gcloud config set project [PROJECT_ID]" to change to a different project.
                @cloudshell:~ (bigqueryml-packt)$ ▮
```

Figure 13.5 – The Cloud Shell environment

3.  We need to authenticate our account for the Google Cloud SDK by running the following command:

    ```
    gcloud auth login
    ```

    A web URL will be shown in the command line. By clicking on this URL, we'll authorize our account to use Cloud SDK. At the end of this process, you'll see a code on the web page that you can copy and paste into your Cloud Shell to complete the authorization process.

4.  Then, we can run the following command to set the current project name in the new PROJECT variable:

    ```
    PROJECT=$(gcloud config get-value project)
    ```

5.  Using the PROJECT variable, we'll create a second variable, BUCKET, that will contain the name of the Google Cloud storage bucket to create, which is where the BigQuery ML model will be exported:

    ```
    BUCKET=${PROJECT}-us-bigqueryml-export-tf
    ```

    The Google Cloud storage bucket name will be a concatenation of the name of our project and the -us-bigqueryml-export-tf string.

6.  Now that we have the name of the bucket stored in a variable, we can create the new bucket by running the following command:

    ```
    gsutil mb -l us gs://${BUCKET}
    ```

> **Important note**
>
> The `gsutil mb` command is used to create a new bucket, while the `-l US` option specifies the geographic location where we want to create the bucket. In this case, the bucket will be created in the United States.

If this is the first time that you are using Cloud Shell to create a Google Cloud storage bucket, then the following banner will appear before the bucket is created:

## Authorize Cloud Shell

gsutil is requesting your credentials to make a GCP API call.

Click to authorize this and future calls that require your credentials.

Figure 13.6 – The Cloud Shell authorization box

Upon clicking on the blue **Authorize** button, the bucket will be created.

7.  Now, let's execute the command that will export the BigQuery ML model into the Google Cloud storage bucket in the TensorFlow SavedModel format. Let's run the following command:

```
        bq extract -m 13_tensorflow_model.bigquery_ml_model_
    to_export gs://${BUCKET}/bqml_exported_model
```

The `bq extract` command is used to extract the BigQuery ML model that's specified after the –m option. The last part of the command indicates the path of the Google Cloud storage bucket where we want to extract the model and the related subfolder; that is, `bqml_exported_model`. As an alternative, it's also possible to export the BigQuery ML model using the following SQL query:

```
EXPORT MODEL 13_tensorflow_model.bigquery_ml_model_to_
export
OPTIONS (URI = "gs://${BUCKET}/bqml_exported_model" );
```

8.  To verify the presence of the exported model, we can browse the Google Cloud Console menu and access the **Browser** functionality under **Storage**, as shown in the following screenshot:

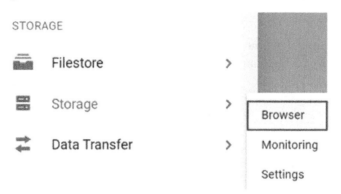

STORAGE

    Filestore            >

    Storage            >     Browser

    Data Transfer    >     Monitoring

                                     Settings

Figure 13.7 – Google Cloud Storage – Browser

Upon accessing the Google Cloud storage bucket we created in *Step 6* and entering the `bqml_exported_model` subfolder, we'll see the exported version of the BigQuery ML model, as shown in the following screenshot:

Filter by name prefix only ▾     ≂ **Filter**  Filter objects and folders

| Name | Size | Type |
| --- | --- | --- |
| 📁 assets/ | – | Folder |
| 🗔 checkpoint | 93 B | application/octet-stream |
| 🗔 graph.pbtxt | 618.7 KB | application/octet-stream |
| 🗔 model.ckpt-1077982.data-00000-of-00002 | 16 B | application/octet-stream |
| 🗔 model.ckpt-1077982.data-00001-of-00002 | 127.1 KB | application/octet-stream |
| 🗔 model.ckpt-1077982.index | 949 B | application/octet-stream |
| 🗔 model.ckpt-1077982.meta | 313.5 KB | application/octet-stream |
| 🗔 saved_model.pb | 118.4 KB | application/octet-stream |
| 📁 variables/ | – | Folder |

Figure 13.8 – The BigQuery ML model exported into the TensorFlow SavedModel format

From this list of the files, we can easily recognize the main components of the TensorFlow SavedModel format that we mentioned in the *Introducing TensorFlow* section of this chapter. We can see the `saved_model.pb` file, which contains the TensorFlow program, the `assets` and `variables` folders, and some additional metadata files.

Now that the model has been exported into the TensorFlow SavedModel format, it's possible to share it with other people and run it on a TensorFlow-compatible environment, outside of BigQuery.

In this section, we learned how to export a BigQuery ML model into a Google Cloud storage bucket by using the TensorFlow SavedModel format. In the next section, we'll learn how to import existing TensorFlow models into BigQuery ML.

# Running TensorFlow models with BigQuery ML

In this section, we'll import the TensorFlow model that we exported in the *Converting BigQuery ML models into TensorFlow* section. Once the model has been imported, we'll use it through the BigQuery ML syntax.

First, we need to remember that our BigQuery ML model has been exported into the folder of a Google Cloud storage bucket. The ML model is stored in the TensorFlow SavedModel format and is in the same format as any other ML model that's been developed by a data scientist using TensorFlow.

If we want to use a TensorFlow model in BigQuery ML, we need to perform the following steps:

1. First, let's run the `CREATE OR REPLACE MODEL` SQL statement. Keep in mind that the path of the bucket – `'gs://<PROJECT_NAME>-us-bigqueryml-export-tf/bqml_exported_model/*'` – is based on the name of your current project, so you need to replace the `<PROJECT_NAME>` placeholder with the name of the project you're working on:

```
CREATE OR REPLACE MODEL `13_tensorflow_model.trip_
duration_tf_imported_model`
OPTIONS (model_type='tensorflow',
        model_path='gs://<PROJECT_NAME>-us-bigqueryml-
export-tf/bqml_exported_model/*');
```

The syntax of the query is composed of the CREATE OR REPLACE MODEL keywords, followed by the identifier of the new ML model; that is, `13_tensorflow_model.trip_duration_tf_imported_model`.

In the OPTIONS clause, we've specified 'tensorflow' in the model_type option. Using the model_path parameter, we've specified the folder where the TensorFlow SavedModel will be stored in the Google Cloud storage bucket.

2.  To verify that BigQuery ML successfully loaded the TensorFlow model, we can browse the BigQuery navigation menu and check that the model is present in the 13_tensorflow_model dataset.

The following screenshot shows that the TensorFlow model has been imported into BigQuery ML. Its name is trip_duration_tf_imported_model:

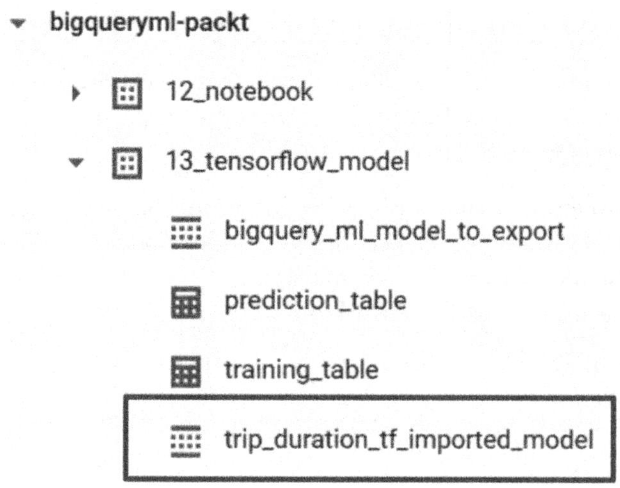

Figure 13.9 – The TensorFlow model imported into BigQuery

3.  If we click on trip_duration_tf_imported_model, we'll be able to access the ML model's details.

The following screenshot shows the details of the imported ML model:

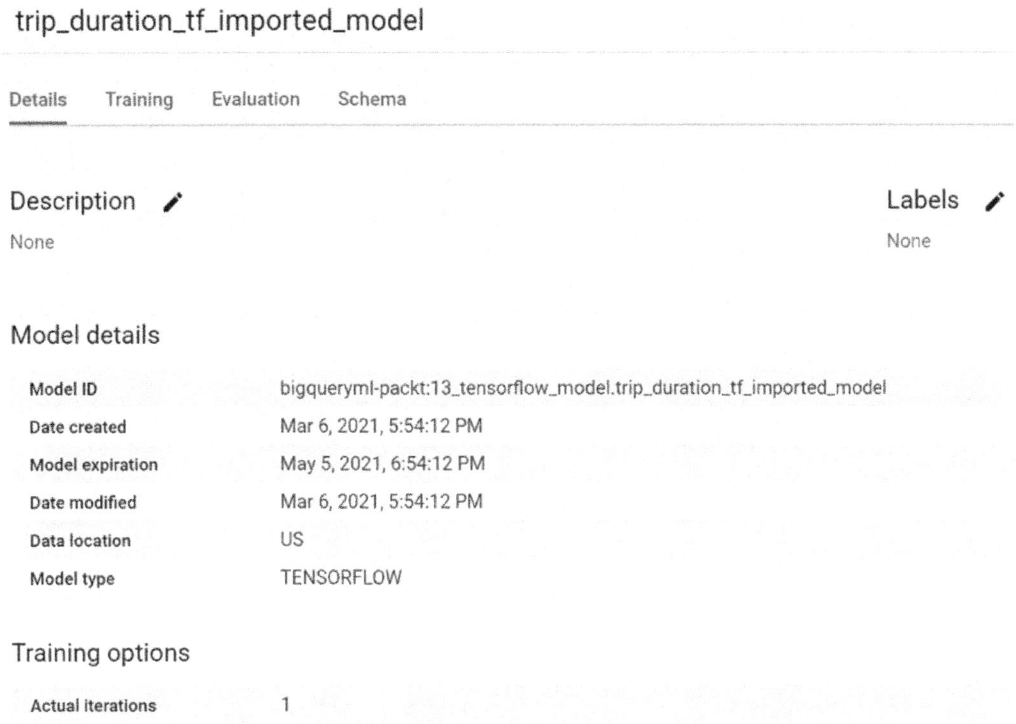

## trip_duration_tf_imported_model

Details    Training    Evaluation    Schema

Description ✏           Labels ✏
None                     None

### Model details

| | |
|---|---|
| Model ID | bigqueryml-packt:13_tensorflow_model.trip_duration_tf_imported_model |
| Date created | Mar 6, 2021, 5:54:12 PM |
| Model expiration | May 5, 2021, 6:54:12 PM |
| Date modified | Mar 6, 2021, 5:54:12 PM |
| Data location | US |
| Model type | TENSORFLOW |

### Training options

| | |
|---|---|
| Actual iterations | 1 |

Figure 13.10 – The details of the ML model we've imported into BigQuery

On the **Details** page of the model, we can clearly see that the model type is **TENSORFLOW**. This feature confirms that, originally, the ML model was in the TensorFlow SavedModel format and has been imported into BigQuery ML.

4.  Now, we can use the imported TensorFlow model with the BigQuery ML `ML.PREDICT` function. Let's run the following SQL statement:

```
SELECT
    *
FROM
    ML.PREDICT(MODEL `13_tensorflow_model.trip_duration_tf_
imported_model`,
        (
        SELECT
            start_station_name,
            end_station_name,
```

```
        is_weekend,
        age,
        tripduration
    FROM
        `13_tensorflow_model.prediction_table`));
```

The result of the query will be presented after a few seconds in the BigQuery UI.

The following screenshot shows the results of executing the query, along with the predictions that were generated by the ML model:

**Query results**          ⬇ SAVE RESULTS     📊 EXPLORE DATA ▾

Query complete (19.5 sec elapsed, 100.5 MB processed)

Job information    Results    JSON    Execution details

| Row | predictions | start_station_name | end_station_name | is_weekend | age | tripduration |
|---|---|---|---|---|---|---|
| 1 | 8.564577102661133 | W 15 St & 7 Ave | W 22 St & 8 Ave | false | 76 | 6.716666666666667 |
| 2 | 10.394192695617676 | Greenwich Ave & Charles St | 8 Ave & W 31 St | false | 67 | 10.216666666666667 |
| 3 | 9.073539733886719 | E 55 St & 3 Ave | E 59 St & Madison Ave | false | 66 | 4.516666666666667 |
| 4 | 22.654930114746094 | Riverside Dr & W 72 St | Riverside Dr & W 72 St | false | 67 | 47.916666666666664 |
| 5 | 48.38661575317383 | Front St & Washington St | W 59 St & 10 Ave | false | 19 | 66.65 |
| 6 | 6.649036407470703 | State St & Smith St | Hoyt St & Warren St | false | 19 | 3.966666666666667 |
| 7 | 14.03892993927002 | 1 Ave & E 30 St | E 17 St & Broadway | false | 70 | 13.566666666666666 |
| 8 | 16.7429141998291 | Kane St & Clinton St | Coffey St & Conover St | false | 19 | 11.833333333333334 |

Figure 13.11 – The predictions that were generated by the TensorFlow model, imported into BigQuery

As we can see, the predicted values are stored in the `predictions` column and represent the predicted trip duration to go from `start_station_name` to `end_station_name` using the bike sharing service.

In this section, we learned how to import a TensorFlow model into BigQuery ML and how to use it by leveraging the BigQuery ML SQL syntax.

# Summary

In this chapter, we learned what TensorFlow is and why it is so important for the ML industry.

First, we analyzed the main commonalities and differences between BigQuery ML and TensorFlow, and we understood that they are addressed to different target personas within the ML community.

Then, we discovered how we can complement BigQuery ML and TensorFlow to get the maximum value by combining these two frameworks.

By taking a gradual and step-by-step approach, we learned how to export BigQuery ML models into the TensorFlow format so that we can deploy them into environments other than BigQuery.

After that, we tested how to import and use a TensorFlow model in BigQuery ML. This approach enables data analysts to easily access and use advanced TensorFlow ML models that have been developed by data scientists and ML engineers. Finally, after importing the ML model, we tested the imported ML model on a BigQuery table to predict the trip duration of a bike ride with the New York City bike sharing service.

In the next chapter, we'll focus on some BigQuery tips and best practices so that we can improve our ML skills further.

# Further resources

- **NYC Bike Sharing Public Dataset**: `https://console.cloud.google.com/marketplace/product/city-of-new-york/nyc-citi-bike`

- **BigQuery ML Create Model for TensorFlow**: `https://cloud.google.com/bigquery-ml/docs/reference/standard-sql/bigqueryml-syntax-create-tensorflow`

- **BigQuery ML Evaluate Model**: `https://cloud.google.com/bigquery-ml/docs/reference/standard-sql/bigqueryml-syntax-evaluate`

- **BigQuery ML Predict**: `https://cloud.google.com/bigquery-ml/docs/reference/standard-sql/bigqueryml-syntax-predict`

- **TensorFlow official website**: `https://www.tensorflow.org/`

# 14
# BigQuery ML Tips and Best Practices

BigQuery ML has the great advantage of democratizing the use of **Machine Learning (ML)** for data and business analysts. In fact, BigQuery ML enables users without any programming experience to implement advanced ML algorithms. Even though BigQuery ML is designed to simplify and automatize the creation of a ML model, there are some best practices and tips that should be adopted during the development life cycle of a ML algorithm to obtain an effective performance from it.

Having a background in data science can help us in further improving the performance of our ML models and in avoiding pitfalls during the implementation of a use case. In this chapter, we'll learn how to choose the right technique for each specific business scenario and will learn about the tools we can leverage to improve the performance of ML models.

Following a typical ML development life cycle, we'll go through the following topics:

- Choosing the right BigQuery ML algorithm
- Preparing the datasets
- Understanding feature engineering
- Tuning hyperparameters
- Using BigQuery ML for online predictions

# Choosing the right BigQuery ML algorithm

In this section, we'll learn why it is so important to define a clear business objective before implementing a ML model, and we'll understand which BigQuery ML algorithm is suitable for each specific use case.

> **Important note**
>
> A **data scientist** is a professional in charge of the collection, analysis, and understanding of large amounts of data. This role typically requires a mix of skills, such as matching statistics and coding.
>
> A **data analyst** is different from a data scientist. A data analyst is more focused on industry knowledge and business processes rather than on coding and programming skills. People in this role have huge experience in data manipulation and visualization and are able to present relevant business insights derived from data.

In order to get meaningful results in ML, it is necessary to define a clear business objective. Before starting on the actual implementation of the ML model, data analysts and data scientists should clearly define the business goal they wish to achieve.

One of the most famous techniques to set up clear goals is known as the **Specific, Measurable, Attainable, Relevant, and Time-based (SMART)** framework. In this paradigm, each letter represents a specific feature that our final goal should satisfy, as outlined here:

- **Specific**: It is necessary to define a clear and precise business objective.

- **Measurable**: In order to understand if a BigQuery ML model satisfies our criteria, we need to select one or more **Key Performance Indicators (KPIs)** such as the **Receiver Operating Characteristic (ROC)**, the **Area Under the Curve (AUC)** value, or the **Mean Absolute Error (MAE)**.

- **Attainable**: We need to analyze the complexity of the use case that we want to solve and set the right expectations—for example, we cannot expect that our BigQuery ML model will predict the right values 100% of the time.

- **Relevant**: We need to focus our efforts on the most important use cases, as it may be that some business scenarios can bring a limited business advantage to our company.

- **Time-based**: As data analysts and data scientists, we have limited resources in terms of time. Focusing on the right goals is fundamental in order to generate value for our company.

We can apply the SMART framework to the ML field to help us in choosing the right use cases and the right BigQuery ML algorithm to use.

As an example, in the following table, you can visualize the SMART framework applied to the use case that we have developed in *Chapter 4, Predicting Numerical Values with Linear Regression*:

| | |
|---|---|
| **Specific** | Predict the trip time, in minutes, of each bike ride for the New York City bike sharing service |
| **Measurable** | Use the Mean Absolute Error (MAE) as the evaluation metric |
| **Attainable** | The Mean Absolute Error (MAE) should be less or equal to 10 minutes |
| **Relevant** | The prediction will improve the customer experience of the New York City bike sharing service providing more affordable information |
| **Time based** | The use case should be implemented by the end of the week |

Figure 14.1 – The SMART framework applied to a ML use case

Once we have defined our business objective using the SMART approach, we are ready to select the best BigQuery ML algorithms that can help us in addressing the business scenario.

According to the business objective that we want to achieve and the training dataset that we can leverage, we can identify the BigQuery ML algorithms that can potentially solve our use case.

In the following table, we can see a summary of all the BigQuery ML techniques that we can use to develop our ML models:

| Labelled Dataset Required | Expected Output | BigQuery ML Algorithm |
| --- | --- | --- |
| Yes | Continuous real numbers | Linear regression |
| Yes | Two discrete classes | Binary logistic regression |
| Yes | Multiple discrete classes | Multiclass logistic regression |
| No | Grouping of the input items | K-means clustering |
| Yes | Couples of linked input items | Matrix factorization |
| Not applicable | Continuous real numbers | Time series - ARIMA PLUS |
| Yes | Continuous real numbers | Boosted Tree - XGBoost - Regression |
| Yes | Multiple discrete classes | Boosted Tree - XGBoost - Classification |
| Yes | Continuous real numbers | Deep Neural Network - Regression |
| Yes | Multiple discrete classes | Deep Neural Network - Classification |

Figure 14.2 – The BigQuery ML algorithms at a glance

In order to achieve our goal, we can navigate to the table represented in *Figure 14.2* and clearly find the BigQuery ML algorithm that can solve our use case. For example, for the business scenario that we've analyzed in *Figure 14.1*, we can assert the following:

- The BigQuery Public dataset that we used in *Chapter 4, Predicting Numerical Values with Linear Regression*, is a labeled dataset because, for each record, it includes the trip duration of the past rides.

- The expected outcome is a continuous real number. In fact, the goal of the use case is to predict the trip duration, expressed in minutes.

By using the table presented in *Figure 14.2*, we notice that we can use one of the following BigQuery ML algorithms to address our prediction use case:

- **Linear regression**
- **Boosted Tree – XGBoost – Regression**
- **Deep Neural Network – Regression**

In this section, we learned how we can set a clear business objective. Then, we understood which BigQuery ML technique we can use to address our business goal. In the next section, we'll focus on preparing the datasets to get effective ML models.

# Preparing the datasets

In this section, we'll learn about which techniques we can apply to ensure that the data we will use to build our ML model is correct and produces the desired results. After that, we'll discover the strategies that we can use to segment the datasets into training, validation, and test sets.

## Working with high-quality data

In this section, we'll understand the characteristics that our datasets should have in order to develop effective BigQuery ML models.

Since ML models learn from data, it's very important to feed our ML algorithms with high-quality data, especially during the training phase. Since **data quality** is a very broad topic, it would require a specific book to analyze it in detail. For this reason, we will focus only on main data quality concepts in relation to the building of a ML model.

> **Important note**
>
> **Data quality** is a discipline that includes processes, professionals, technologies, and best practices to identify and correct anomalies, errors, and defects in data.
>
> This practice is fundamental in supporting business decisions with trusted and affordable data insights.

We can measure the quality of a dataset according to different data quality dimensions.

In the following diagram, you can see the different dimensions used to measure the quality of the data:

Figure 14.3 – The data quality dimensions

We can evaluate the quality of a dataset based on the following dimensions: **Accuracy**, **Completeness**, **Consistency**, **Timeliness**, **Validity**, and **Uniqueness**.

In the following sections, we'll explain each data quality dimension and why it is important for the realization of a ML model.

## Accuracy

**Accuracy** refers to the information that is available in our dataset. If a numerical value is wrong and doesn't reflect reality, this will affect the effectiveness of the BigQuery ML model built on top of it.

Discovering information that is inaccurate is not an easy task, but we can apply some data quality checks to identify relevant issues in the data—for example, we can execute queries to identify and eventually remove records that contain incorrect values.

In the following table, you can see a typical example of inaccurate data, with the presence of a negative value to express the age of a person:

| Name | Age |
|------|-----|
| Bob | 24 |
| Alice | -5 |
| Tom | 35 |

Figure 14.4 – An example of a table with inaccurate values in the Age column

Using MAX and MIN operators in SELECT queries can be a good way to find wrong values in the columns. These records are called outliers because they present very different values from the other records in the same column. Executing some preliminary **Structured Query Language** (**SQL**) queries to extract the maximum and the minimum values of the features and the label can be very useful in helping identify the most relevant errors in the dataset.

For example, in *Figure 14.4*, Alice's age will be identified as an outlier in the **Age** column. In these cases, we can think about filtering out records with non-realistic values.

## Completeness

**Completeness** is focused on the presence of values in the columns of our dataset. If we train the BigQuery ML model on datasets with many missing or NULL fields, these fields will affect the performance of our model.

In the following table, you can see an example of incomplete data:

| Name | Age |
|------|-----|
| Bob | 24 |
| Alice | |
| Tom | 35 |

Figure 14.5 – An example of a table with incomplete values in the Age column

In order to prevent the presence of incomplete records, the most effective solution is to apply specific filters in the query to exclude records with missing values. A typical completeness check is based on adding a WHERE clause when the feature or the label of the model should not be empty and should be different from NULL.

In the following snippet of code, you can see an example of a SELECT statement with completeness checks applied to the <TEXT_FIELD> placeholder:

```
SELECT *
FROM <TABLE_NAME>
WHERE
    <TEXT_FIELD> IS NOT NULL AND <TEXT_FIELD> <> ''
```

In the preceding example, we're applying completeness checks on the table represented by the <TABLE_NAME> placeholder. The quality check verifies that the <TEXT_FIELD> field is not equal to NULL and is not empty.

If a record presents incomplete fields, we can choose to exclude this record from the dataset or to replace missing values with default ones to fill the gaps.

## Consistency

Achieving **consistency** in data is one of the most complex tasks to perform. In enterprise contexts, the same data is usually stored in multiple locations and may be expressed with different formats or units of measurement. When a column presents a value incompatible with the values in other columns of a dataset, the data is inconsistent.

For example, we can imagine a table with a column that contains a temperature expressed in °C and another column with the same temperature in °F. If the two values should represent the same temperature but are not well calculated, the table will present an inconsistency.

In the following table, you can see that the second record presents an inconsistency in the temperature values:

| City | Temperature in Celsius | Temperature in Fahrenheit |
|---|---|---|
| New York | 10 | 50 |
| Paris | 15 | 2 |
| Sydney | 25 | 77 |

Figure 14.6 – An example of a table with inconsistent values in the Temperature columns

In *Figure 14.6*, the second record—which corresponds to the temperature measured in **Paris**—presents an inconsistency between the °C and the °F scale.

To check the consistency of the data, we should usually apply validation checks on multiple fields that can reside in the same table or in different tables.

## Timeliness

**Timeliness** is particularly important when we need to use a BigQuery ML model. When we train a ML model, we need to be sure that all the features used during the training stage will be available when the ML model is executed.

In the business scenario of *Chapter 4, Predicting Numerical Values with Linear Regression*, we used the start and stop stations of a bike rental company to predict the trip duration. In this case, we've trained the BigQuery ML model leveraging the start and stop station, but if the stop station is not available at the prediction time, the ML model becomes inapplicable and worthless.

To avoid this common error, we need to check that all the features used to train the model will also be available during the prediction phase when the ML model will generate the predictions.

## Validity

The **validity** of a value is strictly related to the expected format that a field should have. If a column contains date values expressed in the format *DD/MM/YYYY* and one of the records presents the format *DD-MM-YYYY*, the validity of the record is compromised.

In the following table, you will notice that the second record presents a non-valid value for the **Birth Date** field:

| Name | Birth Date |
|------|------------|
| Bob | 02/05/1985 |
| Alice | 05-07-1984 |
| Tom | 27/10/1997 |

Figure 14.7 – An example of a table with invalid values in the Birth Date column

To meet this dimension, we must check that all the values of a column are stored in the same format and in a homogeneous way. In order to check the exact format of each field, we can apply regular expressions to the values in the columns.

## Uniqueness

**Unique** information means that there is exactly one record in a table to represent a specific item. Data duplication can happen due to several reasons, such as bugs in the data ingestion process, or uncontrolled interruptions and restarts during data loading.

In order to prevent these errors, we need to know the fields that compose the **Primary Key (PK)** of our records, and we need to check that the **PK** matches one—and only one—record.

> **Important note**
> In a table, the **PK** is the minimum set of columns that uniquely identify a row.

The presence of duplicated records can lead the ML model to learn from occurrences that are not actual but generated by technical errors.

Now that we've discovered all the data quality dimensions to check before implementing our BigQuery ML model, let's take a look the techniques we can use to segment the datasets into training, validation, and test sets.

# Segmenting the datasets

In this section, we'll learn how to easily segment the datasets to support the training, validation, and test phases of a BigQuery ML model.

For most BigQuery ML algorithms, we need to split the initial dataset into three different sets, as follows:

- The **training** dataset represents the sample of data that we'll use to train our BigQuery ML model.

- The **validation** dataset is different from the training dataset and we can use it to evaluate the model's performance. We perform validation on completely new data that is different from the sample data used in the training stage. In this phase, we can also tune the hyperparameters of the model.

- The **test** set is the dataset used to finally apply the model and verify its results and performance.

Splitting the initial dataset into these three subsets can be cumbersome, but if you have enough data, you can apply the following rule of thumb:

- 80% of the data for the training set.

- 10% for the validation set.

- The remaining 10% for the test set.

- If we're working on large amounts of data, we can reduce the percentage of observations used for the validation and test sets.

In the following screenshot, you can see a graphical representation of the optimal splitting strategy:

Figure 14.8 – The 80/10/10 splitting strategy for ML

In order to achieve the best results, the split procedure should be as random as possible.

In the following code block, you can see how to apply this rule of thumb by using the MOD function:

```
SELECT
  CASE
    WHEN MOD(<RECORD_KEY>, 10) < 8 THEN 'training'
    WHEN MOD(<RECORD_KEY>, 10) = 8 THEN 'evaluation'
    WHEN MOD(<RECORD_KEY>, 10) = 9 THEN 'test'
  END AS dataframe
FROM
  <TABLE_NAME>
```

In the example, the records stored in the table represented by the placeholder <TABLE_NAME>, are split into three different sets according to the value of the field dataframe. In this case, the MOD function returns a value from 0 to 10. Using this function allows us to group the records into three different sets. By leveraging the clauses MOD(<RECORD_KEY>, 10)<8, MOD(<RECORD_KEY>, 10) = 8 and MOD(<RECORD_KEY>, 10) = 9, we can split the records into the 'training', 'evaluation' and 'test' sets.

Now that we've understood how to segment the datasets according to our needs for training, validation, and testing, let's look at the understanding of the feature engineering techniques.

# Understanding feature engineering

In this section, we'll understand which techniques we can use to improve the features of a BigQuery ML model before the training stage.

> **Important note**
>
> **Feature engineering** is the practice of applying preprocessing functions on raw data, to extract features useful for training a ML model. Creating preprocessed features can significantly improve the performance of a ML model.

By design, BigQuery ML automatically applies feature engineering during the training phase when we use the CREATE MODEL function, but it also allows us to apply preprocessing transformations as well.

In order to automatically apply the feature engineering operations during the training and the prediction stage, we can include all the pre-processing functions into the TRANSFORM clause when we train the BigQuery ML model.

As we can see from the following code example, we need to use the TRANSFORM clause before the OPTIONS clause, and after the CREATE MODEL statement:

```
CREATE MODEL <MODEL_NAME>
TRANSFORM(<TRANSFORM_CLAUSES>)
OPTIONS
  (<OPTION_CLAUSES>) AS
<TRAINING_TABLE>
```

In BigQuery ML, there are two different types of feature engineering function, outlined as follows:

- **Scalar** functions apply on a single record
- **Analytic** functions calculate the results on all the rows

In the following list, you can take a look at the most important feature engineering functions that you can apply in BigQuery ML:

- ML.BUCKETIZE: This is used to convert a numerical expression into a categorical field—for example, you can use this function to convert the age of a person into *Young*, *Middle*, or *Old* buckets.

- `ML.FEATURE_CROSS`: This is used to combine two features into a unique feature. For example, if in a dataset we have the gender and the place of birth of a person, we can combine these two features to simplify our BigQuery ML model. This technique is particularly indicated when we've correlated features and we want to include both the information in our ML model.

- `ML.QUANTILE_BUCKETIZE`: This is very similar to the `ML.BUCKETIZE` function. In this case, the function is analytic and applies on all records in the dataset. The splitting of records into buckets is based on the quantiles of an entire set of records.

> **Important note**
> The **Quantile** is the specific portion of a dataset. For example, it identifies how many values are above or below a certain threshold value.

- `ML.MIN_MAX_SCALER`: This is an analytic function that returns a value from zero to one according to the distribution of the values in the entire record set.

- `ML.STANDARD_SCALER`: This is an analytic function that allows us to use the standard deviation and mean of the record set.

For an entire list of feature engineering and preprocessing functions, you can visit the official BigQuery documentation at the following link: `https://cloud.google.com/bigquery-ml/docs/reference/standard-sql/bigqueryml-preprocessing-functions`.

Now that we have learned about feature engineering, let's move on to hyperparameter tuning.

# Tuning hyperparameters

In this section, we'll discover the most important hyperparameters that we can tune in BigQuery ML.

> **Important note**
> **Hyperparameter tuning** is the practice of choosing the best set of parameters to train a specific ML model. A hyperparameter influences and controls the learning process during the ML training stage.

By design, BigQuery ML uses default hyperparameters to train a model, but advanced users can manually change them to influence the training process.

In BigQuery ML, we can specify the hyperparameters in the OPTIONS clause as optional parameters. The most relevant hyperparameters, depending on the model, that we can change before starting the training of a BigQuery ML model are listed here:

- L1_REG: This is a regularization parameter that we can use to prevent overfitting by keeping the weights of the model close to zero.

- L2_REG: This is a second regularization parameter that we can use to prevent overfitting.

- MAX_ITERATIONS: This represents the maximum number of iterations that BigQuery ML will perform to train the model.

- LEARN_RATE: This is a parameter that affects how much the model changes according to the error of the previous iteration.

- MIN_REL_PROGRESS: This is the minimum improvement that is necessary to continue the training after an iteration.

- NUM_CLUSTERS: This is used for K-Means algorithms and represents the number of clusters that the model will create.

- HIDDEN_UNITS: This is used in **Deep Neural Networks (DNNs)** and represents the number of hidden layers in a network.

For a complete list of all the hyperparameters that you can apply with BigQuery ML, we suggest visiting the official documentation at `https://cloud.google.com/bigquery-ml/docs/reference/standard-sql/bigqueryml-syntax-create`.

# Using BigQuery ML for online predictions

In this section, we'll understand how we can use a BigQuery ML model in a synchronous and online manner.

BigQuery ML represents a huge opportunity to democratize ML techniques for business and data analysts. When BigQuery ML is trained and ready to use, we can invoke it directly in BigQuery using a SQL query or we can export it into TensorFlow format.

The requirements of each use case drive the prediction type that we should adopt, as outlined here:

- We use **online prediction** when we want to enable request-response applications and when getting an immediate prediction is critical.

- We adopt **batch prediction** to process large volumes of data when we don't need immediate predictions—for example, scheduling daily or weekly jobs that calculate predictions on the data collected since the last job execution.

While using BigQuery SQL statements is more suitable for batch predictions on a large number of records stored in a BigQuery table, the possibility of exporting BigQuery ML models into TensorFlow opens new opportunities in terms of applications.

In the following diagram, you can see the life cycle of a BigQuery ML model from the training phase to the deployment phase:

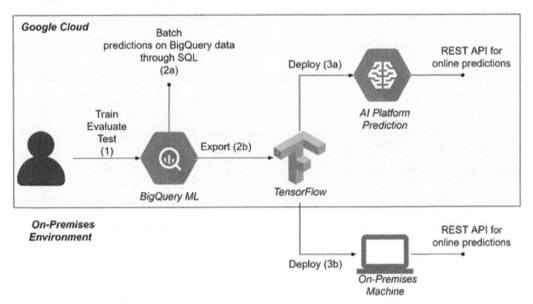

Figure 14.9 – Using a BigQuery ML model for online predictions

From the preceding diagram, we see that in the first step **(1)** of the BigQuery ML model life cycle we train the ML model by leveraging the training dataset stored in BigQuery. In this first step, the ML model goes through the three main stages of the development cycle, as follows:

- **Train**: In this stage, the BigQuery ML model learns from the training data.

- **Evaluate**: In this step, we evaluate the KPIs of the model and we can tune the hyperparameters.

- **Test**: In this last phase, we finally test the BigQuery ML model on the test dataset to get the predictions.

When the BigQuery ML model satisfies our expectations in terms of performance, we can do the following:

- Use the model in BigQuery **(2a)** through SQL by leveraging data that is already stored in tables. This approach typically works well for batch predictions—for example, we can periodically run the BigQuery SQL statement to execute the model every day or every week by generating the new predictions.

- Export the model into the TensorFlow `SavedFormat` **(2b)**, as we described in *Chapter 13*, *Running TensorFlow Models with BigQuery ML*. This second approach is particularly suitable for running the ML model outside of BigQuery on other TensorFlow-compatible platforms. The same approach can be adopted by exporting the ML model into the XGBoost Booster format.

When we've exported the BigQuery ML model, we can deploy the ML algorithm to one of the following:

- **Google Cloud AI Platform Prediction (3a)**: With this Google Cloud module, we can deploy trained ML models in the cloud and leverage the cloud infrastructure to serve the model and generate online predictions. This cloud service automatically provisions and manages the infrastructure resources to run the ML model and can scale up according to the number of requests that come from client applications. The deployment on Google Cloud AI Platform Prediction automatically generates a **Representational State Transfer** (**REST**) endpoint that can be used to invoke the model through **HyperText Transfer Protocol** (**HTTP**) requests.

This kind of approach is particularly useful when we have multiple client applications that should interact with our ML model and we don't want to have to worry about the infrastructure maintenance of the service. As a prerequisite, we need to consider that we can only use this kind of approach if an internet connection is available. In fact, to invoke the REST **Application Programming Interface (API)** exposed by the cloud platform, we need to perform HTTP requests from the client applications to the cloud.

- An **on-premise machine** where it can be deployed using containers **(3b)**. TensorFlow models, in fact, can be deployed using containers by leveraging a **TensorFlow Serving Docker** container. To understand the deployment steps of a TensorFlow model in a **Docker** container, you can check out the documentation at `https://www.tensorflow.org/tfx/serving/docker`.

> **Important note**
>
> A **container** is a virtualization mechanism that runs on top of a single operating system. **Docker** is a container engine used to deploy containerized applications. The container engine allocates the hardware resources for each application and manages the scalability of the virtual infrastructure.

We can use this approach when the ML model needs to run under specific conditions, such as during an absence of internet connectivity, or on sensitive data. In fact, when we deploy the on-premise machine ML model, the cloud infrastructure is no longer involved in the predictions and there is no data transfer between the on-premise environment and the cloud.

In both deployment scenarios, the ML model can be invoked by using HTTP requests, passing the input parameters in the request payload. At the end of the ML model execution, the predictions are returned into the response payload.

# Summary

In this chapter, we've learned the most important tips and best practices that we can apply during the implementation of a ML use case with BigQuery ML.

We've analyzed the importance of data preparation; we started looking at the data quality aspects; then, we've learned how we can easily split the data to get balanced training, validation, and test sets.

We then looked at how we can further improve a ML model's performance using BigQuery ML functions for feature engineering.

After that, we focused our attention on tuning hyperparameters. When we train a model, BigQuery ML allows us to choose different parameters, and these variables influence the training stage.

Finally, we have understood why it is so important to deploy BigQuery ML models on other platforms so that we get online predictions and satisfy near-real-time business scenarios.

Congratulations on finishing reading the book! You should now be able to use BigQuery ML for your business scenarios and use cases. I suggest you continue to keep constantly informed about this topic, which is so interesting and is evolving so quickly.

## Further resources

- **BigQuery ML Create Model**: `https://console.cloud.google.com/marketplace/product/city-of-new-york/nyc-citi-bike`

- **BigQuery ML preprocessing functions**: `https://cloud.google.com/bigquery-ml/docs/reference/standard-sql/bigqueryml-preprocessing-functions`

- **BigQuery ML `CREATE MODEL` statement for importing TensorFlow models**: `https://cloud.google.com/bigquery-ml/docs/reference/standard-sql/bigqueryml-syntax-create-tensorflow`

- **BigQuery ML `ML EVALUATE` function**: `https://cloud.google.com/bigquery-ml/docs/reference/standard-sql/bigqueryml-syntax-evaluate`

- **BigQuery ML `ML PREDICT` function**: `https://cloud.google.com/bigquery-ml/docs/reference/standard-sql/bigqueryml-syntax-predict`

- **Exporting a BigQuery ML model for online prediction**: `https://cloud.google.com/bigquery-ml/docs/export-model-tutorial`

Packt.com

Subscribe to our online digital library for full access to over 7,000 books and videos, as well as industry leading tools to help you plan your personal development and advance your career. For more information, please visit our website.

## Why subscribe?

- Spend less time learning and more time coding with practical eBooks and Videos from over 4,000 industry professionals

- Improve your learning with Skill Plans built especially for you

- Get a free eBook or video every month

- Fully searchable for easy access to vital information

- Copy and paste, print, and bookmark content

Did you know that Packt offers eBook versions of every book published, with PDF and ePub files available? You can upgrade to the eBook version at packt.com and as a print book customer, you are entitled to a discount on the eBook copy. Get in touch with us at customercare@packtpub.com for more details.

At www.packt.com, you can also read a collection of free technical articles, sign up for a range of free newsletters, and receive exclusive discounts and offers on Packt books and eBooks.

# Other Books You May Enjoy

If you enjoyed this book, you may be interested in these other books by Packt:

**Hands-On Artificial Intelligence on Google Cloud Platform**

Anand Deshpande, Manish Kumar, Vikram Chaudhari

ISBN: 978-1-78953-846-5

- Understand the basics of cloud computing and explore GCP components
- Work with the data ingestion and preprocessing techniques in GCP for machine learning
- Implement machine learning algorithms with Google Cloud AutoML
- Optimize TensorFlow machine learning with Google Cloud TPUs
- Build an end-to-end machine learning pipeline using Cloud Storage, Cloud Dataflow, and Cloud Datalab
- Build models from petabytes of structured and semi-structured data using BigQuery ML

**Automated Machine Learning**

Adnan Masood PhD

ISBN: 978-1-80056-768-9

- Explore AutoML fundamentals, underlying methods, and techniques
- Assess AutoML aspects such as algorithm selection, auto featurization, and hyperparameter tuning in an applied scenario
- Find out the difference between cloud and operations support systems (OSS)
- Implement AutoML in enterprise cloud to deploy ML models and pipelines
- Build explainable AutoML pipelines with transparency
- Understand automated feature engineering and time series forecasting
- Automate data science modeling tasks to implement ML solutions easily and focus on more complex problems

# Packt is searching for authors like you

If you're interested in becoming an author for Packt, please visit authors. packtpub.com and apply today. We have worked with thousands of developers and tech professionals, just like you, to help them share their insight with the global tech community. You can make a general application, apply for a specific hot topic that we are recruiting an author for, or submit your own idea.

# Leave a review - let other readers know what you think

Please share your thoughts on this book with others by leaving a review on the site that you bought it from. If you purchased the book from Amazon, please leave us an honest review on this book's Amazon page. This is vital so that other potential readers can see and use your unbiased opinion to make purchasing decisions, we can understand what our customers think about our products, and our authors can see your feedback on the title that they have worked with Packt to create. It will only take a few minutes of your time, but is valuable to other potential customers, our authors, and Packt. Thank you!

# Index

_Drenel N1_

_– recently dynamic tree_